Bought for 'Spike'.
Resc

1991

C000213283

- S + K - Best

- SPIKE - LOVED THIS STAFF.

- JACK - My one in a million
very special.

- PIP. - 100 mph. midget.

-

The Staffordshire Bull Terrier

POPULAR DOGS' BREED SERIES

BASSET HOUND	*George Johnston*
BEAGLE	*Thelma Gray*
BOXER	*Elizabeth Somerfield*
CAIRN TERRIER	*J. W. H. Beynon, Alex Fisher and Peggy Wilson*
CAVALIER KING CHARLES SPANIEL	*Mary Forwood*
CHIHUAHUA	*Thelma Gray*
COCKER SPANIEL	*Veronica Lucas-Lucas and Joyce Caddy*
COLLIE	*Margaret Osborne and Aileen Speding*
DACHSHUND	*E. Fitch Daglish, Amyas Biss and Jeff Crawford*
DALMATIAN	*Eleanor Frankling, Betty Clay and Marjorie Cooper*
DOBERMANN	*Fred Curnow and Jean Faulks*
FOX TERRIER	*Elsie Williams*
GERMAN SHEPHERD DOG	*J. Schwabacher, Thelma Gray and Madeleine Pickup*
GOLDEN RETRIEVER	*Joan Tudor*
GREAT DANE	*Jean Lanning*
IRISH SETTER	*Janice Roberts*
LABRADOR RETRIEVER	*Lorna, Countess Howe and Geoffrey Waring*
MONGREL	*Angela Patmore*
OLD ENGLISH SHEEPDOG	*Ann Davis*
POODLE	*Clara Bowring, Alida Monro and Shirley Walne*
PUG	*Susan Graham Weall*
ROTTWEILER	*Judy and Larry Elsden*
SCOTTISH TERRIER	*Dorothy Caspersz and Elizabeth Meyer*
SHETLAND SHEEPDOG	*Margaret Osborne*
SHIH TZU	*Audrey Dadds*
SPRINGER SPANIEL	*Dorothy Moorland Hooper and Ian B. Hampton*
STAFFORDSHIRE BULL TERRIER	*John F. Gordon*
WELSH CORGI	*Charles Lister-Kaye and Dickie Albin*
WEST HIGHLAND WHITE TERRIER	*D. Mary Dennis and Catherine Owen*
YORKSHIRE TERRIER	*Ethel and Vera Munday*

THE STAFFORDSHIRE BULL TERRIER

JOHN F. GORDON

POPULAR DOGS
London Sydney Auckland Johannesburg

Popular Dogs Publishing Co. Ltd

An imprint of Century Hutchinson

Brookmount House, 62–65 Chandos Place,
Covent Garden, London WC2N 4NW

Century Hutchinson Australia (Pty) Ltd
88–91 Albion Street, Surry Hills, NSW 2010

Century Hutchinson New Zealand Limited
191 Archers Road, PO Box 40–086, Glenfield, Auckland 10

Century Hutchinson South Africa (Pty) Ltd
PO Box 337, Bergvlei 2012, South Africa

First published 1971
Revised editions 1971, 1972, 1975, 1978, 1980,
1983, 1984, 1986, 1989

Copyright © John F. Gordon 1971, 1972, 1975, 1978,
1980, 1983, 1984, 1986, 1989

Breed Standard Copyright © The Kennel Club

All rights reserved

Set in Baskerville by Deltatype, Ellesmere Port

Printed and bound in Great Britain by
Mackays of Chatham PLC, Chatham, Kent

British Library Cataloguing in Publication Data

0 09 166090 4

CONTENTS

	Author's Introduction	10
1	Origin and History	15
2	The 'New Breed'	34
3	The Standard	45
4	Character and Conformation	64
5	Choosing a Puppy	82
6	Training and General Management	90
7	Breeding and Stock Rearing	107
8	Shows and Showing	139
9	The Final Stages	145
10	Ailments	152

APPENDICES

A	Kennel Club Registration Totals	159
B	Breed Clubs	160
C	List of Champions	164
	Bibliography	204
	Index	208

‘The wisest dog I ever had was what is called the Bulldog-Terrier. I taught him to understand a great many words, insomuch that I am positive that the communication betwixt the canine species and ourselves might be greatly enlarged . . .’

SIR WALTER SCOTT

From Capt. Thomas Brown’s *Biographical Sketches and Authentic Anecdotes of Dogs*, 1829

ILLUSTRATIONS

Between pages 32 and 33

Ch. Hurricane of Judael and Hurricane Freya
Judael owned by James Edward and Mary Pringle and daughter
Freya owned by James Edward and Mary Pringle

Ch. Reckless Lass
Bred by S. Shepherd. Owned by Edward and Iain Williams

A Bull-and-Terrier. Painting by James Ward, 1820

Billy, Rose and Tumbler, the property of F. Redmond. Old English Bulldogs, ancestors of the Stafford

Jem Burns' Four Pets. The kennel boy, Jack Shepherd, and the Bulldogs, Duchess, Cribb and Ball. From an original oil painting by T. Clayton, 1843

The Bull and Mastiff. After Howitt by Dubourg, 1813

The Bulldog of 1798, by Howitt

Dog-fighting. From the original hard ground etching by Henry Alken, *c.* 1820

Between pages 64 and 65

Badger-baiting. From the original hard ground etching by Henry Alken, *c.* 1820

The Bulldog Mars. From the original oil painting by J. Pollott, *c.* 1848

Alpaka Alf's Fancy
Owned by Alf Tittle

Ch. Skerry Dhu of Dumbriton
Bred by R. A. Chesson. Owned by Danny Gilmour and Neil MacLean

Ch. Eastaff Noire-Fille
Owned by Mrs Joyce Shorrock

Ch. Topcroft Toreador
Bred and owned by H. Latham

Ch. Orchid Beauty
Bred and owned by V. H. Pounds

Ch. Ashstock Black Maria
Owned by Alec Waters

Between pages 96 and 97

American Staffordshire Terrier Ch. Indian Doc
Owned by Mrs D. M. Archer

Ch. Boldmore Black Sabbath
Bred and owned by Mr and Mrs M. Clarke

Ch. Langport Spearhead
Owned by K. C. Langdon

Ch. Ginnells Black Tuskyanna
Owned by Mr and Mrs P. Shoulder

Ch. Rapparee Lady Luck
Owned by Mr and Mrs J. Bolton

Ch. Curfews White Orchid
Owned by B. Barnes

Bandits Fawn Dandy
Owned by K. C. A. Davies

Ch. Indiana Acid Queen
Bred by Mr and Mrs T. Curd. Owned by Haraway and Carol

Between pages 128 and 129

Ch. Jolihem Dreadnought
Bred and owned by L. Hemstock

Ch. Duke of Ducks Hill
Bred by Mrs Membry. Owned by Mr and Mrs J. H. F. Ward

Constones Yer Man
Bred and owned by Mr and Mrs A. M. Lee and Mr A. W. A. Cairns

Ch. Eastaff Guardian

Owned by Mrs Joyce Shorrock

Ch. Wallace the Wizard

Bred by Squires. Owned by Wood and Hedges

Ch. Fearless Red of Bandits

Owned by the author

Lioness, dam of Tough Guy

Owned by H. Mellings

Constones Tuscaloosa Sam

Bred by Mr and Mrs A. M. Lee and Mr A. W. A. Cairns. Owned by Mrs C. J. H. Lee and Mrs B. Greaves

IN THE TEXT

1819 broadsheet for Eccles Wakes announcing a bull-bait *page* 22

Chart showing the evolution of the Staffordshire Bull Terrier and allied breeds 42

Figure 1 Points of the Staffordshire Bull Terrier 52
2 Head profiles 54
3 Ears 54
4 Mouths 56
5 Fronts 57
6 Hindquarters 57
7 Body 58
8 Body plan 58
9 Tails 59
10 Stifles 59
11 Feet 59
12 Pasterns 60

AUTHOR'S INTRODUCTION

Over the last thirty years I have observed with enthusiasm and no little pride the Staffordshire Bull Terrier's rise from his humble beginnings as a show dog to the successful bencher he is today. At one time among the least admired breeds—through no fault of his own, but due to his gladiatorial background from which he had barely emerged when the twentieth century began—he is now one of dogdom's most popular Terriers. He can claim to be a breed to be reckoned with, not only outside the show ring but firmly within it. In recent months, a Staffordshire, Champion Wystaff Warfare, was made Best in Show All Breeds at the Leicester Abbey Park Championship Show—a rare accolade indeed, but certainly the forerunner of others which will grace the breed's future.

Such a book as this cannot be produced without the help of others—even the Staffords themselves by virtue of their successful campaigning in the show world have created a demand for more literature to further their interests! My thanks to them, also to Arthur Hill ('Kinderlee') for his valuable help in compiling the list of champions and to Glan Williams for his lucid diagrams, not forgetting those who so kindly sent me pictures of their excellent dogs.

1971 J.F.G.

Arrangements having been made to reprint this book, it is only fitting that the list of champions (Appendix C) should be extended to the date when the second edition goes to press. This has been done, and one or two small alterations and amendments which have been brought to my notice have received attention.

This now seems an admirable opportunity to thank the many breed enthusiasts who have written to me since the first edition was published to express their appreciation for what they have generally and kindly termed my 'best book' on the breed.

1972

J.F.G.

It is gratifying to learn that a third edition of my book has been arranged. It has not proved necessary to alter the text, but amendments and alterations have been made to the Appendices, with additions to the list of champions bringing this up to date.

Staffordshire Bull Terriers are, according to the Kennel Club 1974 list of annual registrations, the third most popular Terrier breed in the United Kingdom. What progress has been made! What a far cry from the pitiful figures of 1935 and the early post-war years when the breed was getting itself known and established. Now we can claim its emancipation and be proud of the way the Stafford has endeared itself to the public, not only here but throughout the world, and especially in the United States of America where it is becoming an important breed.

1975

J.F.G.

Since the third edition appeared in 1975 there have been some changes in the fees and pattern of registration at the Kennel Club; the names and addresses of some club secretaries have altered and Appendices A and C, which refer to registration totals and champions, have been extended.

Naturally, I am pleased to have achieved a fourth edition and take this opportunity of thanking the many Staffordshire Bull Terrier enthusiasts who have written me or conveyed in some form their appreciation of this book on their chosen breed.

1977

J.F.G.

I have been asked to contribute a brief author's note to this fifth edition of my book. What can I say but express delight that my book has gone to every corner of the earth where there exists an interest in our wonderful breed. It is indeed very fitting that the book's continuing success is being marked in 1980, the year in which the breed's own success is marked by achieving top Terrier entry at Cruft's. The reader will find the list of champions and appendices up-dated in the usual way and I hope new readers will enjoy my book as others appear to have done.

1980 J.F.G.

Staffordshire Bull Terriers have progressed in numbers and quality to an almost unbelievable extent over the last few years. We are currently involved with a pedigree breed which has set its indelible mark on dogdom. The Stafford's great worth as a useful and formidable guard to home and property in these somewhat troubled social times has not gone unnoticed by the general public, resulting in the dog's general appeal going far beyond the exhibition ring.

This is the sixth edition of my book, brought up to date with the changing fees and list of champions and other small items. My thanks to the many readers and breed concerns who have expressed their appreciation for the book's usefulness and guidance.

1983 J.F.G.

The continued success of this book can only confirm that many more fanciers are becoming involved with Staffordshire Bull Terriers and experiencing, no doubt, the delight, reward and even surprise which this breed is able to bestow upon the intelligent and understanding owner. May such progress long continue—the breed deserves it.

1984 J.F.G.

Now we are into the eighth edition and again, with up-datings in various parts of the text, the book is going to all parts of the world and must surely be encouraging the expansion of love for our wonderful breed. My appreciation to the innumerable fanciers who have sent their congratulations and best wishes.

1986 J.F.G.

Naturally, I was pleased to learn from my publishers that a ninth edition was planned for 1989. I have many complimentary comments from fanciers in almost every land, all expressing their appreciation for the book's usefulness. This I find very gratifying and may I wish these and all breed enthusiasts great success in their endeavours.

1989 Romford, Essex J.F.G.

1

Origin and History

The Staffordshire Bull Terrier, looking very much as he does today, apart from explained and accepted variances in size, weight, and name, has existed in Britain for the best part of 175 years. Written and pictorial history allows us reasonable grounds for believing this, and the fact that our sporting breed can claim to have sprung from English dog stock so long ago entitles him to the honour of being listed as a genuine 'Old English' dog. This is an accolade for which few canine varieties can qualify today.

Unfortunately, whereas we have some licence to formulate an opinion about the Staffordshire Bull Terrier's 'manufacture', which began somewhere during the terminal years of the eighteenth century, the authentic story of his development is hidden. This is due to the fact that no one bothered (as far as we know) to keep records about dogs in those days. They bred and fashioned their dogs to suit particular sports or functions, but matters like pedigree, so important to us, were disregarded completely. This indifference to written pedigree and mating records persisted in the Staffordshire Bull Terrier even beyond the first quarter of the twentieth century. The old dog-fighting fraternity, rather like the bull- and bear-baiting devotees, believed the best way to produce good fighters was to mate dog and bitch of proven courage. Considerations like colour and fancy points were despised and, therefore, ignored. Due to this attitude, which had persisted in the Black Country when the breed was accepted for registration by the Kennel Club in 1935, few Staffords in Britain had what might be termed an authentic family tree. Most dogs and bitches were known just by their pet names, which showed scant variation and imagination. In fact, one Darlaston street in 1934 boasted five Staffordshire Bull Terrier dogs and four bitches, yet only two names, 'Mick' and

'Bill', were shared between the dogs and all the bitches answered to 'Nell'. Little wonder in such circumstances that early pedigrees proved confusing and often useless.

Early Progenitors

To discover from what type of early dogs our Staffordshire Bull Terrier evolves it is necessary to travel well back through the centuries. Many of Britain's invaders were met on the beaches by fighting dogs, which were of immense size, either Mastiffs or forerunners of that noble breed, now a rarity, unfortunately. Such animals were probably introduced to these islands by the trading Phoenicians, long before the Christian era, became domiciled here, and were trained by the ancients to help them in battle. That these fearsome beasts distinguished themselves in warfare is revealed in Roman writings, and they are referred to as the 'Pugnaces' and 'broad-mouthed dogs' of Britain. Many were shipped back to Italy by the *Procurator Pugnacium*, an official appointed by Rome to keep the amphitheatres adequately supplied with fierce animals. There they were pitted against creatures from the jungle, against armed men and other huge dogs. That they achieved fame at these bloodthirsty sports is evident from the way these dogs spread to almost every land in Europe and Asia, especially where the Romans held power. As these big dogs became domiciled in the new countries they interbred with others, and new varieties were formed. It is certain that many modern breeds, some perhaps that have become extinct in passing years, owe their type and great size to the old fighting Mastiffs.

Jesse in his *Anecdotes of Dogs*, 1858, describes this dog as 'a dog of gigantic size, of a yellowish colour, with a black muzzle'. The description seems to tally with that of another huge canine from the past—the Molossus, so named because he was bred in Molossi, a town in Epirus, Ancient Greece. Although the name Molossus (or Mollossus) was used generically to encompass several of the heavy, herding dogs of divers sorts that existed in Sparta and the Balkans, the variety that concerns us is one not unlike the Mastiff. There is a plaster reproduction of his kind in the Metropolitan Museum of Arts, New York, executed about

400 B.C. by an unknown artist. Riedel's famous illustration in *Icones Animalium*, 1780, can be inspected in the British Museum. In much the same way as Spain, even today, produces its special fighting bulls for the bull-ring, these big Greek Mastiffs were bred solely for arena sports, although their ancestry has a history of the hunt, where they were used as heavy dogs of the chase. Assyrian bas-relief of 600 B.C. and drawings found on the excavated tombs of certain Egyptian pharaohs depict these Molossians, which were capable of pulling down, and probably able to kill, even the king of the beasts, although bears and wild asses were the usual quarries. Remains have been found of these big dogs, yet alongside the fossils have been those of dogs, similar in construction and conformation, yet smaller.

Oddly enough, this disparity of size in Mastiff bloodstock has persisted down the centuries. No one bothered much to comment on it until the fifteenth and sixteenth centuries, when writers described Mastiff types of two sizes—one big and ponderous, used for baiting sports in Tudor England, the other a dog of more modest girth, although powerful and solid, used for guard work and domestic purposes. That this dog spent most of his life chained up in a yard probably accounted for his name—Bond-dog or Bandogge. It would seem that the smaller Mastiff was the forerunner of our modern Bulldog, which, if true, shows the close affinity between the two breeds. An interesting feature of the Bulldog's breakaway from the main Mastiff stem is his inheritance of the bigger breed's coat colours. Early pictures and prints show the Mastiff in a variety of coat colours, many liberally splashed with white—in fact, typical of the coats now sported by our Bulldogs. On the other hand, the coat of the modern Mastiff, when seen, as well as his close relation the Bullmastiff, is of the more modest hues of fawns and brindles.

In the fifteenth century we are introduced to the Alaunt or Alan. The name appears in *The Master of Game*, written by Edward, Second Duke of York, between 1406 and 1413. A dog of large Bulldog proportions it is described as 'short-headed, pugnacious and inclined to hang on to anything attacked'. Chaucer, too, in his *Knight's Tale*, tells us of Alaunts belonging to the King of Thrace:

Aboute his chaar ther wenten whyte alaunts,
Twenty and mo, as grete as any steer,
To hunten at the leoun or the deer,
And folwed him with mosel faste y-bounde,
Colered of gold, and touettes fyléd rounde

Of course, 'grete as any steer' must not be taken too literally, although doubtless these dogs were of impressive size. Nothing further was heard of them, at least by that name, although the Spanish Bulldog, a variety employed successfully in the bull-ring, was called *Alano* in early Spanish. Descendants of the *Alano* were actually imported from Spain into England during the first half of the last century with the idea of introducing greater size (the Spanish dogs weighed about 90 lb) and exaggeration of fanciers' points with which the foreigner seemed well blessed. Whether these imports of the old Alaunt blood proved worth while to British stock development remains unconfirmed.

The first serious attempt to classify dogs and make a proper division of the breeds according to their function, appearance, and names occurred in 1570. This was by Dr Johannes Caius (founder of Caius College, Cambridge, and Physician-in-Chief to Queen Elizabeth) in *De Canibus Britannicus*, and written in Latin. Six years later, Abraham Fleming translated it into English in *Of Englishe Dogges*, where the Mastive or Bandogge is described as 'an huge dogge, stubborne, eager, burthenous of body, and therefore of but little swiftness, terrible and fearful to behold, and more fearse and fell than any Arcadian curr'. It seems that almost any dog that was large-bodied in Caius' day would have been termed a Mastiff. In Old English 'masty' meant 'fat', and no doubt the word is akin to 'massive', for in the sixteenth century dogs were named according to their appearance as well as their function in life. Obviously, dogs in this group descended from the Old European Mastiff, forerunner of the Old English Mastiff, bull-baiter extraordinary in the Elizabethan age, and close kin to the Bandogge and Bulldog from which our kind of Bull Terrier descends. Today we call him the Staffordshire Bull Terrier. That a Terrier breed or breeds of Old English vintage were used with the Old English Bulldog to produce him, we are ready to believe. His very name confirms that Bull and Terrier crossings took place. Maybe the early and slenderer Bulldogs, too, were bred on more Terrier-like lines than breeders want in Bulldogs today. If they were, then in the century that has passed, the two distinct paths of development will have met and fused in the passing years. We in the breed are content in the knowledge that we have a grand, vigorous, and upstanding breed bred from solid, traditional British dog-stock. Whether its last hundred years of development was influenced by unadulterated bloodlines of Bulldogs or even if a vast concourse of Terriers set their seed to the Staffordshire Bull Terrier's destiny, it does not matter. The finished dog is one to be proud of; certainly he rates highly in dogdom today.

Bear-baiting

'What folly is this to keep with danger
A great mastiff dog and foul ugly bear
And to this anent, to see them two fight
With terrible tearings, a full ugly sight.'

ROBERT CROWLEY, 1518–88

This comparatively slow-moving yet extremely barbarous sport is one of ancient vintage. Its heyday was in the Tudor period when bloodsports were rife in Britain, especially in London. Here, bears were actually bred and maintained to keep up the supply to the bear-pits and itinerant bear wards. The latter took their valuable bears all over the country, attending fairs and feast days, boasting of their animals' prowess in battle, and allowing the owners of dogs to run their charges against the bear for a small fee. The dogs used were usually of Bulldog or Mastiff type, often termed Bandogges in those days, seldom less than 70 lb in weight and invariably ferocious. Often, five or six of them at a time would be loosed at the bear, who would crush a dog in one hug and disembowel another with ease. The bait would proceed until the dogs had either been maimed and dispersed or one of the dogs had 'pinned' the bear by sinking his teeth into its face or body. The event was seldom, if ever, continued to the bear's demise, not only because of that animal's value and scarcity, but because of his superiority in the contest.

In Henry VIII's reign a bear-garden was opened at Bankside in Southwark, London. The place, known as Paris Gardens, quickly gained an unsavoury reputation. It held about a thousand people, each of whom paid a penny for admission. On baiting days it was crammed with spectators, the sport quickly becoming one of London's most fashionable pursuits. Some bears, by virtue of their ferocity or skill in coping with the dogs, became famous and their careers were followed eagerly by devotees of the game, much as noted sportsmen receive public adulation today. Bears were often named, and one, Sackerson, is mentioned by Shakespeare. Other ursine notabilities such as Tom of Lincoln, Blind Robin, and Ned of Canterbury, while not so honoured in the literary field, at least achieved fame in the bear-pits. The Bankside was frequented by royalty and many visiting foreign dignitaries, anxious to savour the English 'sport'. Queen Elizabeth I was a keen participant; she had her own Chief Master of the Bears, who could impound at will any bears, bulls, or dogs he wanted. It is said that the Queen became so perturbed at the increasing predilection of the public for theatre-going that she called for legislation to prevent the production of plays on Thursday, this being baiting day.

When James I became king, the bear-garden came under royal protection, a Master of the Bears and Dogs being appointed at an official fee of a farthing a day. In actual fact, the job netted its holder, Edward Alleyn, about £500 per annum, no mean sum in those days. The office was abolished in 1642. After the Restoration, bear-baiting returned to favour until the reign of Queen Anne, when it began to decline. By 1750 it had more or less disappeared from the English pastoral scene, although London interest was maintained intermittently into the early years of the nineteenth century.

Bull-baiting

This sadistic pastime is said to have started in England during the reign of King John, although it was known here and on the Continent during previous centuries. It is sometimes referred to as bull-running, for the wretched bull would be chased through village streets and across the fields by hordes of screaming people, bent on its blood. Finally, it would be baited by savage dogs of the Mastiff and Bulldog varieties and either killed that way or bludgeoned to death by local butchers. The man whose name has gone down to posterity for starting the game was William of Warenne, then Lord of Stamford in 1209, who saw possibilities in it, and forthwith leased some of his acreage to the butchers, provided they supplied a 'mad' bull for baiting every year six weeks before Christmas. Traditionally, Stamford had its bull-running for another six hundred years, some of the events proving macabre orgies of cruelty, the bull eventually being thrown into the River Witham, then cut up and its flesh distributed to the poor. It was avowed that meat so 'coursed' became more succulent than that from a pole-axed beast, and this belief persists even today in some hunting circles.

The dogs used in bull-baiting were, at first, big dogs such as were employed in bear-baiting, but these were found rather ponderous for what was a fast-moving sport; also they were shown to be more vulnerable to goring and tossing than a fleeter, more nimble, lower-to-ground dog. Even when bull-baiting became more localised as a sport, i.e. when the bull was tethered by a 30 ft chain to a post in the ground, it was clear to the sporting fraternity that a 'new look' in dogs was needed to liven up the proceedings. It was not until the early part of the nineteenth century that smaller dogs were produced, not only by selection of smaller varieties of the Bulldog, but also by crossing the Bulldog with game Terriers of various kinds. Most interest in bull-baiting was in Elizabethan days, the sixteenth century being the most active period, bull-rings cropping up everywhere and the game even coming under royal patronage and being accorded the benefits of certain ancient laws. The bull was often able to dig a hole with his front feet, into which he could lower his nostrils away from the dogs who sought to 'pin' him with their jaws. Some bulls became most proficient at the sport and many good dogs were killed, few being unscathed at the end of the bait. Dogs would be tossed high into the air, to descend on the hard ground with back or limbs broken; unless, of course, they had been caught in the outstretched aprons of their butcher-owners or had received the succour of a long pole

Eccles Wake

Will be held on MONDAY and TUESDAY, the 30th, and 31st of August; and on WEDNESDAY and THURSDAY, the 1st, and 2d of September, 1819.

On MONDAY, the ancient Sport of

BULL BAITING,

May be seen in all it's various Evolutions.

Same Day,

A DANDY RACE,

For a PURSE of SILVER—the best of heats—The second-best to be entitled to 5s.

Same Day,

A FOOT-RACE for a HAT,

By Lads not exceeding Sixteen years of age.—Three to start, or no race.

On TUESDAY,

A JACK-ASS RACE,

For a PURSE of GOLD, value £50.—The best of three heats—Each to carry a feather.—The Racers to be shewn in the Bull-ring exactly at 12 o'clock, and to start at 2.—Nothing to be paid for entrance: but the bringer of each *Steed* to have a good Dinner gratis, and a quart of strong Ale, *to moisten his clay.*

Same Day,

A FOOT-RACE for a HAT,

By Lads that never won a Hat or Prize before Monday.—Three to start.

Same Day,

An APPLE DUMPLING Eating,

By Ladies and Gentlemen of all ages: The person who finishes the repast first, to have 5s.—the second, 2s.—and the third, 1s.

On WEDNESDAY,

A PONY RACE,

By Tits not exceeding 12 hands high, for a CUP, value £50.—The best of heats.—Three to start, or no race.

Same Day,

A Foot-Race for a Hat, value 10s. 6d.

By Men of any description.—Three to start.

Same Day,

A Race for a good Holland Smock,

By *Ladies* of all ages: the second-best to have a handsome Satin Riband. Three to start.

On THURSDAY,

A GAME AT PRISON-BARS.

Also,

A GRINNING MATCH through a Collar.

For a Piece of fat Bacon.———No *Crabs* to be used on the occasion.

Same Day,

A YOUNG PIG

Will be turned out, with his Ears and Tail well *souped*, and the first Person catching and holding him by either, will be entitled to the same.

Smoking Matches, by Ladies and Gentlemen of all ages.

To conclude with a grand FIDDLING MATCH, by all the Fiddlers that attend the Wake, for a Purse of Silver.—There will be prizes for the second and third-best—Tunes; "O where, and O where does my little Boney dwell. Britons strike home—Rule Britannia—God save the King." May the King live for ever, huzza!

N. B. As TWO BULLS in great practice are purchased for diversion, the Public may rest assured of being well entertained. The hours of Baiting the Bull, will be precisely at 10 o'clock in the Morning for practice, and at 3 and 7 o'clock for a prize. The dog that does not run for practice is not to run for a prize.

The Bull-ring will be stumped and railed all round with Oak Trees, so that Ladies or Gentlemen may be accomodated with seeing, without the least danger.—Ordinaries, &c. as usual.

☞ The Bellman will go round a quarter of an hour before the time of Baiting.

GOD SAVE  ***THE KING.***

JOHN MOSS, Esq. } STEWARDS.
T. SEDDON, Esq. }
T. CARRUTHERS, Clerk of the Course.

J. Patrick, Printer, Manchester.]

1819 broadsheet for Eccles Wake announcing a bull-bait *(Courtesy K. F. Woolfenden)*

thrust beneath their loins on the downward journey, to break their fall. If a dog did take hold, however, he was very difficult to dislodge. Stories have been told of owners amputating parts of the hanging dog, boasting meanwhile of the good breeding, the gameness and 'bottom' of the animal because he would not loose his hold. Such atrocities are hardly credible, but writers of the time assure us they are true. Sometimes a dog impossible to shift in spite of the bull's ranting and roaring to shake him off, would be removed from the scene by the simple expedient of taking a sharp knife and cutting round the piece of flesh he had taken hold of. Such incidents are sickening, but they show the stuff these old Bulldogs and Bull-and-Terriers were made of. It is what breeders seek in their dogs today, but seldom get. Too many decades have passed in which opportunities for maintaining such gameness have been lost to the breed. No civilised person wishes to see baiting sports again—and let it be said that the following pastime of dog-fighting played its part in perpetuating good temperament in the Pit Bull Terrier—but what now? Milder forms of field sport, like ratting, help to keep a Staffordshire's temperament well endowed, but the tonic can work on just a few dogs, not the breed as a whole, and this is where our dog is at a disadvantage.

By the end of the eighteenth century much interest had been lost in bull-baiting. The aristocracy had long since dismissed it as a vulgar sport, and in 1802 a call was made to prohibit it. The subsequent debates were little more than political and class arguments, but when, in 1835, the Society for Prevention of Cruelty to Animals (now the RSPCA) held a successful test case at Lincoln Assizes, the end was in sight. It is interesting to relate that Stamford, first in the field with the sport in England, was last out. Two years after the Lincoln result it was still running its annual bull, but when the cavalry and a draft of London police were moved into the town and its mayor was presented with a bill for £600, all concerned felt the cost too high, and no more bull-baiting took place.

Dog-fighting

The *real* fighting dog is a Bull Terrier of the kind we are proud to know today as a Staffordshire Bull Terrier. Dog-fighting did not become popular as a pastime until the last century, and although it had been conducted frequently alongside the more spectacular events of bear- and bull-baiting, it did not come into its own until those pastimes disappeared from the public scene. Of course, dog-fighting and cock-fighting should have gone with them, but being more adaptable to hole-and-corner staging they were less affected by the prohibitions of the 1835 Act. In fact, both received an impetus which, in the case of dog-fighting at least, carried its activities through even into the first quarter of the present century. Today it is virtually extinct as a sport, but even in the 'forties matches were staged, mainly in the Birmingham area.

A wide variety of sizes and weights of dog have been used in dog-fighting. Pure-bred Staffordshire Bull Terriers have for the most part evolved from a mixed ancestry of pit dogs, ranging from little scrappers of 12 lb up to heavyweights of 60 lb and more. It was usual to match dogs in the pit, pound for pound. Not many owners were stupid enough to allow a 24 lb dog to fight against one that was 6 lb heavier. Weight is telling in a contest that might last between half an hour and two hours. When dogs were evenly matched in weight and fighting skill some fights went on for much longer, and matches lasting six hours have been reported, although these were rare. It must be remembered, too, that dogs were fought at 'fighting weight'. This meant bringing them down to iron-hard condition, no spare fat and with their ribs showing. A show dog such as we know today at perhaps 40 lb could be pared down in this way to about 31 lb, and in this condition he would be not only fit to fight, but ready, too. Of course, the real old-timers in the Black Country, one or two of them alive today, knew how to bring their dogs into superb 'nick', as they say. Sometimes this meant feeding the dog on prime raw beef while the family made do with offal. Large bets were made on the dogs, £200 a side not being an unusual wager. The dogs changed hands a lot, especially if they lost their owners' money. They were lucky in such cases to live, for losing dogs, like dogs that lacked gameness, were not wanted on the scene. Either they were left to the mercy of a winning adversary or, with a brick for company, put into a sack and flung into the canal.

Dog-fighting had its own rules and regulations, which were adhered to rigidly, although one or two of the northern counties adopted their own interpretation of procedure. The rules were maintained for well over a hundred years, and the following form of agreement that was used is reproduced here for interest.

ARTICLES OF AGREEMENT

ARTICLES OF AGREEMENT made on the ______ day of ________ 18____ ________ agrees to fight his ______ dog ____ pounds weight against ______ dog ____ pounds weight, for £____ a side at ____ ______ on the ____ day of ______ 18____.

The dogs to be weighed at ____ o'clock in the ______ and fight between ______ o'clock in the ______.

The deposits to be made as in hereinafter mentioned; to be delivered to ____________ (who is to be the final Stakeholder), namely, the first deposit of £____ a side at the making of the match; the second deposit of £____ a side, on the ______ of ______ at the house of ____________; third deposit of £____ on the ____ of ______ at the house of __________; fourth deposit of £____ on the ______ of ______ at the house of __________; fifth deposit of £____ on the ______ of ______ at the house of __________; which is the last.

RULES

1. To be a fair fight ____ yards from the scratch.
2. Both dogs to be tasted before and after fighting if required.
3. Both dogs to be shewn fair to the scratch, and washed at their own corners.
4. Both seconds to deliver the dogs fair from the corner, and not leave until the dogs commence fighting.
5. A Referee to be chosen in the pit; one minute time to be allowed between every fair go away; fifty seconds allowed for sponging; and at the expiration of that time the timekeeper shall call 'Make Ready', and as soon as the minute is expired the dogs to be delivered, and the dog refusing or stopping on the way to be the loser.
6. Should either second pick up his dog in a mistake, he shall put it down immediately, by order of the Referee, or the money to be forfeited.
7. Should anything pernicious be found on either dog, before or after fighting in the pit, the backers of the dog so found to forfeit,

and the person holding the battle money, to give it up immediately when called upon to do so.

8. Referee to be chosen in the pit before fighting, whose decision in all cases to be final.
9. Either dog exceeding the stipulated weight on the day of weighing, to forfeit money deposited.
10. In any case of a dog being declared dead by the Referee, the living dog shall remain at him for ten minutes when he shall be taken to his corner if it be his turn to scratch, or if it be the dead dog's turn the fight shall be at end by order of the Referee.
11. In any case of Police interference the Referee to name the next place and time of fighting, on the same day if possible, and day by day until it be decided, but if no Referee be chosen, the Stakeholder to name the next place and time; but if a Referee has been chosen and then refuses to name the next place and time of fighting, or goes away after being disturbed, then the power of choosing the next time and place be left with the Stakeholder and a fresh Referee to be chosen in the pit, and the power of the former one be entirely gone.
12. In case of Police interference and the dogs have commenced fighting they will not be required to weigh any more; but if they have not commenced fighting they will have to weigh day by day at lb. until decided at the time and place named by the Referee, or if he refuses and goes away, then the Stakeholder has to name the time and place.
13. The seconder of either dog is upon no consideration to call his adversary's dog by name while in the pit, nor to use anything whatever in his hands with which to call off his dog.
14. To toss up the night before fighting for the place of fighting, between the hours of ____ and ____ o'clock at the house where the last deposit is made.
15. The above stakes are not to be given up until fairly won or lost by a fight, unless either party break the above agreement.
16. All deposits to be made between the hours of ____ and ____ o'clock at night.
17. Either party not following up or breaking the above agreements, to forfeit the money down.

____

____

WITNESSES ____________________ SIGNED ____________________

____________________ ____________________

The fights were staged in a regulation pit, an area—not necessarily bounded on all sides such as one sometimes sees in the old prints—across the centre of which was drawn a chalk line. This division was known as the 'scratch', and each contestant had to pass across this line in order to attack his adversary in the opposite corner. The old bare-knuckle pugilists had a similar system, and it may be from this word 'scratch' came the phrase 'come up to scratch' which we use today when we imply that a person has come forward to face up to his obligations. A famous dog-fighting pit was the Cock Pit, Duck Lane, Westminster, and middle nineteenth-century London abounded with these dens. Many matches were, of course, staged in private, pub cellars being a popular rendezvous, and in the old days, in the provinces, Walsall was notorious for the pastime. One oddity in the sport was the function of the taster, whose job, prior to the fight, was to go over the coat of every dog with his tongue. If anyone had doctored the coat of a dog with some such substance as tobacco water or alum that was likely to blister the mouth of his opponent, the taster would be able to detect it. For this unsavoury job he would receive the sum of a shilling for each fight. When the match was about to begin, the whole place would be shuttered and barred and no one would be allowed to leave until the fight was over. In the event of the police turning up, the organisers had handy a few rats and a good Terrier or two in order to effect a speedy change of scene into a harmless rat-killing contest.

The method of fighting with these dogs is interesting. Both dogs were 'played' in their respective corners by their seconds. One would be released and would be expected to go straight across the 'scratch' line to bring his opponent out of his corner. It was this rule that caused dissent between the Birmingham and Yorkshire factions of the game, for it allowed, in effect, a dead dog to win a fight. This might seem incomprehensible, but it is true: a dog might be disabled, even lying dead in his corner, with the other dog's turn to scratch. The living dog, maybe because he had had enough fighting, his courage was exhausted, or he was just too weak to move to the centre of the pit, just could not scratch over the chalk line. Due to this inability he became the loser. This was an old Birmingham rule and was not used in London and Yorkshire bouts. Any hesitation to scratch meant that a dog had lost his fight; a contestant only half-hearted in his urge to do battle might, for example, stop to lift his leg at the side of the pit. Such indifference to the job in hand was judged to be tantamount to cowardice, and cowards were dealt with very summarily in dog-fighting circles. However, the real ones knew how to fight. Pit dogs, if ever they became veterans at the game, developed great cunning. Some would let a newcomer almost eat them for several rounds, then turn and finish him off in a few minutes when he tired. Dogs had their own special tactics in battle: some preferred the head, others the throat; foolish and inexperienced battlers took a shoulder hold; the clever ones went for the legs. An opponent is not much good with a broken leg and if his stifle has been crushed his fight is as good as lost, for he is unable to push in against his tormentor.

A 'fair go away' is dog-fighting parlance used when the heads and forelegs of both contestants fall in opposite directions. This ends the round, and both dogs can be picked up by their seconds and returned to their corners to be sponged down — from the same bucket. The dog that 'goes away' first is the one obliged by the rules to come up to scratch in the following round, provided it is a fair pick-up by the seconds. Should it not be a fair pick-up, then each dog comes up to scratch alternately in subsequent rounds. At the pick-up, should one dog grab the other, as often happened, both have to be put down to continue the fight and the seconds have to wait for a 'fair go away' as before. If a dog 'turns' or loosens his hold to take breath, the seconds will take their dogs to the corners. One minute is allowed between rounds, and when the timekeeper calls 'let go', the dog due to scratch is expected to leave his corner immediately or he loses his match.

No one makes the real Staffordshire Bull Terrier fight. The pit dogs of those days wanted to fight because the urge was bred deep in them. Maybe the owners, who encouraged them to do battle, were at fault, especially as the game was tied up with heavy wagering. Unfortunately, from the mid-1980s, this unhealthy sport has recrudesced in Britain and organised dog-fights are reported frequently by the media. Such activities are viewed with grave concern by the public and Government alike. Every effort is being made by the RSPCA to stamp it out and punish the offenders.

Ratting

The use of a small Bulldog or Bull-and-Terrier for killing rats in a pit was classed as a permissible, even a legitimate, sport or fancy up to 1912. In that year, however, the RSPCA successfully prosecuted a notorious Leicester rat-pit owner, and the pastime was driven underground, much to the chagrin of its followers who claimed that not only was this the last remaining 'poor man's' sport, but that Bull Terrier temperament would suffer with its going.

One can hardly argue that the Victorian method of throwing scores of rats into a four-sided pit at the mercy of a 'live-wire' Bulldog or Bull Terrier possessed even the rudiments of humanitarianism. A well-trained dog would pick the rodents up one by one in rapid succession, breaking their backs with a series of nips, dozens being destroyed within a few moments. Dogs who lacked speed or carried a kill round in their mouths were unpopular, for wagers were won or lost according to the greatest number of rats killed in the fewest minutes. Celebrated canines like Billy, in 1823, despatched 100 rats in five minutes; one dog called Jacko was noted for his marathon performance at which he killed a thousand rats in one hour forty minutes. Dogs, which averaged about 12 lb in weight and, from the old prints, looked like miniature Staffords or Black-and-Tan Terriers, but often went under the name of Bulldogs, were frequently bitten on the lips by rats. It is reported that many died from a 'cancer' contracted thereby. Even the handlers had to make sure their trousers bottoms were tied-up before they entered the rat-pit in case the creatures ran up their legs.

Henry Mayhew, in *London's Labour, London's Poor*, 1851, and Augustus Mayhew, in his contemporary novel *Paved with Gold*, 1858, wrote vivid accounts of the rat-killing matches of the period. These affairs were attended not only by the rougher elements in the town, but by titled people, too. The rats, when released from traps or sack, would pile themselves up into a mound in one corner of the pit. A popular way of dispersing the mound before the dog entered the pit was to blow on them, which some spectators did to amuse themselves. However, as soon as the dog was thrown in he would rush straight for the pile of rats and thrust his head right into it, extracting and killing one after the other. Soon the horde of rodents would be rushing about trying without success to escape the Bull Terrier's champing jaws. Soon, all would be dead. Occasionally, ferrets were used instead of dogs, but it was said that some of these so-called ratting contests were staged solely as a cloak for the more nefarious sports of dog-fighting and badger-drawing.

Badger-drawing

This was a decidedly unpleasant diversion, and it is believed that clandestine badger matches are not entirely unknown even today. The badger comes off very badly in these events, nor can anyone envy the dogs. It is a great test for gameness in dogs, and many a well-thought-of dog has disgraced himself by refusing to face up to a fearless badger.

The procedure in badger-drawing was to catch a wild badger and house him in a box or crate about 2 ft square. The top of the box was either lidded or roofed with wire netting. Attached to one side of the box was a tunnel, usually made of wood, of varying lengths up to perhaps 10 ft. A light was suspended over the netted roof, and the dog would be run down the tunnel at the badger. Once he reached the box he would try to grab the animal and draw him down the tunnel into the open. Meanwhile, the sadistic onlookers would be watching his progress through the top of the box and egging him on or making side bets on his chances. The badger is a very tough customer. Not only is his hide thick and almost impenetrable but, also, he is very hard and fast biting, able to inflict serious wounds on a dog, sometimes taking off a nose, as many a good Stafford has known to his cost. Unfortunately, because of his ability to deal harshly with a dog, he has been treated atrociously at times. It is said that some of the old 'sportsmen' would cut away the lower part of a badger's jaw to prevent his damaging a dog, or stake his tail to the ground to restrict his movements. With such treatment, and the continual drawing by fresh dogs, the badger stood very little chance and succumbed very quickly. Sadly, there were always plenty of replacements in the old days, and as a result this game mammal suffered a good deal of persecution. Today, because his natural domain is becoming restricted by developing towns, he is becoming increasingly rare.

Other baitings

Although records exist to tell us that all manner of animals were baited by dogs in the old days, events in which lions, tigers, and apes on horseback featured were rare. More frequent, perhaps, were matches staged between a Bull Terrier and a monkey. A noted contest of this description was held at the Westminster Pit between a dog of 20 lb (the property of a nobleman) and Jacco Maccacco, a celebrated fighting monkey who beat many good fighting dogs in his day. It is said that at one of his contests a ringside watcher handed the ape a metal rod with which he immediately belaboured his surprised opponent. The monkey was said to be so fierce that even his owner had to protect his legs by keeping a shield of sheet metal between himself and the animal.

Appearance in art

Although early artists devoted much of their time to dogs, delineation was, in the main, restricted to animals owned by famous people of their day. Nevertheless, some attention was given to the forbears of the Staffordshire Bull Terrier. The nineteenth century holds for us the richest store of Bulldog and Bull Terrier art from which to draw our impressions, probably the most famous picture being 'Crib and Rosa', painted by Abraham Cooper, RA, about 1816. It shows two fine specimens in piebald coat, described as Bulldogs, but which apart from their distinct laybacks could be taken for early Staffordshire Bull Terriers. 'Rosa', particularly, has the outline, pump-handle tail and stance of a Stafford, and yet both she and 'Crib' were closely referred to by the people who formulated the Bulldog Standard. Other animal painters were George Townley Stubbs, RA, who did a wonderful painting in oils of a brindle and white Bull Terrier in 1812, and H. B. Chalon, who painted the memorable Wasp, Child, and Billy group at about the same time. Unfortunately, nearly all the good subjects available seem to have been described as Bulldogs. That they were, we cannot dispute, for generally their names can be found in Jackson and Bowers' *Bulldog Pedigrees*, 1892–8, described as 'A List of All Known Bulldogs and their Reputed Ancestors'. However, as we have suggested elsewhere, Bulldogs and Bull-and-Terrier sorts lived side by side in the vital period of their emancipations, and it is doubtful if even doggy folk then knew or cared very much about true nomenclature. Be this as it may, Staffordshire Bull Terrier people have to be content with art that featured these ferocious-looking Bull-types, purported to be Bulldogs, but which may just as easily have been ancestors of the Stafford. Other artists who have depicted the Bull Terrier include James Ward, Ben Marshall, and the Wolstenholmes, not forgetting engravers like John Scott, Cruikshank, J. Clark, and William Ward, who was Engraver Extraordinary to HRH the Prince of Wales and Duke of York. The best known of bull-, bear- and badger-baiting studies come from Henry Alken's work, and the coloured aquatint engravings of J. Clark. The pictures appeared in Henry Alken's *National Sports of Great Britain*, 1820.

In literature

The back numbers of *The Sporting Magazine* contain many references to the sporting Bulldog or Bull Terrier types that lived in the years that immediately preceded and followed 1800. Among them we can read about Lord Camelford's fighting dog Trusty, a fawn or fallow specimen with Chippendale legs noted for his 'fifty pitched battles', also of Bulldog and monkey fights, and much about baitings and rat-killing. Other publications of the day such as *Sporting Anecdotes*, 1804, similarly illuminated London and national life in those days.

We learn a lot of the Bull Terrier from Pierce Egan. He lived

Ch. Hurricane of Judael and daughter Hurricane Freya

Ian Tully

Ch. Reckless Lass

Courtesy George Ainscough

'A Bull-and-Terrier', painting by James Ward, 1820.
Note closely cropped ears

Courtesy F. Potts

'Billy, Rose and Tumbler', the property of F. Redmond.
Old English Bulldogs, ancestors of the Stafford

Courtesy Gerald Massey

'Jem Burns' Four Pets'. The kennel boy, Jack Shepherd, and the Bulldogs, Duchess, Cribb and Ball. From an original oil painting by T. Clayton, 1843

Historic Dog Features

'The Bull and Mastiff', after Howitt by Dubourg, 1813

Historic Dog Features

The Bulldog of 1798, by Howitt

Historic Dog Features

Dog-fighting. From the original hard ground etching by Henry Alken, *c.* 1820

and wrote in the sporting age that comprised the first few decades of the last century. His *Sporting Anecdotes*, 1820, covers all the 'manly' sports from archery to cock-fighting, with records of dog-fights in the notorious Amphitheatre (or Cock Pit), Duck Lane, Westminster and other haunts. Many celebrated dogs are mentioned, and in *Life in London*, 1821, there are some wonderful coloured plates by I. R. and G. Cruikshank. Later, in 1822, when he wrote in *Annals of Sporting*, the 'Bull-Terrier' was mentioned for what is believed to be the first time. Captain Thomas Brown's contribution to the Bull Terrier by according it a paragraph to itself in his *Biographical Sketches and Authentic Anecdotes of Dogs*, 1829, published in Scotland, is recorded in Chapter 2, but Jesse in his *Researches into the History of the British Dog*, 1866, and his somewhat earlier *Anecdotes of Dogs*, 1846, are valuable to the Bull Terrier student, as is James Watson's *Dog Book*, 1906. In *Dogs*, 1840, by C. H. Smith, a coloured plate of a Bull-and-Terrier appears, probably the first of its kind.

Elizabethan authors such as Blount, Nichols, Holinshed, Stow, and the German Hentzner, as well as Pepys, are worthy of study at least for the bloodsports of their day, vivid pictures being drawn from their writings. Strutt in his *Sports and Pastimes of the People of England*, 1801, and Hackwood who wrote, a century later, his *Old English Sports*, 1907, reveal the atrocities of the era in which the Bull Terrier played, through no fault of his own, such an inglorious part.

More recent contributions to the field include the valuable books and booklets of Mr Joseph Dunn, and Count V. C. Hollender's *Staffordshire Bull Terriers*, 1952. Mr H. N. Beilby's *Staffordshire Bull Terriers*, 1943, was published at a time when the breed was just beginning to make its mark on public fancy, and Jack Barnard's various booklets on the breed are still sought after. The author's own title *The Staffordshire Bull Terrier Handbook*, 1951, was reprinted, then revised to satisfy the demand for breed information, and his other titles *Staffordshire Bull Terriers*, 1964, and *The Staffordshire Bull Terrier Owner's Encyclopaedia*, 1967, have been produced meanwhile. George Armitage's *Thirty Years with Fighting Dogs*, 1935, is now out of print, but those who have read it found it fascinating, although perhaps a little stark.

2
The 'New Breed'

No one knows really how the Staffordshire was 'manufactured' or produced. One can only surmise, for the dog days of the early nineteenth century were clouded with indifference to such matters, things like pedigrees and mating records being non-existent, as far as we know. Sporting writers of those days gave the clue to crossings having taken place between Bulldogs and Terriers by their use of the name Bull Terrier. The first to mention the dog by this name was Pierce Egan, in *Annals of Sporting* (Vol. 1), 1822. He says: 'The true bred Bulldog is but a dull companion and the Terrier does not flash much size, nor is sufficiently smart or cocking—the modern mixed dog includes all of these qualities and is of a pleasant airy temper.' Later in his *Biographical Sketches and Authentic Anecdotes of Dogs*, 1829, Captain Thomas Brown gave the Bull Terrier a chapter to himself.

What we cannot disregard when considering the Staffordshire Bull Terrier's evolution is the existence then of Bulldogs that looked like present-day Staffords. For example, look at Billy, whom most readers know as the famous rat-killing dog of 1823. He is purported to have despatched 100 rats in five-and-a-half minutes, an all-time record, no doubt. This dog is stated to be a Bulldog on the original aquatint engraving in the author's possession, and even details of his breeding appear in the legend. But was he a Bulldog in name only just because in those days people in the game were casual in their nomenclature? It seems extremely likely that dogs like Billy, and even C. C. Stockdale's Top who lived about thirty years later, lie on a direct line of ancestry to the modern Staffordshire Bull Terrier, being developed as Bulldogs on lighter, perhaps rangier style than present-day Bulldog fanciers would accept, but acceptable enough to the dog-fighting fraternity whose needs were for a more athletic variety. These sorts developed eventually, not only on their Bulldog line but also in conjunction with the Bulldog-Terrier cross-breeds of the century, to form the dog we accept today as the Staffordshire Bull Terrier. This dog emerged into the twentieth century with an unsavoury reputation for fighting and violence, which was not redeemed much by the 'sportsmen' who kept the game going with dog-fight matches in barns and pub cellars, even into the middle 'thirties. The Staffordshire Bull Terrier was unfortunate that his kind became associated with ruffians and people who cared little for him as a dog, owning him, instead, for what he could win for them by fighting. It took a long time for him to become free of stigma, meanwhile his cousin, the sleek, streamlined white English Bull Terrier, evolved by Hinks in the middle nineteenth century, had secured a firm foot-hold, not only as a stylish and elegant breed with Corinthian flavour, but in the show ring. The Bulldog proper had long since made its own niche in exhibitors' preference. The 'pushed-in' face of Elizabethan days, generally considered to be the real Bulldog, was 'cornered' by enthusiasts and developed into the show Bulldog we know today. A lot of the extreme ferocity possessed by the breed was bred out and, unfortunately, a good deal of exaggeration of physical points was bred in, to the Bulldog's disadvantage, no doubt. One could hardly imagine the present-day dog doing a job of work in the pit or roughing-up his traditional adversary, the bull. But we are not much concerned with Bulldog evolution here, other than its contribution to the making of our own breed, the Staffordshire Bull Terrier.

We believe, then, that the breed is the result of Stafford-like Bulldogs being bred on more Terrier-like lines, also from factual crosses between the Old English Bulldog and various Terrier breeds; and that these two sources would have fused some decades before the turn of the twentieth century and produced a fighting Bull Terrier breed that went under a variety of names including Brindle Bull, Pit Bull Terrier, Pit Dog, and so on.

His emancipation

Most of our dog's fighting career took place in the Black Country. The chainmakers and miners were very partial to the breed, for apart from the occasional match that won or lost them a few pounds, they admired its fearless and pugilistic temperament. These men took their dogs to the foundries, chaining them to posts while they worked at the furnaces. Lunchtime would mean boasting of a dog's prowess in the pit, and many a working break would be enlivened with an impromptu match. This was the fighting Bull Terrier's life up to the early 1930s. No one ever visualised him as a show dog or a dog to be bred for anything other than fighting ability. The fact that certain factions believed that he should be bred for 'beauty', which is no more than another word for type, in dogdom, seemed to the majority incomprehensible, and even insulting to a breed with such a warlike heritage from the past. However, dog-showing was beginning to make heavy impact on the community: some people saw the commercial opportunities, others were more earnest in their endeavours to benefit the breed. Dogs, generally, were being improved and 'beautified' around this period, seldom-seen varieties like the Boxer were being campaigned at the shows and it is small wonder that the Black Country lovers of the Stafford wanted to give him his opportunity too.

To Mr Joseph Dunn of Cradley Heath should go much of the credit for putting the Staffordshire Bull Terrier 'on the map'. His pioneer work and that of his associates started about 1932. At first, he suffered a good deal of derision from the fighting pit-dog cliques, but determined to see his project through successfully he persisted with the Kennel Club until he obtained permission to include the breed in the Any Variety Terrier Class of a four-class Exemption Show, held at Cradley Heath in the spring of 1935. The late Fred Holden (Freden) judged, with authorisation to award four placings to our breed regardless of the official placings in the Terrier Class. In an atmosphere of intense interest, for breed history was being made that day, from twenty-six exhibits present the following placings were made:

1. Birch's Monty (later renamed Vindictive Monty)
2. Shaw's Jim (later renamed Jim the Dandy)
3. Pegg's Joe (later renamed Fearless Joe)
4. Mallen's Cross Guns Johnson

Nos 2 and 3 above were later used as typical examples of the breed to weave the breed Standard. Nearly all the other dogs and bitches present formed the nucleus of our present-day breeding.

The name?

During 1935 a good deal of argument took place about the name of the breed. The name 'Bull Terrier' was already taken by the owners of the white and coloured varieties of today. That these varieties were first in the field of show work and breeding there can be no denial. That the breed should be given the name of Bull Terrier is understandable, but that their owners should object to the use of the word 'Bull' when the name Staffordshire Bull Terrier was put forward is not. However, in July 1935, with Kennel Club approval, the Staffordshire Bull Terrier Club was formed for the purpose of holding shows and sponsoring the breed. Because its founders knew their dog was the *original* Bull Terrier, and therefore traditionally entitled to the name, at least, they refuted any move to prevent the use of its rightful title. The county name of Staffordshire is now a source of pride to owners, many of whom enjoy an occasional trip to the outskirts of Birmingham where, in places like Cradley Heath and Quarry Bank, they can meet breed old-timers with a good selection of Staffords of ferocious aspect upon which to feast their eyes. There they get the atmosphere of their chosen breed, so steeped in English tradition.

The first breed club

The Staffordshire Bull Terrier Club was proud to have as its president the late Jack Barnard (Chestonion), new owner of Jim the Dandy. Jack was a good friend of the author and his death in 1959 was a sad loss. Mr Maurice Smith was the club's first chairman, and Mr Joe Dunn its honorary secretary. Joe Dunn was later responsible for introducing the author to the breed, and his opinion on Staffordshire Bull Terriers and breed matters is considered unchallengeable and unique. Mr Dunn guided the club efficiently for seven years, when the post was taken over by Mr Matthew Weaver. It is interesting to record the names on the first committee. They were: Harry Pegg (owner of Fearless Joe, also Dee's Pegg, dam of Ch. Fearless Red of Bandits), Joe Mallen (owner of Ch. Gentleman Jim, Cross Guns Johnson, Good Lad, and The Great Bomber), Jack Birch (Vindictive Monty), S. W. Poole (Lassomine), A. Forrest (Dinkie), C. Grosvenor (Lady Rose), G. Williams (Lestom Boy and Brindle Thelma), Miss M. Hill and Mr Maurice Smith. Club members, too, comprised people who made their mark on the breed in the years to come. People like Jack Dunn (Triton Judy, dam of Jim), B. Hardwicke (Cinderbank Beauty), A. Slater (Annie's Pal), A. Griffiths (Ardblaster), H. Boxley (Vindictive Montyson), Horace Priest (Nance the Fearless and Dee's Pegg), also Messrs T. B. Bishop, G. A. Dudley (Wychbury), A. Foxall, S. Grew, F. W. Holden (Freden), L. E. Homer, H. Hough, W. Shakespeare, F. Silvers and J. W. Wood, with many others, put the Stafford on the right path in its early days.

Mr Phil Dee followed Jack Barnard to the presidency of the club. Like Arthur Heald of Horton, who wrote, in 1934, the privately circulated treatise on the breed, *Make Ready*; Mike de Courcy Boxill and Lew Prince of Kensington all were reminiscent of Corinthian sporting bucks from the pages of Pierce Egan. They enjoyed sport with Staffords, preferring the small ones of about 25 lb weight. Dee himself was keen on badger- digging and could recount many exploits where the Stafford often came off second-best, for Brock is no mean adversary when he is fit and on his own ground. Some grand dogs have been killed at or died following these 'digs', and the noted Fearless Joe was one. The sport is not indulged in much these days, in Britain at least, although it has its participants in Ireland where they like a good sporting dog properly qualified in the field.

Mr Harry Melling was the next president. He died young, but his memory and that of the dogs he owned, Lioness and the

Westall-bred Tough Guy, winner of a challenge certificate, remain. The position was then filled by Mr H. N. Beilby, BSc, who owned the celebrated c.c. winner Tackle. Mr Beilby's book *The Staffordshire Bull Terrier*, 1943, was the first cloth-bound breed monograph and did much to instruct early enthusiasts. Following him came Mr H. Meldrum and Mr G. H. (Snowy) Dunn, who held office up to 1946.

The club held its initial meetings at Joe Mallen's pub, the Old Cross Guns, Cradley Heath. This pub name was later to become Joe's official affix. The hostelry itself was famous for its breed atmosphere. Old and interesting pictures adorned the walls and appeared at times from Joe's inside pockets. He was a mine of information, sometimes had a macabre turn of humour, and he had a wonderful warmth of friendship for breed people, for whom his house was always open. The loss of his wife Lily in February 1968 was a severe blow to him and a loss to the breed by which she was greatly respected. Joe Mallen was a chainmaker, standing well over six feet. He could wield a hammer that few could lift and, apart from running the pub, he lived in a world of fighting dogs, fighting cocks, and testy badgers! He owned many good Staffords, none so famous as Ch. Gentleman Jim, the first dog champion in the breed. This dog (born 1937, died 1947) sired many champions. He is the popular 'maker' of the M-Line, completely outshining other sons of Brindle Mick who, in effect gave the initial of *his* name to the Line.

Making the Standard

Making the Standard was one of the first duties that fell to the SBTC. It was gone into thoroughly by a body of experts, men with years of experience and ownership in the breed. Two good current dogs were set up as excellent examples of the breed. They were Harry Pegg's Joe (Fearless Joe) and Mrs J. Shaw's Jim (Jim the Dandy), the former a fawn, the latter a brindle. Their anatomy and structural points were examined, and a lot of old sketches, prints and photographs discussed. It will be understood that in any breed, provided a number of examples are available, some features will be more or less uniform or common to the majority. Assuming that these characteristics are sound ones they can then be accepted as being typical of the breed. Some difficulties were at first experienced in the discussions, for a wide range of types and sizes existed in Staffords in those days. It was natural that those who owned the big bulldoggy types claimed theirs were the right type, while those with the long-muzzled lightweights supported theirs. It needed a lot of tact and discretion on the part of club officials to convince these enthusiasts who was right and who was wrong, while still retaining their interest, to say nothing of their memberships. Clearly, the Stafford as a fighting dog had natural physical attributes expected of a combatant canine. Where these were found common to a number of dogs they were accepted as desiderata in the breed, and eventually a Standard was formulated and passed to the Kennel Club for approval. For some time argument was rife in Staffordshire towns like Walsall, Darlaston, and Cradley Heath, each of which had different ideas as to what constituted a good Stafford. However, as their opinion in the main of a good Stafford was one that fought and won, they were hardly qualified to pass worthwhile comment of any kind on what constituted a good type for exhibition.

Family connections—old and 'new'

The Blue Paul

This was a breed domiciled in Scotland for most of the nineteenth century, the last-known specimen being exhibited by a Mr James B. Morrison of Greenock in 1889. It was used mostly for fighting on the west coast and around Glasgow. Some important bouts were staged in the middle 'sixties, the Scottish gipsies and tinkers being keen followers of the sport. The Blue Paul was believed to have taken its name from the pirate Paul Jones, who is credited with having introduced the breed from abroad. However, this is unconfirmed, although rarely seen pictures of the dog resemble a certain type of Spanish Bulldog. Clearly, the breed has the conformation of a Stafford, but it was much larger, running to at least 60 lb in weight. That it had some common link in ancestry with the

Stafford there can be no doubt, but its colour was blue, similar to that seen in some Greyhounds. Unfortunately, the breed is now extinct, although its colour sometimes appears in modern litters, suggesting that the Blue Paul and the Staffordshire Bull Terrier were interbred as well as matched when heavyweight bouts were held.

The Bull Terrier

The white English Bull Terrier was evolved by the noted Birmingham dog breeder James Hinks, being introduced to the dog fancy early in the 1850s. Hinks had experimented for some years previously, and although his 'secret' in making this smart new breed has never been authenticated, it is believed that the old-type Bull Terrier (now the Staffordshire) was used in crossings with the Old English White Terrier, now extinct, and possibly with infusions of Dalmatian. The Bull Terrier was bred and developed solely as a show dog, as he is today, although Hinks was able on occasions to prove his new breed lacked nothing in gameness. Unfortunately for Staffordshire fanciers in later years, it was able to claim by its prior establishment as a show dog the name 'Bull Terrier', which some of our pioneers would have preferred as their breed's denomination.

The Coloured Bull Terrier

This breed, apart from its colours, which resemble the various coats found in the Staffordshire Bull Terrier, is more or less identical in type and shape to the Bull Terrier. The variety was formed in the first decade of the present century by crossing back the white Bull Terrier to his progenitor the Staffordshire.

Both Bull Terrier varieties are larger and heavier than the Stafford. There are other differences, too, the major one being in the cast and style of the head. The Bull Terriers have been bred for streamlined head and downface, erect ears, triangular-shaped eyes, and flat cheeks, their gait also being quite distinct from that of the Stafford.

There is a small counterpart of the coloured form known as

CHART SHOWING THE EVOLUTION OF THE STAFFORDSHIRE BULL TERRIER AND ALLIED BREEDS

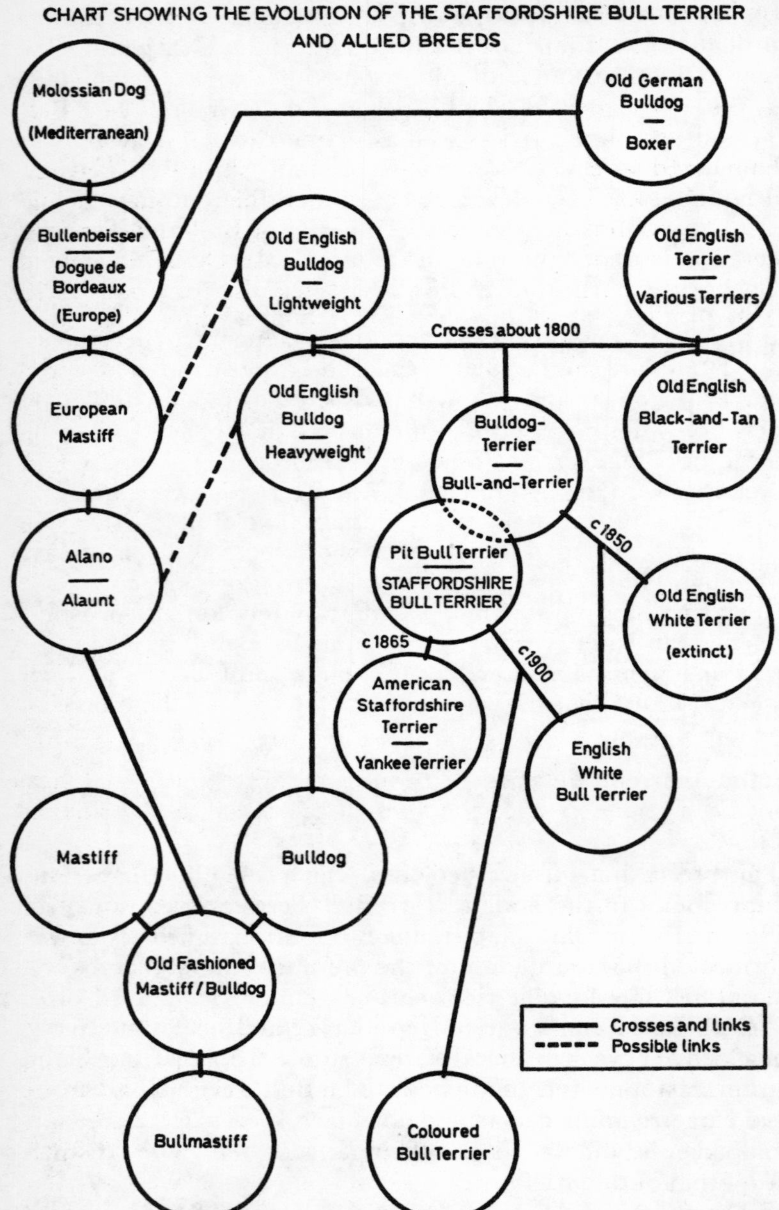

the Miniature Bull Terrier, a breed achieving some popularity in Britain today.

The Staffordshire Terrier of America

This breed is related closely to the Staffordshire Bull Terrier, although it has been developed on rather different lines, being 15 to 25 pounds heavier. Early imports of Bull-and-Terriers were made about the time of the American Civil War when 'Cockney' Charlie Lloyd took over a number of English Pit Dogs in 1865. These included the famous Paddy, Pilot, and Rafferty which, with others, were interbred with Bull Terrier types already in the States. At first these dogs were called Pit Bull Terriers and Pit Dogs, being almost entirely in the hands of the sporting fraternity and used for fighting. Later they became known as American Pit Bull Terriers, and even today the United Kennel Club in Kalamazoo registers dogs under this name. Then, thanks to Captain Will Judy, the publisher, the dog became known as the Yankee Terrier, prior to the present denomination of Staffordshire Terrier being accepted by the American Kennel Club in late 1936.

Some wonderful sporting strains exist and are maintained along the lines of our old Pit Dogs. In the show-bench world the Staffordshire Terrier becomes increasingly popular. It is a handsome breed, shown mostly with cropped ears. Its Standard (reproduced here by permission of the AKC) has not been changed since the start of the breed, and reads as follows:

General impression: The Staffordshire Terrier should give the impression of great strength for his size; a well-put-together dog, muscular, but agile and graceful, keenly alive to his surroundings. He should be stocky but not longlegged or racy in outline. His courage is proverbial.

Head: Medium length, deep through, broad skull, very pronounced cheek muscles, distinct stop; and ears are set high.

Ears: Cropped or uncropped, the latter preferred. Uncropped ears should be short and held half-rose or prick. Full drop to be penalised.

Eyes: Dark and round, low down in skull and set far apart. No pink eyelids.

Muzzle: Medium length, rounded on upper side to fall away abruptly below eyes. Jaws well defined. Under jaw to be strong and have biting power. Lips close and even, no looseness. Upper teeth to meet tightly outside lower teeth in front. Nose definitely black.

Neck: Heavy, slightly arched, tapering from shoulders to back of skull. No looseness of skin. Medium length.

Shoulders: Strong and muscular with blades wide and sloping.

Back: Fairly short. Slight sloping from withers to rump with gentle short slope at rump to base of tail. Loins slightly tucked.

Body: Well-sprung ribs, deep in rear. All ribs close together. Forelegs set rather wide apart to permit chest development. Chest deep and broad.

Tail: Short in comparison to size, low set, tapering to a fine point; not curled or held over back. Not docked.

Legs: The front legs should be straight, large or round bones, pasterns upright. No semblance of bend in front. Hindquarters well muscled, let down at hocks, turning neither in nor out. Feet of moderate size, well arched and compact. Gait must be springy but without roll or pace.

Coat: short, close, stiff to touch, and glossy.

Colour: Any colour, solid, parti, or patched is permissible, but all white, more than 80 per cent white, black-and-tan, and liver not to be encouraged.

Size: Height and weight should be in proportion. A height of about 18 to 19 in. at shoulder for the male and 17 to 18 in. for the female is to be considered preferable.

Faults: Faults to be penalised are Dudley nose, light or pink eyes, tail too long or badly carried, undershot or overshot mouths.

3

The Standard

The original Standard of the Staffordshire Bull Terrier up to 1987 is reproduced by kind permission of the Kennel Club.

Characteristics: From the past history of the Staffordshire Bull Terrier the modern dog draws his character of indomitable courage, high intelligence, and tenacity. This, coupled with his affection for his friends, and children in particular, his off-duty quietness, and trustworthy stability makes him the foremost all-purpose dog.

General appearance: The Staffordshire Bull Terrier is a smooth-coated dog. He should be of great strength for his size and, although muscular, should be active and agile.

Head and skull: Short, deep through, broad skull, very pronounced cheek muscles, distinct stop, short foreface, black nose.

Eyes: Dark preferable, but may bear some relation to coat colour. Round, of medium size, and set to look straight ahead.

Ears: Rose or half-pricked and not large. Full drop or prick to be penalised.

Mouth: The mouth should be level, i.e. the incisors of the bottom jaw should fit closely inside the incisors of the top jaw, and the lips should be tight and clean. The badly undershot or overshot mouth to be heavily penalised.

Neck: Muscular, rather short, clean in outline and gradually widening towards the shoulders.

Forequarters: Legs straight and well boned, set rather wide apart, without looseness at the shoulders, and showing no weakness at the pasterns, from which point the feet turn out a little.

Body: The body should be close-coupled, with a level topline wide front, deep brisket, well-sprung ribs, and rather light in the loins.

Hindquarters: The hindquarters should be well muscled, hocks let down with stifles well bent. Legs should be parallel when viewed from behind.

Feet: The feet should be well padded, strong, and of medium size.

Tail: The tail should be of medium length, low set, tapering to a point and carried rather low. It should not curl much, and may be likened to an old-fashioned pump handle.

Coat: Smooth, short, and close to the skin.

Colour: Red, fawn, white, black or blue, or any of these colours with white. Black-and-tan or liver colour not to be encouraged.

Weight and size: Weight: dogs, 28 to 38 lb. Bitches, 24 to 34 lb. Height (at shoulder), 14 to 16 in., these heights being related to the weights.

Faults: To be penalised in accordance with the severity of the faults: Light eyes or pink eye-rims. Tail too long or badly curled. Non-conformation to the limits of weight or height. Full drop and prick ears. Undershot or overshot mouths. The following faults should debar a dog from winning any prize: Pink (Dudley) nose. Badly undershot or overshot mouth. Badly undershot—where the lower jaw protrudes to such an extent that the incisors of the lower jaw do not touch those of the upper jaw. Badly overshot—where the upper jaw protrudes to such an extent that the incisors of the upper jaw do not touch those of the lower jaw.

Note: Male animals should have two apparently normal testicles fully descended into the scrotum.

The foregoing is the Standard by which Staffordshire Bull Terriers were judged. It is not the first breed Standard the pioneers drew up in the 1930s but, in the main, there are only minor variations between the two. The amendments were made at a meeting of the delegates from the breed clubs on 9th October 1948, in Wolverhampton. This convention was arranged by the now defunct Staffordshire Bull Terrier Clubs Advisory Council and its findings were approved by the Kennel Club in 1949 and ratified by that body in January 1950. The amendments are tabulated below and it will be seen how they compare with the phrasing of the original document.

Point	1935 *Standard*	1948 *Standard*	*Comment*
Eyes	Dark	Dark, but may bear some relation to coat colour.	Probably allows too much freedom of interpretation.
Ears	Prick ears acceptable, but no size for ears mentioned.	Prick ears to be penalised. Ears should be small, neat and tidy.	A good and progressive amendment.
Colour		Blue coat is added.	Breed people generally require more information about Blues.
Height	15 to 18 in.	14 to 16 in.	Has helped to get better balanced specimens.
Mouth and Nose	Penalised badly undershot and badly overshot mouths, also the Dudley nose.	Penalisation is amended to debarment from prize winning.	Progressive step, virtually allowing disqualification of specimens affected.

Further, in common with other breeds, the original Standard has an associated Scale of Points. These are detailed below if only for their 'antique' interest. The system of points is not generally approved today either officially or by the breed. Some novice judges have tried to use points when placing exhibits but most have foundered hopelessly with the method, which has no merit except as a rough guide. Alongside the 1935 Points have been entered the 1948 Points recommended by the Advisory Council. As far as is known, no one has ever employed them, although it is interesting to note how the breed, after thirteen years of exhibition life, began to show interest in movement and balance.

To understand the Standard and visualise the dog it describes it needs to be read and studied with a good dog standing near. If the breed Standard of the Staffordshire Bull Terrier were to be given to someone who had never set eyes on a Stafford and he was told to sketch what he pictured from the

Scale of Points	1935	1948
General appearance, coat and condition	15	10
Head	30	25
Neck	10	10
Body	25	25
Legs and feet	15	15
Tail	5	5
General movement and balance		10
Total	100	100

words, it is unlikely that the drawing would look anything like the dog we know, even if the man were a good artist. The Standard is intended as a guide only, and it has to be interpreted correctly if it is to prove useful. There is always talk in the breed about revising or modifying the Staffordshire Standard. No doubt the existing provisions do not suit everybody, but some owners seem inclined to set their dogs up as ideals and then shape the Standard to fit them instead of using the Standard to shape their dogs. Often, the demands for Standard revision includes alteration of the height and weight clause, for Staffordshire Bull Terriers are still inclined to turn up in a variety of sizes, although this tendency has diminished a lot recently, as compared with the early post-war years. In those days good ones from opposite ends of the scale turned up consistently, and although over-38-pounders were frowned upon, the classes for the lightweights of under 32 lb were quite well supported. Today the breeder aims conscientiously for dogs that 'fit' the Standard. Our Standard states its terms of reference quite clearly, having been prepared by breed experts who were fully aware what was wanted in a Stafford. The majority of breeders, comprising the backbone of the fancy, use this Standard as their *vade mecum* and base their efforts in producing good dogs on the description it imparts. By doing this they hope their aim at the target (which is the Standard) will prove a good one and will result in a home-bred champion. If someone alters the Standard or, in effect, moves the target suddenly to one side, the shot will go wide and the aimer or breeder will get disheartened and soon lose interest. Altering Standards, like changing boats in midstream, is a risky manoeuvre, and provided the working Standard is a good one and has proved itself a competent guide in the production of typical and sound Staffordshire Bull Terriers, it should not be altered merely to please a minority.

However, the opinion has been held for some time that breed Standards in all breeds needed tidying and trimming of superfluous description and the wording condensed. Thus in 1987, revised Standards (the Staffordshire Bull Terrier's among them) were issued by the Kennel Club. The following is the *current* breed Standard, reproduced by kind permission of the KC. Official copies are available at the Club's London address (see page 160) on payment of a nominal fee.

The 1987 Standard

General appearance: Smooth coated, well balanced, of great strength for his size. Muscular, active and agile.

Characteristics: Traditionally of indomitable courage and tenacity. Highly intelligent and affectionate especially with children.

Temperament: Bold, fearless and totally reliable.

Head and skull: Short, deep through with broad skull. Very pronounced cheek muscles, distinct stop, short foreface, nose black.

Eyes: Dark preferred but may bear some relation to coat colour. Round, of medium size, and set to look straight ahead. Eye rims dark.

Ears: Rose or half pricked, not large or heavy. Full drop or pricked ears highly undesirable.

Mouth: Lips tight and clean. Jaws strong, teeth large, with a perfect, regular and complete scissor bite, i.e. upper teeth closely overlapping the lower teeth and set square to the jaws.

Neck: Muscular, rather short, clean in outline gradually widening towards shoulders.

Forequarters: Legs straight and well boned, set rather wide apart, showing no weakness at the pasterns, from which point feet turn out a little. Shoulders well laid back with no looseness at elbow.

Body: Close coupled, with level topline, wide front, deep brisket, well sprung ribs; muscular and well defined.

Hindquarters: Well muscled, hocks well let down with stifles well bent. Legs parallel when viewed from behind.

Feet: Well padded, strong and of medium size. Nails black in solid coloured dogs.

Tail: Medium length, low set, tapering to a point and carried rather low. Should not curl much and may be likened to an old-fashioned pump handle.

Gait movement: Free, powerful and agile with economy of effort. Legs moving parallel when viewed from front or rear. Discernible drive from hindlegs.

Coat: Smooth, short and close.

Colour: Red, fawn, white, black or blue, or any one of these colours with white. Any shade of brindle or any shade of brindle with white. Black and tan or liver colour highly undesirable.

Size: Weight: Dogs 28 lb to 38 lb. Bitches 24 lb to 34 lb. Desirable height (at withers) 14 to 16 inches, these heights being related to the weights.

Faults: Any departure from the foregoing points should be considered a fault and the seriousness with which the fault should be regarded should be in exact proportion to its degree.

Note: Male animals should have two apparently normal testicles fully descended into the scrotum.

The Standard interpreted

It is best to accept the breed Standard simply as a template or pattern that defines in detail the perfect Staffordshire Bull Terrier. That such a paragon has not yet been born we are all aware, but what many may not know is that even the best dogs in the breed seldom, if ever, reach 75 per cent of the total requirements of the Standard. This means that the breed has still a long way to go before perfection is achieved.

The interpretation of the Standard, of course, often differs according to the individual enthusiast. No two people read the same novel and visualise its characters identically, and even with a semi-technical tabulation of virtues and faults like the Staffordshire Bull Terrier Standard there must occur variations of concept. It is important, therefore, that the people who administer the breed, meaning its breeders and judges, should be more or less in agreement as to the formula needed to picture the perfect specimen. There is little room for the faddists who approve diverse and extreme types as well as exaggerated physical features: nor is there room for the breeder who tries to shape the Standard to fit his dog rather than the reverse. Such rebels exist in every breed and need to be guarded against. The Stafford is an old variety as far as its history is concerned, but as a breed for show work it can claim not much more than thirty-five years. Little can be achieved in the way of uniformity in so short a time, which is probably less than twenty-five generations, quite apart from the fact that not much of the planning involved can be proved skilful or productive of superlative stock. Even today not many breeders could recite the Standard correctly—and they should be able to. The ideal state is that all conscientious breeders should be guided along the same path towards Staffordshire Bull Terrier perfection. That everyone should be expected to acquire the same mind's eye picture of the perfect Staffordshire is not feasible, but it is reasonable to expect the enthusiast to *understand* it when he reads and applies it to a first-class living model specimen of the breed. Such a dog should be of an excellence that cannot be denied because of the consistency of his top award-winning career under adjudicators whose knowledge and integrity are beyond question. Find such a dog and read the Standard as you survey him. Implant in your mind the words of the Standard as you examine the physical part or point the phrase defines. Absorb a mental picture of the excellence you look at with the written description that has been contrived to give you that understanding. Remember, though, it is not possible to word a Standard, even in our bountiful English language, so that its details will define precisely the perfect Stafford. Type for instance; this is virtually indefinable. Poise; you have to *see* it to know it is right. Personality, too; this becomes apparent only when it is displayed. No one can put these attributes into adequate words, yet all are essential to a Staffordshire Bull Terrier if he is to qualify as a top-flight example of his breed.

Most of the sections in the Standard have been interpreted in the section on Conformation, and a special part covers his character. However, some features remain to be discussed and these include the following.

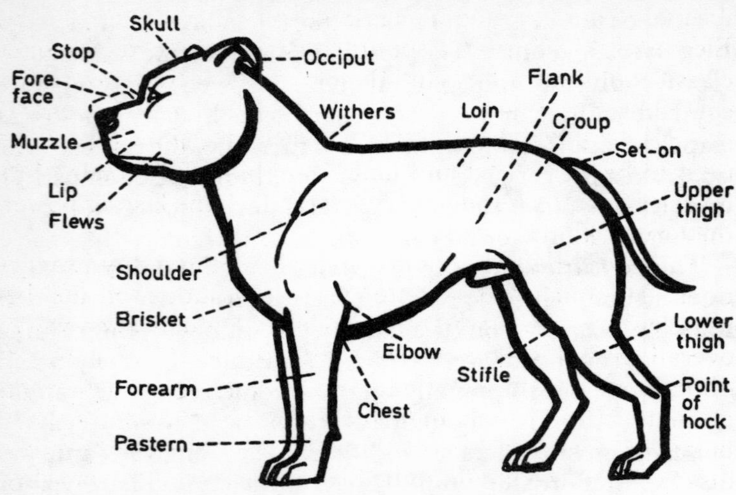

Figure 1 Points of the Staffordshire Bull Terrier

General appearance. The way the dog presents himself, in fact. Of course, he must have the basic attributes to look good to start with, and apart from well-formed physical features he must have *pedigree nobility.* To be really good, a Staffordshire Bull Terrier must have this; it encompasses Type, too, that quality essential to a dog if he is to represent the ideal example of his breed. Some people term this *quality.* It does not matter what it is called; if a dog has it, then it will stand out just as surely as one lacking it must fail in general appearance. Expression is important, too. A dog lacking correct breed outlook is usually one whose eyes are wrongly set in his head; maybe they are too small, too large, or wrong in colour. The Staffordshire Bull Terrier is a bold, fearless dog and his expression should conform thus. A 'varminty' expression is alien to the breed; this is for rough-coated and little earth-entering Terriers only. Eyes too light in colour spoil his expression. The eyes should be dark, such as the Standard prefers, and, frankly, the darker they are the better. If they have to bear some relation to coat colour, let them not stray too much towards lightness, for so often light-eyed dogs are shrewd rather than intelligent, and yellow eyes are not wanted. Bad expression can arise from indifferent health, too—any of these reasons could militate against his general appearance. Elegance is essential also; it comes from correct balance, classical outline, and sound deportment. Good bone structure contributes to this as does proper muscle distribution. The muscles on an athletic dog like the Staffordshire Bull Terrier need to be well toned and long, as opposed to bunchy, bulky muscles which, although very strong, lack the lasting power of the former kind.

To be well balanced, a dog must be without any exaggerations. He must have complete co-ordination of the body muscles to give him a natural, flowing action coupled with his overall conformation. His lateral, vertical, and horizontal dimensions should integrate to make a pleasing whole, so that no matter from which angle he is viewed he is seen to be well balanced. Even the Staffordshire Bull Terrier's head, which we discuss later and is said to be his major feature (it was always given most points when a Scale of Points existed), should not be exaggerated. Further, all components of the dog's physical make-up, his head, neck, shoulders, body, hindquarters, tail, feet, and foreparts, should be properly coupled. This means that they should fuse or flow into each other to produce a pleasing finished specimen. A dog can be the possessor of a wonderful head and body, yet the neck joins them together in an ugly, untidy fashion. His front and forequarters can well be ideal but the front feet might well seem those of another Stafford. Dogs so constructed are always unsound. They have no value in the breeding field, for the tendency to lack integration is transmittable. The degree of unsoundness will be shown when the animal moves. Some badly affected specimens, looking veritable pictures when standing or posed for exhibition, are revealed as hopelessly unsound as soon as they move, and although the impression of good general appearance might weigh well in a dog's favour initially, the importance of seeing him move both ways becomes obvious.

Ears. The Staffordshire Bull Terrier's ears, when correct, contribute substantially to his general appearance. Ears that are untidy, i.e. too large, neither up nor down, and 'flying', prove a disadvantage to the dog. The ideal ear formation is the rose shape. The ear should be small, thin, neatly made and folded back slightly to expose part of the inner 'burr'. The

Figure 2 Head profiles: (a) dish-faced; (b) down-faced, too long in muzzle; (c) weak underjaw; (d) strong foreface, short muzzle, typical

organ is carried to the side of the head, the tip falling back to rest, tucked away where the occiput joins with the neck's upper end. Ears so made and shaped, being small, accentuate the size of the Stafford head and skull, which is to be desired. Ears should respond readily to sound and coordinate at such times with expression, adding to an exhibit's general appearance by giving him vibrancy and verve.

Half-pricked ears are acceptable to the Standard, although they are viewed in most breed circles as 'second best'. Provided they are small they look all right, but heavily made examples look ugly, and the extreme form of tulip ear is no more than an unwanted heritage from the past. The extra thickness of cartilage where the ear sets on to the skull is responsible for semi-erect shape; in the old days it did not matter what the shape of the ears was—they just cropped them to suit the fashion demanded in the local dog pit. They cannot crop ears today because it is a criminal offence, so if rose ears are preferred to semi-erect or half-prick then the latter kind must be bred out. Full prick ears, such as the noted Iron Jack had in the pre-war years, are no longer acceptable, although, frankly, one seldom encounters them today.

Mouth. No one subject in Staffordshire Bull Terriers has provoked so much argument and ill-feeling as that of mouths. The Standard says the mouth should be level, that is, the incisors of the lower jaw should fit closely inside the incisors of

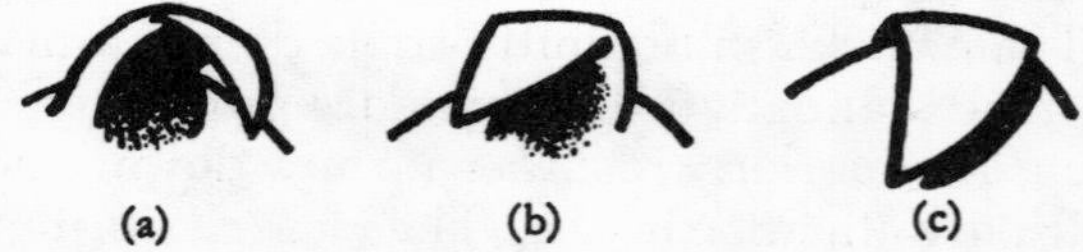

Figure 3 Ears: (a) rose shape, typical; (b) semi-erect, correct but second grade; (c) hound or button type

the top jaw, and the lips should be tight and clean. The badly undershot or overshot mouth has to be heavily penalised. A full complement of teeth is usually forty-two, although sometimes a particularly short-faced specimen will be found with forty-four. In the upper jaw there are six incisors, followed by two canines and four pre-molars and two molars on each side. The lower jaw is similarly furnished but with an extra molar on each side; the upper jaw contains twenty permanent teeth, the lower jaw twenty-two.

To assess mouth quality in a Stafford, his entire dentition should be examined, inspecting both teeth and gums. Any irregularity in formation or missing teeth should be penalised, for such a dog's biting efficiency is impaired, a serious matter in one bred for fighting. His teeth should be big, strong, and white. Small teeth in a Stafford are undesirable for they break easily and lack holding power.

It is inevitable that the undershot mouth will persist in the breed for generations to come. It is a legacy from the Old English Bulldog, progenitor of the Staffordshire Bull Terrier. The fact that undershot mouths are less frequently seen today than a decade ago suggests that breeders are mastering the fault, but meanwhile it must be remembered that no good dog should be damned merely because he lacks a perfect mouth. The undershot jaw, and other faulty mouths for that matter, should be penalised only in relation to the dog as a whole.

Sectional diagrams showing the various mouth formations to be encountered in Staffordshire Bull Terriers today, together with explanatory text, are reproduced here.

Colour. The breed Standard permits a wide range of coat colours; in fact, only black-and-tans and liver colour are undesirable. No one can be certain why these two coats are ostracised, but it is believed that black-and-tan especially, if allowed to persist in the breeding field, would speedily become the dominant coat. At this stage it is worth recording that the black-and-tan markings Stafford people do *not* want are those as found in the Manchester Terrier and its smaller counterpart, the English Toy Terrier. Most people know the breeds; they are jet black with rich mahogany tan on the muzzle to the nose, tan spots on the cheeks and above each eye. The underjaw and throat are tanned with a 'V' and tanning is seen on the

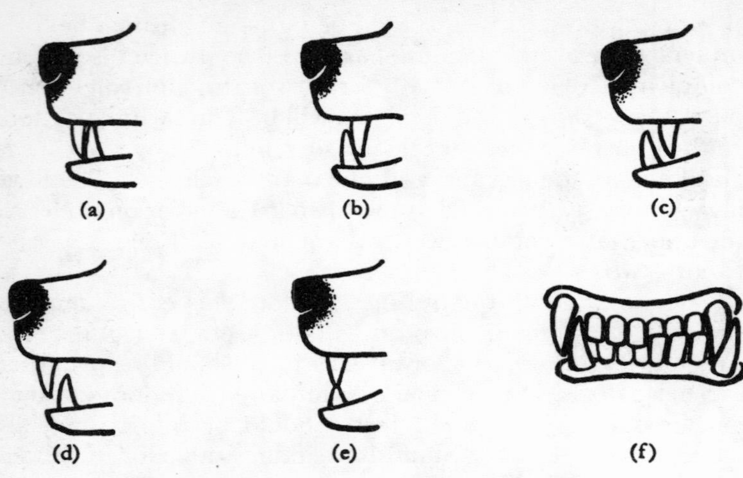

Figure 4 Mouths: (a) level or terrier mouth, correct. The six upper incisors project only *slightly* beyond those of the lower jaw, sitting closely over and on the latter and making a perfect scissor bite; (b) slightly undershot mouth, incorrect. In effect the exact reverse of (a), but lacks potency in battle as a dog strikes down and sideways to take hold, and he would secure inferior grip; (c) badly undershot mouth: seriously incorrect. The lower incisors jut out acutely beyond the upper ones with visible space between. Such a dog would be handicapped in taking hold, his bite would be more bruising than cutting, according to the degree of fault. Bad examples are often called 'grinners'; (d) badly overshot mouth, seriously incorrect. A very weak mouth, often associated with a snipey muzzle and sometimes referred to as 'pig-jaw'. In its moderate form, when upper teeth protrude only slightly, it is frequently unobserved and confirmed as a level mouth; (e) flush mouth, sometimes referred to as 'dead level' or 'even'. This is quite useless as it has no bite, no strength because it cannot intermesh scissor-wise. Unfortunately it is often 'allowed' by judges; (f) wry mouth: seriously incorrect. The incisors of the upper jaw meet crosswise with those of the lower jaw. Not only does it lack clean bite and efficient scissor action, but dentition becomes cracked and damaged after a few years

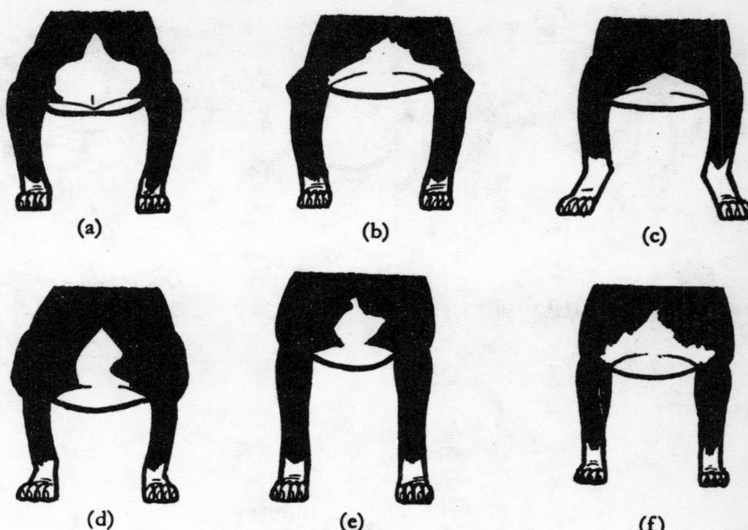

Figure 5 Fronts: (a) Bulldog front, loose shoulders; (b) out at elbows, the elbows point outwards; (c) poor bone, Chippendale effect, weak front; (d) overloaded at shoulders, light bone; (e) tight front, high on leg; (f) good sturdy front, slight turn-out at pasterns typical

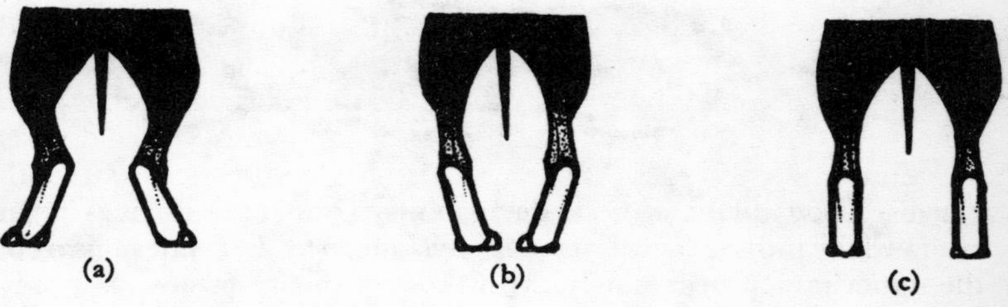

Figure 6 Hindquarters: (a) cow-hocks; (b) in-toes; (c) typical, correct

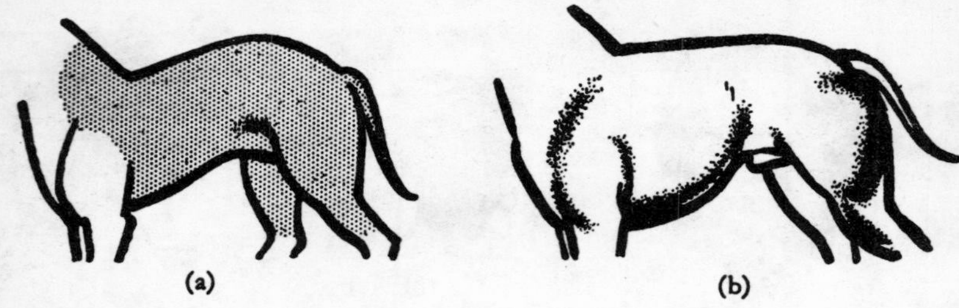

Figure 7 Body: (a) sway back, dip behind shoulders, roach back, shallow body; (b) typical, correct

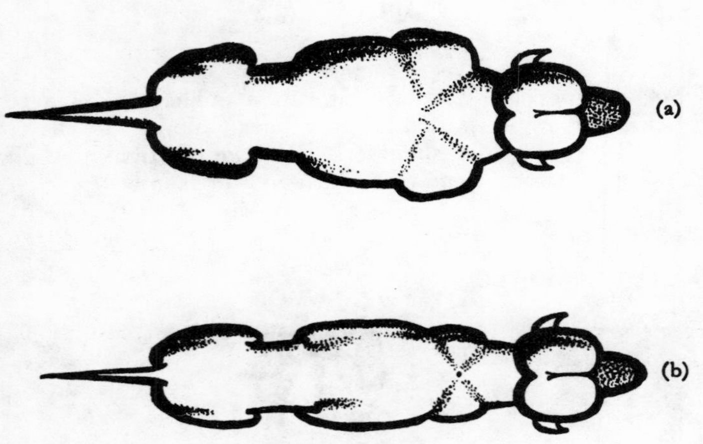

Figure 8 Body plan: (a) good development, broad shoulders, big rib cage, waisted-in, general strong physique; (b) flat sides, narrow shoulder development, shelly

Figure 9 Tails: (a) ring or hook tail; (b) gay tail, a tail carried above the level of the back; (c) typical tail, carried like an old-fashioned pump handle

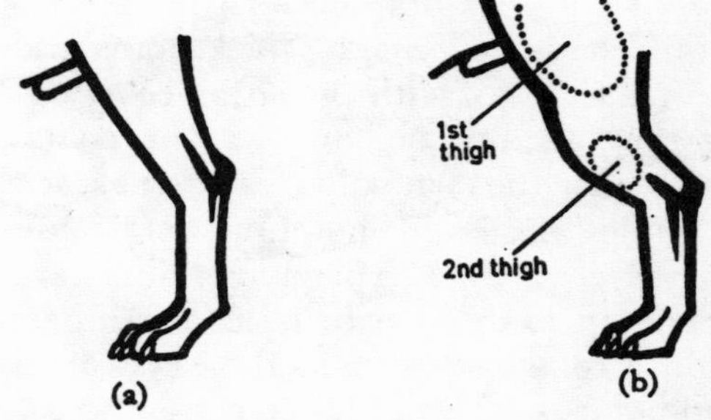

Figure 10 Stifles: (a) straight stifle, weakness at pastern; (b) well-bent stifle showing first and second thighs

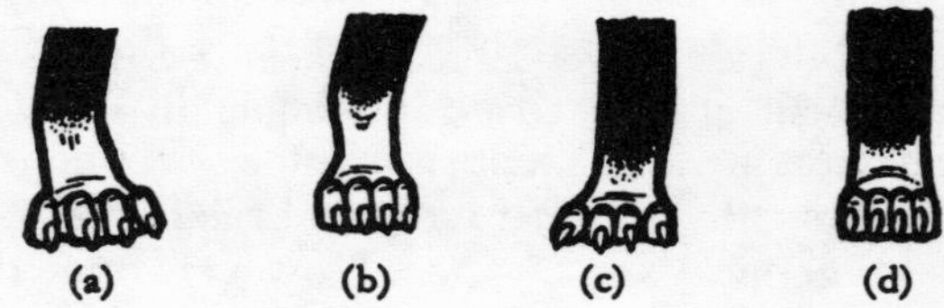

Figure 11 Feet: (a) weak bone, open or splayed feet; (b) well-knuckled but bent at pastern, seen in the Chippendale-type front; (c) flat, 'plate' feet; (d) weel-knuckled, compact feet: typical

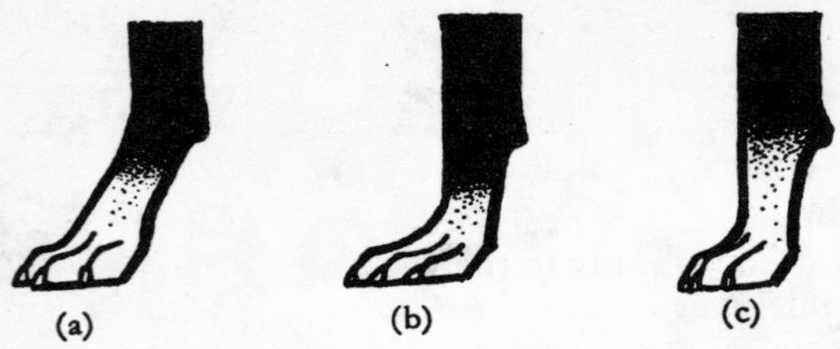

Figure 12 Pasterns: (a) weak pastern, slopes forward from above foot; (b) flat foot, weak bone; (c) firm, well-knuckled, typical

breeching and knees downward. This describes the marking generally, but in the Stafford, the 'tan' is often found to be a powdery fawn, and the black a smudgy black, although examples have been seen that are just as dense and defined as in a true Manchester Terrier. The important thing is that to disqualify as a show exhibit because it is black-and-tan, a Stafford should have at least the back, loins and parts of his head black or nearly so, with throat, cheeks, legs, breeching, and under the tail tan or fawn. Liver coats are usually displeasing because the coat colour is often associated with the unwanted Dudley nose and matching eye shades. Stud dogs with liver coat seem always to produce youngsters that abound in the same colour. Mahogany brindles are sometimes assessed as livers, quite erroneously, provided the eyes are dark, the nose is black, and points such as lips, eye-rims, and toenails remain black.

Blue is a coat colour only introduced when the Standard was revised in 1948. True blues are all right; in fact, the breed has seen some very good specimens since 1935, but too frequently 'wishy-washy' blues are brought out for exhibition. The sad thing is that no one can rightly oust these doubtful blues from the award cards, for there is nothing specifically phrased in the Standard to justify their exclusion. Such specimens, even if they are good physically and attractive in breed type, can be faulted perhaps on general appearance. However, once they begin to win prizes they more often than not become involved in breeding, producing stock with mottled coats even less attractive than themselves, and difficult to eradicate. It has become essential to know what is meant by a good blue, and breed leaders should attempt to decide this as soon as possible by securing an approved specimen to put on display at discussion groups so that enthusiasts can be educated in the matter.

White is a coat 'colour' not generally popular, although many of the early dogs in the breed were white. The antipathy to white is due probably to the way it brings a Stafford into the English Bull Terrier 'camp'. Admittedly, a white Stafford looks akin to a poor Bull Terrier and, conversely, a coarse-skulled Bullie might well be mistaken for a Stafford at a distance. On the other hand, we have had some wonderful all-white Staffordshires in the list of champions since 1935 and most of these have proved good stock-getters. Congenital deafness, at one time to be found in white Bull Terriers and other predominantly white breeds, has never been encountered in Staffords.

Brindles and fawns appear in a wide range of shades. Brindles can be found lightly marked on grey and fallow grounds, known as grizzles, then through a variety of colour depths to black. However, the blacks are never entirely black, some brindling is invariably to be found on the flanks. Fawns appear from lemon to deep chestnut red, and all these coats, both brindle and fawn, are found with white markings; alternatively, a dog that is mainly white can have patches of these colours. A Stafford with a coat half white and half dark brindle is termed a pied or piebald; when the brindling is of light colour he should be termed a skewbald. The main coat colour should be referred to first; thus, a white dog with brindle patches is a white and brindle, one with fawn patches a white and fawn. 'Red' is not an accepted Staffordshire Bull Terrier colour technically—it is correctly termed fawn.

It is most important that all coat colour is dense. Pigmentation must be good and pure. It can normally be checked at the 'points' of the dog, these being toenails, eye-rims, and nose and lips. On coloured dogs these points should be black, or at least very dark, some concession being allowed on white dogs or where the points are adjacent to white coat. Then it might be found that the black toenails are interspersed with paler horn colours. Likewise, eye-rims on an all-white specimen or one with white around the eyes will seldom be black, and although the Standard asks for some penalisation of rims that are pink, the wise judge will make allowance for white dogs when appraising them.

A fawn dog looks particularly smart when sporting a dark mask and such a marking often indicates the specimen is of good pigmentation. A fawn bred from one or more brindle parents sometimes has a dark trace of brindling running down the backbone to tail tip, or perhaps a spot of brindle 'thumb mark' halfway down his tail. Such dogs are frequently well blessed with pigment and make useful factors in breeding for depth of colour.

Weight and size. Modern Staffords descend from a wide range of weights and sizes in their ancestry. Even in the early 'thirties it was usual to find Staffords of 15 lb running with litter brothers weighing 30 lb more. Many well-known dogs of the early post-war years stood 18 and 19 in. at the shoulder, and 50 lb was not unusual, although most owners tried never to admit their dogs went above 38 lb. These days, the weights are more uniform and 16 in. at the shoulder and 38 lb weight seems to come naturally to most show-bred specimens. The 1945 classes that catered for the 'under 32 lb' would find little support now. The present Standard holds a tighter rein on weight and size, and this is to the good for it gives breeders a clearer target at which to aim. It is to be expected that a specimen of 16 in. and 38 lb (some concession is usually allowed to 40 lb) would be well balanced, producing a fairly small-framed dog but bulky, with hard muscle and latent power. The present desired dimensions appear adequate, and breeders seem to have settled down to producing stocky, type-filled specimens that please the eye. It is to be hoped that the accepted size and weight of the Stafford will be maintained. No one wants to see them getting too small, too low on the leg, and too weighty in head, giving the 'tadpole' effect. Once a Stafford gets too small he loses caste. He was made to be a fighting dog, a canine warrior without fear and with great strength and stamina. The sport he was bred for and the physical attributes with which he was endowed suit a dog of substance and good size rather than a lightweight. The latter fitted better into the work of the rat-pits, where sharpness and agility coupled with Terrier determination made him an expert killer.

Faults. The main faults, certainly those that concern us most, are structural faults, skeletal weaknesses. Poor heads, ewe necks, long and slack backs, upright shoulders, straight stifles and weak pasterns, all these are serious, as is deficiency in breed temperament. However, they become the responsibility of the breeder and the judge and are dealt with according to the section of the Standard into which they fall, proper temperament and character being bred to as required.

The 'lesser' faults such as light eyes, pink eye-rims, the Dudley nose and tails which are either too long or badly curled, can be eradicated by selective breeding. The mere fact that specimens with bad faults seldom if ever receive prize cards soon precludes such animals from use in any worthwhile breeding programme. The badly undershot jaw is, however, a more difficult fault to counter. Even after thirty or more years of scientific breeding in Staffords, with the belief in most fanciers' minds that this is the paramount fault, it is only in recent years that a certain modicum of success has been achieved in removing it. Nowadays, really serious undershot mouths are seldom seen, although slightly undershot formation of the jaw is still encountered, of course, and far too frequently. Bad ear form and carriage are easy enough faults to correct in breeding; in fact, most deficiencies can be erased from a strain if skill and patience are devoted to a few generations of careful breeding.

4

Character and Conformation

Character

The Standard tells us that, apart from the Staffordshire Bull Terrier's 'indomitable courage, high intelligence and tenacity', he is affectionate with his friends, especially infants, and his character generally is one of trustworthiness and stability. No one who has owned a Stafford can deny him this reference, although, as in all breeds, there are individuals who will default due to adverse environment in puppyhood or some other cause that may impair, even obliterate, some desirable feature.

Staffordshire Bull Terrier character, when understood correctly, is recognised to be somewhat complex. However, it is fairly termed 'honest', because the dog's true nature is one that is positive and straightforward, being intelligent rather than shrewd. For well over a century at least, old writers decried the brain power of the breed, which existed under a variety of names such as Bull-dog, Bull-and-Terrier, Pit-dog, Brindle Bull, and so on. Many feared, yet despised these fighting dogs, forbears of the Staffordshire Bull Terrier, considering them mentally backward. In *The Dog in Health and Disease*, 1887, J. H. Walsh (Stonehenge) attributes to F. Cuvier, the French naturalist (1773–1838), the assertion that 'this dog has a brain smaller in proportion than any other of his congeners', which is no compliment to his sagacity. Other authorities from the same period describe him as 'stupidly amiable', 'not capable of much attachment', 'rarely, if ever, teachable', and so on. All are depositions we know today to be quite untrue. Rather than being retarded mentally, the breed is a stubborn one, a trait commonly mistaken for low intelligence. The old Bulldog needed stubbornness and tenacity for his job of baiting the bull and the bear—of this there can be no doubt. The same

Historic Dog Features

Badger-baiting. From the original hard ground etching by Henry Alken, *c.* 1820

The Bulldog Mars, owned by Capt. Henry Bethune. Note the 'tulip' ears. This dog, a likely ancestor of the Staffordshire Bull Terrier, was by Capt. Nelson's Turk out of Ashburnham Bulley's Venom. The original oil painting by J. Pollott, *c.* 1848, is in the author's possession

Alpaka Alf's Fancy

Ch. Skerry Dhu of Dumbriton

Gibbs

Eastaff Noire-Fille winning the bitch C.C. at the Western SBTC 1988 show; handled by Alan Hedges, judge Joan Bywater

Ch. Topcroft Toreador

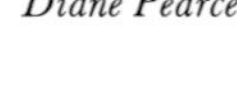

Diane Pearce

Ch. Orchid Beauty

Ch. Ashstock Black Maria

attributes have been passed down to the modern Staffordshire Bull Terrier, and by being so endowed it may be that he will need a firmer hand and greater patience in training than other breeds which are, perhaps, less staunch in their character.

The breed is a very determined one. What the Stafford sees and thinks he should do, he usually does. Such actions are seldom restrained and may well be difficult to anticipate at times by an owner who has not taken the trouble to train himself to the job. Recommendations of training methods to suit this breed will be found in a later chapter, and he who wishes to enjoy the ownership of a Stafford to the full and at the same time have the dog enjoy him as an owner, should read it.

Few Staffordshires feel or accept fear. Because of this, a fair number get run over, and it is wise never to unleash one on a road where traffic passes. The characteristic of indifference to fear and to pain, for many seem totally unconcerned with this, too, is well exampled by H. N. Beilby, BSc, in *The Staffordshire Bull Terrier*, 1943. He tells of a Stafford used to crossing the road early every morning to visit his favourite lamp-post. One morning, a car beat him to it halfway across the street. Down he went, cracking a couple of ribs and being well abrased, but he was up on his feet in a moment, staring balefully after the vehicle. Then, with a shake, he continued his walk to the opposite pavement, where he calmly lifted his leg. Actually, this casual attitude to pain is one of the dangers with the breed. It is no exaggeration to say that an injury capable of reducing the member of a lesser breed to a coma because of its pain, will have no such merciful effect on a Staffordshire, who seems to bear suffering with more than ordinary courage. Fortitude is another characteristic which comes to him, of course, as a legacy from his sporting ancestors. In those old days, callous owners bred their dogs to treat pain as something to be shrugged off rather than deter their efforts in the affray. We have read horrific tales of Bulldogs while hanging on to the bull's head having their limbs amputated by these 'sportsmen', just to prove to the onlookers how well the stock was bred for gameness and tenacity. Oddly enough, these misused creatures so often proved their owners' boasts by continuing to lay hold. It is a pity they did, for it must have encouraged the experimenters to even more frightful atrocities.

Nevertheless, we have inherited a fine breed with gameness and great endurance in its blood. We seek at all times to maintain these features, and one particular bloodline in the breed is reasonably well charged with fire and spirit, which it more often than not passes on to its issue. The stud dogs representing this strong line are, of course, highly prized and their worth is such that they contribute more to their breed than any fine show-ring champion with less measure of inherent valour in his procreative powers.

Let it not be thought that the Staffordshire Bull Terrier is a dog that wants to fight all the time. Such a dog would be a menace to the community. Actually, the *real* Stafford seldom seeks a fight. Unfortunately, a fight is often forced on him, and when this happens, who can blame him for rough-handling his attacker? This he *can* do and usually does in no uncertain way, thereby frequently finding himself accused of ruffianism. Far from being a lout, he is really a genial, mild-mannered canine, boisterous at times and ready for rough play or gentle affection, as the situation demands. Too often, however, a dog of this temperament, which combines kindliness with strength, is challenged by others less endowed with such positive characteristics. It is not unusual, if one owns a Stafford and one is out with him on the leash, to be rushed at by some free-running big dog, barking insults and threats. It is no less unusual to hear the dog's owner call out, 'It's all right—my dog won't hurt yours!' The next moment, the barking dog has got rather too near and, having been grabbed by the hitherto calm Stafford, sensing attack, is being pushed into the ground for his trouble. Now, of course, the situation is reversed. The Stafford is the 'aggressor' (even on his leash) and the barking nuisance, no longer barking, is the aggrieved victim. Hard words are uttered, coupled with a few threats, and the Stafford at once becomes an object of vilification. This situation and others like it are to be avoided at all costs. They do neither the breed nor the nerves any good, quite apart from the fact that no Stafford deserves to be blamed for an unpleasant incident that is not of his making.

With small children, the Staffordshire Bull Terrier is marvellous. He makes a wonderful nursemaid—even the toughest, roughest dog instinctively moderates his movements and acts decorously when tiny tots are about. Jack Barnard, first president of the Staffordshire Bull Terrier Club, told an amusing tale that illustrates the Stafford's protective spontaneity with youngsters. He owned a big skewbald dog—to be truthful, the terror of the neighbourhood as far as strangers were concerned. The dog adored Jack's daughter, then aged about four years, and a great affinity had developed between the two. The dog was kept in his kennel and run at the end of the garden and was more or less unapproachable in much the same way as an autocratic ruler is by his fearful subjects. However, protocol was not for the little girl, for every time her nurse went to collect her at bedtime, she eluded the woman and ran for the kennel. There, she put herself behind the dog who at once became so menacing that no one dared enter to secure the child. This performance took place almost nightly until Jack hit on the notion of keeping the dog indoors instead of outside, whereupon domestic discipline was restored. Perhaps at this stage, it is opportune to advise on the joint ownership of dogs and children.

All creatures, be they human or otherwise, are beset at times with doubts and jealousy. It is not fair to cherish and fuss a dog for years, only to ignore and humiliate him when a baby comes along. Too many families fail to realise the unhappiness they bring on the domestic dog, just for want of a moment's thought. At times, a jealous dog about the house is a dangerous acquisition; for this reason when a baby arrives on the scene, the dog should be fussed and petted even more than usual to ensure that he does not feel neglected or out of favour. He will soon learn to love the child intensely and guard it with his life, if necessary. Should it be desired to have dog and baby grow up together, it is wise to get a small puppy, perhaps two or three months before the baby is expected. This will allow a reasonable interim period for the dog to become house-trained and manageable; also, he is agog with pre-natal bustle. In due course, the child will be crawling around and the puppy will have grown and acquired some sense of responsibility and know better how to conduct himself. Avoid buying a mature dog to rear with a newborn child. For one thing, buying older stock is often a chancy business; one can seldom learn the exact and true reasons for its being available. More likely, the dog will have no experience with very small babies and may not welcome routine in a home so established, where affections and attentions need to be shared.

The Staffordshire Bull Terrier is able to change ownership, usually with little or no fuss. In fact, it is frequently the parting owner who seems to suffer more remorse when such an exchange occurs. The equanimity shown by the dog is another heritage from the past, when baiting the bull or in the combat pit, he might change hands for a comparatively large sum. Alternatively, if he disappointed an owner by losing a fight or displaying some defect of courage, he would be sold for a pittance, even given away. At worst, he would be pushed into a sack with some chain-link and consigned to the bottom of a Black Country canal, so intent were these early owners to preserve only their gamest stock to procreate its kind.

Conformation

The perfect Staffordshire Bull Terrier has yet to be born, but in recent years, with the great upsurge of popularity accorded the breed in Britain and abroad, some extremely fine specimens have been developed by the leading kennels. These dogs and bitches have usually been honoured by becoming show champions at the hands of competent judges. Nevertheless, they have *not* been perfect—just *excellent* Staffordshire Bull Terriers, no more. The perfect one remains still 'just around the corner' in the Staffordshire world, as indeed it does with most breeds, which accounts for the intense competition that exists to produce the perfect specimen. The breed is an 'old-young' one; old in that it was developed in Bulldog-Terrier form a century and a half ago; young so far as its breeding for show-beauty and conformation is concerned, for it has been bred scientifically only from the mid-1930s when it was 'recognised' by the Kennel Club. Three and a half decades are few enough years in which to breed a paragon. In some breeds perhaps a 'sport' or chance good one near to this model of perfection will appear, but it is unlikely to occur in Staffordshire Bull Terriers just yet, because the breed conformation we seek and which could be pronounced perfect by our standards today has hardly had time to superimpose its particular line, substance, and type on breed background. This applies as the breed exists today, although, generally speaking, improvement takes place from generation to generation, albeit slight. Too frequently, we witness in current stock the effect of ancestry that was either too light in build or indeterminate in its conformation. Sometimes we see youngsters reverting to early types that were too coarse or much too bully in their make-up for aesthetic acceptance as true Staffordshire Bull Terriers. Until these undesirable influences from the old Terrier and Bulldog progenitors have been completely submerged into the breed's background and are unlikely to reappear, even in reversionary form, we must wait a little longer before we can expect to breed dogs that come consistently true in type, size, and conformation.

Today, in the show world of Staffordshire Bull Terriers (and one assumes among non-show-going Staffords too), a better type of stock is developing due to the dedication of our breeders. As the generations of these 'improvements' pass on they pave the way to the day when breeders will be able to plan their matings with much less uncertainty as to their outcome.

The Staffordshire Bull Terrier's conformation was designed for a purpose. The old-time breeders who evolved him sought to overcome the shortcomings of the heavy, large and cumbersome Bulldog, which was too slow for the lethal sports of their day, and those of the little Terrier, whose lightness and varminty verve made scant impact on the game. As was stated in the opening chapter, they solved their problem by interbreeding the varieties to produce a dog which, by virtue of his temperament and conformation, was ideally equipped for the fighting sports of the day; hence the structure and conformation of the Staffordshire Bull Terrier (whose very name reveals the ingredients of his mixture). Whether we like the idea or not, if we like the Staffordshire and want him to do well in dogdom, we must consider him physically and temperamentally as a fighting dog. The fact that we do not fight dogs or set them on bulls and bears these days matters little. We have to breed the dogs as though we do. We must preserve the right conformation (as well as temperament) to suit the work for which the Staffordshire was originally required.

Soundness. This comes first, always. What is soundness? It is the ability of the dog to do his job properly with the entire physical support. It means that every part of his body should work in unison to an effective end which, in turn, means perfection of movement. If this is faulty, the reasons for it need to be explored. Unsoundness can be inherited or acquired. Anatomical unsoundness is shown in skeletal faults such as upright shoulders, which would give the Staffordshire an untypical or mincing gait, or a sloping croup, which would affect adversely his propulsion. Cow-hocks, when the points of hocks turn in to each other, caused by structural and/or muscular weakness, are often inherited, although they *could* be acquired by a dog badly reared in puppyhood or kept in an unfavourable environment. Certainly, a dog affected by genetic faults will pass the defect on to his progeny, whereas an animal with induced or acquired characteristics of unsoundness will not. Nevertheless, when the individual exhibit is affected by either kind of fault he is unsound on the day of the show, and by this rule alone must he be assessed. A fighting dog would have to be completely sound to last out the combat; one handicapped by cow-hocks could not use his hindquarters effectively to push in at an adversary; and a dog with straight stifles, therefore one with poor rear angulation, would be badly encumbered and likely to lose a fight against an opponent with whom he was otherwise equally matched. Soundness encompasses temperament too, and a vicious untenable dog or one lacking breed character can be rightly deemed unsound.

Taking the components of the physical dog and assessing the individual conformation of each, we have:

The Head. This is the major feature of the Staffordshire Bull Terrier, certainly first in the opinion of most judges and fanciers. Of unique cast, the true Stafford headpiece is one of blocky, solid strength, yet chiselled without exaggeration and coarseness. Good balance in the head is essential. The great, capacious skull needs ample breadth and depth, is squarish in conformation, and bounded on either side of the face with bumpy, muscular cheeks. The muzzle itself is of vital importance to the 'beauty' of the head. It should be short, strong, broad yet clean cut, and with good depth. The ideal ratio to aim for in skull and muzzle proportions is 2:1 respectively. If the muzzle is too narrow, too short, too long, or too shallow, true conformation is lost. No matter from which angle the muzzle is viewed it must always appear correct in its proportion to the skull. Correct balance would be lost if the stop (the indentation made where the muzzle joins the skull in front of the eyes) is too shallow. This step-like formation should be deep and distinct, for it gives the head power and proper breed character. The surface of the face below the eyes should be well filled up and with well-bolstered tissue. In profile, the conformation of the muzzle is firm, bold and determined in aspect. The repandus, or bent-upward part of the underjaw, is 'squarish'; it must not be shallow or receding, for these are negative features, and weak. The muzzle topline must be straight. If it slopes down at an angle from the stop (down-face) or tilts up so that the tip of the nose is slightly higher than the point of stop (dish-face) these are faults of conformation and liable to penalty in the ring.

The Body. The Staffordshire Bull Terrier's body is the classic example of *multum in parvo*. The strength, athletic prowess, and spring of a much bigger canine is crammed in his frame. His back is strong, muscular, firm and well put together with no significant arching. When viewed from the side, the length of the back from the withers (where the neck joins the body) should be approximately the same dimension as that of a line drawn from the withers down the foreleg to the ground. Thus, the actual body on legs should make roughly a square when in profile. The chest should be deep, allowing maximum expansion, and from the same viewing position the lower line of the chest should then extend to the rear, rising up under the flanks and supporting the loins which in the Staffordshire Bull Terrier are light, yet strong with dry musculation, as though sculpted. Where the line reaches the stomach there will be some evidence of tuck-up, but this must be slight and essentially of muscular tautness and flatness in the belly region. It must never appear as a drawn-up contraction of the area, suggestive of abdominal pain. The Staffordshire Bull Terrier's spine, although firm, is very flexible throughout its length, important in a dog bred for fighting and needing to turn, twist, and arch his back continually when in action. The dorsal section, extending from the base of the neck to the beginning of the lumbar region, is made up of thirteen interlocking bony segments having attached to them an identical number of ribs, the 'cage' thus formed housing and protecting the dog's heart and lungs in particular. Of these thirteen ribs, nine join to the sternum or breastbone (these being termed true ribs) and the remaining four, which are not so attached, being called false or floating ribs. In the Stafford, the ribs should be well-rounded and quite deep, for a capacious rib-cage will allow generous lung room and unhampered chest expansion during bouts of extreme physical exertion. The term 'barrelled' when applied to a Stafford's ribs, seen in some show reports, is perhaps a little misleading. A better term would be 'well sprung', for a barrel-shaped rib-cage, being round and already fully expanded, would permit no further dilation when required. The ideal rib formation is rotund with depth, the great spring being maintained noticeably towards the rear of the chest. Lung capacity is normally decided by length rather than depth of chest, however, and a dog so well endowed would be referred to as having a 'well-ribbed back', the development being assessed from the lowest point of the back to the body underline rather than from the withers to the brisket.

The Neck. This is supported by the seven segments of the cervical vertebrae, running in an upward and bending line from rather low down between the shoulder blades (and joining the dorsal vertebrae) to a point at the rear of the dog's skull. The conformation of the Staffordshire Bull Terrier's neck is an example of strength and beauty. It is fairly short, yet not so restricted in its length as to lack some elegance. It should be massively developed, the upper line of the neck especially being arched or crested with hard flexible muscle. From leaving the contours of the shoulder region, the neck should taper only gently towards the back of the head in order to give the dog enough spring and power necessary to administer the armament of his head when in combat. The fighting dog uses his head effectively, striking forward with it like a hammer blow. A neck that is too short will vitiate the potency of such a blow; likewise it is prone to the coarse accoutrements of dewlap and wrinkle. The opposite fault, that is, an extended 'drain-pipe' or ewe neck, lacks strength, therefore has scant striking power. Both are unwanted characteristics of conformation because they would be impediments to a dog bred for fighting and contend against aesthetic balance in the show dog.

The Shoulders. The neck and shoulders are significantly linked. A dog possessing an over-long neck will usually evince a tendency for too much length throughout his entire spinal column, even the coccygeal or tail bones being extended more than is desirable in the Staffordshire Bull Terrier. Such a specimen would normally be termed 'rangy' and would be penalised in the show ring. However, it is a fact that a dog so made is often the owner of good shoulders. Just as easily, a dog with fair length of neck, but with a short back (such as required in the Stafford) could have well-constructed shoulders. In the past, and to some extent still, some breeders have striven to produce *very* short necks in their stock in the mistaken notion that extra shortness is required. Ultra-short cervical formation does not lend itself to the production of well-laid-back shoulders (the converse is true also, and shoulder construction will influence the set of neck). This means that the pleasing fusion between neckline and withers is lost. Correctly, when viewed in profile, the upper neckline or crest should be continuous and unbroken down to and through the withers into the topline of the dog's body. When the neck is too short and cylindrical, lacking elegance and without pleasing graduation in its width from top to bottom, it either makes a visible angle at the withers, appears 'stuck on', or too deeply set into the body, so that crest and topline seem almost horizontal. Dogs bred like this, without curves in the upper and lower lines of the neck, must fail in shoulder formation. A dog must hold his head erect, the neckline flowing smoothly into the body.

The Staffordshire Bull Terrier's shoulders should be fairly well laid back. The term 'laid back' means that the scapula (shoulder blade) is of correct good length as required in the breed, that it is broad and set obliquely so that its upper broad end is laid back as far as possible against the dorsal vertebrae to which it is joined. At its lower end, it joins and articulates with the arm-bone or humerus, making an angle of about 90 degrees. When the upper end of the scapula lies forward, i.e. in a perpendicular position with its head nearer to the base of the neck, it is said to be upright, because the angle formed with its lower end and the upper end of the humerus becomes obtuse. The shoulder joint so formed will adversely affect the dog's forward action and, at the same time, detract from the expected muscular development of his upper chest, which assumes a flat aspect. It is clear from this that a dog too short in the neck and too 'cobby' in body, with short thoracic structure, is unlikely to move well. A dog so made would carry the weight of his foreparts on his elbows, which under pressure may well be forced outwards, causing looseness, therefore unsoundness in front. In effect, a well-laid-back shoulder is a good shock-absorber in the dog, allowing him to run, jump and indulge in strenuous exercise without suffering jarring symptoms to his forequarters. It is also necessary to ensure correct movement, which in the Staffordshire is unique, being bold and positive, with spring, ample stride and easy rhythm. An upright shoulder will reduce the length of distance of his step to a mince, even a hobble when the formation is extreme, and in a breed noted for its athletic ability this would be disastrous.

Usually, impaired musculature goes with faulty bone construction, and the desirable conformation of the Staffordshire is lost due to overloading of muscles in the shoulder region. In some working breeds this is unimportant, but in the show ring and in a sphere where streamlining and sleek contours are required, it becomes objectionable. When the shoulder blades are well laid back, the muscles covering them are usually well distributed but when the scapula is short and upright the muscles are usually massed over a more confined area of the shoulders, which at once seem to stand out in bumps. This looks coarse and does, in effect, detract from the pedigree refinement of the dog. The Bulldog is a good example of this characteristic, which in the breed is correct. His Standard requires that the shoulders should appear 'tacked on'; such shoulders in the Staffordshire would be termed 'loaded' or 'bossy' and are far from the breed's ideals; in fact, any specimen displaying them in the show ring is unlikely to achieve much success. Alternatively, a narrow scapula is often accompanied by musculature that is too weak to support the shoulders properly, the blades becoming distinctly contoured at the withers under the skin and the entire shoulder framework being 'loose'.

Front and forequarters. Probably what we want most to see in the Staffordshire Bull Terrier's front is an impression of straightness, at least as far as the fore limbs are concerned, which should be parallel down to the pasterns, at which point the feet turn out a little. There should be ample width across the brisket and chest and the dog should give the impression of being 'on his toes', alert, and ready for anything. The entire aspect of the Stafford when seen in this position should be positive, and impressive, evincing great strength and solid framework and bone. Fronts that are 'tight', often due to upright shoulders, accompanied by shallow chest development, are typical of the Terrier family, but not a Terrier characteristic that should be built into the Stafford. 'Chippendale' fronts, showing forelegs bowed and bent like the furniture that bears that name, are undesirable and, fortunately, not often encountered these days. 'Pin-toes' are not uncommon, however; these are feet that turn inwards, often accompanied by elbows that turn outwards. The propensity for this fault is a structural one, although it is capable of being self-induced. Some dogs use it as a way of 'digging in' their feet when trying to thwart the pull of their leash. Allowed to become an effective habit when exercising or in the show ring, it can persist and is likely to be adopted at inconvenient times.

The forelegs need to be well separated, provided the width is conducive to proper balance in the particular specimen. This will allow development of ample width and depth in the chest. The legs must be of average length, for a dog standing too high will lack class and balance, whereas one too low to ground will not only lose out on balance, but be restricted in agility. Some weakness remains in the elbows of Staffordshire Bull Terriers. Too often, they point outwards instead of being drawn in close to the sides. The Stafford's elbows should be braced well into the sides of his chest by firm pectoral muscles which at one end are joined to the sternum or breastbone, and at the other to the humerus or armbone and beyond into the flesh of the armpit. When a dog is in good physical condition and generally well conformed, the elbows will lie firmly and naturally in to his sides. A young exhibit is frequently seen with unstable elbows when moving. This can be due to youthful undevelopment or lack of adequate exercise. A judge sometimes comments that such a specimen needs to 'tighten up', suggesting that he will improve with age and added exercise and perhaps better feeding.

Below the elbow come the separate parallel bones, the radius and ulna. These support the forearm and run down the legs from elbow to knee, the upper ends articulating at the elbow joint with the lower end of the humerus. The three bones mentioned are very readily affected when a puppy has rickets due to adverse foetal environment or faulty rearing. Although it is possible that a rickety puppy's limbs may strengthen as he matures and is exercised, there can be no hope of a complete cure, and his conformation will always be impaired.

The pastern, which is equivalent to the wrist in man, lies below the knee joint in the lower part of the leg. It is not uncommon to find weakness at this point in the young Staffordshire, especially if his rearing have been casual. The breed calls for great girth and a reasonably heavy body weight for its size, therefore any deficiency in the supporting bone structure or joints, such as the pastern, will cause sag. Again, if the tendon behind the pastern is slack or the regulating muscles above lack strength, then the dog is certain to be 'down' in pastern. Hard, daily exercise on a cinder track or similar rough going will often remedy the condition, but the cure is frequently an extended one before enough strength can be developed in the muscles to straighten the pastern.

The Hindquarters and Rear. The rear end of the dog is represented by the seven lumbar bones of the spinal column, followed by the sacrum, a triangular bony formation, at which point the tail is set on. The lumbar vertebrae pass through the region of the loins and have certain significance in that, if too long (and it is a fault in the Stafford to look long), the specimen concerned will look as though his rear half is estranged from his front. Because of this he will be branded as long in the back. A dog long in dorsal vertebrae is (strictly speaking) long in back, at least as far as the Staffordshire Bull Terrier is concerned. The *impression* of extra length in back is gained from the coupling space formed between the dog's last rib and the pelvic projection emplaced just above the hip joint. This space is provided by the over-long lumbar vertebrae, consequently the corporal parts lying immediately below that region, i.e. loins, flank, and belly, will also take on extra length, giving an illusory effect of length to the back. Thus, when a judge says a Staffordshire is too long in back, it is just possible that he may mean it is too long in loin. When considering this region of the loins and sacrum, it is important that the Stafford's topline is level throughout, although some *slight* muscular arching over the loins is to be seen. On the other hand, the 'Roach Back' is a serious and transmittable fault in the breed. It is shown by a convex arching of the spine from the withers to tail, notably over the loins. The fault is usually accompanied by upright shoulders, the dog, in a thoroughly untypical manner, thrusting out his head when moving, as well as carrying his tail too low. This last charactertistic is caused by the sloping line of the croup which covers the sacrum at the set-on of tail.

The Staffordshire Bull Terrier's hindquarters should be well developed with muscle on buttocks and legs. The hocks should be well let down and the stifles nicely bent. Their general conformation will be discussed later, but it is important to know that this area is just as vital to the fighting dog as the armament of his head. With powerful and well-angulated hindquarters he was able to propel himself against and push in at an adversary. The great thrust required for this could come only from dynamic muscular hind power, which a well-made Staffordshire Bull Terrier possesses. That this propelling machinery needs to be maintained, even improved on, if that is possible, is obvious to the conscientious breeder. The importance lies in the position of the croup, the correct length of the bones, their proper shape, the manner of articulation, and the distribution and quality of the muscles that abound in the hind-parts. In effect, the sound dog must have perfect angulation, for good rear action depends on it.

The pelvic bone should be angled at about 30 degrees from the spine, and according to its true angle from the horizontal, it will influence the emplacement of the hip joint, the femur (first or upper thigh bone) and the tibia (second or lower thigh bone). These two bones, the latter in conjunction with the fibula, articulate at the stifle. The angle they make decides the quality of the joint upon which good movement depends. A wide or obtuse angle, giving a steep formation and stilted action is undesirable, and the dog is said to be straight in stifle. The backward thrust he needs to propel himself forward is weakened according to the degree of straightness, and in a Staffordshire Bull Terrier the straight stifle is a serious fault.

We have shown how the fighting dog would be at a disadvantage with it, and the modern dog would suffer, too. It would impede free and effortless action and prevail against his store of stamina over long distances. Likewise, boisterous play, running and jumping would quickly exhaust him. No Staffordshire with a straight stifle can expect to move with any major degree of boldness and ease—certainly he could never produce the gait typical of his breed.

The stifle joint is notorious for its tendency towards unsoundness. Being a fairly loose union of the lower end of the femur with the upper end of the tibia, it is wedged or padded with cartilages held secure by ligaments. When, as often happens with weighty breeds, these ligaments are stretched beyond their usual and normal tautness, the gristle or tissue becomes loose and rubbed. This causes irritation, then lameness, and although it is usually of a temporary nature it can become chronic if ignored. Whereas the condition is common to mature dogs of five years and more, younger Staffords and puppies are likely to suffer from patella luxation (slipping patella). This is a small pebble-like bone that performs a similar function to the human knee-cap. It is lodged in the muscles that abound around the front of the upper thigh and it is contrived to glide over the grooved lower extremity of the femur when controlled by these muscles. Whereas the two projecting smooth ridges of bone (the trochlea) which provide the groove should offer ample depth for the small bone to move, it may happen that due to hereditary reasons the channel is too shallow or degenerate in its form. In dogs so affected the patella may slip to the inner side of the limb, as there is nothing to prevent this. The knee at once becomes locked and the dog will do a sort of hop, skip and a jump as he moves forward. The lameness is usually temporary and some youngsters will cast off the infirmity as they mature and develop their thigh muscles, thereby improving their movement. However, the breeder is recommended to take note of individual dogs so affected, espectially mature ones he encounters, and avoid including them in his breeding programme.

Good turn of stifle in the Stafford is a valued asset. However, good angulation must be supported by first-class musculature in the hind region, especially with muscles and bones of correct substance, quality, and length on either side of the stifle joint, notably on the upper and lower thighs. The dog's propelling ability is dependent on the controlling force he can muster to straighten the hind limb from its state of angulation into a state of complete extension. The major contribution to achieve this comes from a well-developed lower or second thigh. The muscle development there is also essential for perfect strong, forceful and effortless action, although excess muscle will tend to hamper his fluid movement unless the thigh is rather long, which means that the hock must be low, or well let down. Long or high hocks are other factors that adversely affect a dog's stride, making it short and without resilience. All muscles should be of refined quality. Coarse, bumpy muscles might be effective over short distances, but a lasting muscle is a long and well-toned one and will allow a Stafford to get maximum effect from his reserve of stamina.

Occasionally, a dog that seemingly is of good, sound hind construction when standing will bring his lower hind legs together when moving away, in extreme cases even aligning or crossing his back feet in their tracks. Such a dog demonstrates a structural fault in the nether region and the effect of good balance is destroyed. The cause is usually due to a tight pelvic girdle or limbs that are loosely articulated at the hip, or again, slightly incurved so that they converge either from the hip or the stifle to the hock when the dog moves. A dog with variable gait, i.e. one who rolls when moving, could also be loose at the hip joints, or be poorly articulated at the stifles, which would cause them to 'punch out', especially when at the trot. Such a fault is frequently accompanied by cow-hocks, i.e. when the points of hock turn in to each other, making the back toes turn out.

To produce perfect action, a Stafford must move his hind legs in true parallel to each other throughout their length, i.e. from hip to foot, showing firm flexion at the points of stifle and hock. Between the two limbs ample space should exist to provide complete freedom of movement, which should be positive and with steady stride in order to maintain the picture of pleasing balance throughout his body.

The Tail. The breed standard says that the Staffordshire Bull Terrier should carry his tail 'rather low', that it should be 'low set', 'of medium length', and look like 'an old-fashioned pump-handle'. The fact that the tail is required to be low set should not be taken so literally that its set-on is visualised as similar to that of the Greyhound, Great Dane, and Alsatian. The root of the Stafford's tail should be a strong one; and it should be remembered that the coccygeal or tail bones are a continuation of the spinal vertebrae, the set-on being placed at the sacrum. This means that any thin or inferior growth of the tail bones is likely to indicate similar inferiority in the bone of the spine and skeleton generally. A very low-set tail is undesirable, and any fault in the set-on will be due to inferior emplacement of the sacrum in relation to the spine, for where the sacrum finishes the tail begins. As shown in the section on hindquarters, the pelvic bone, being joined to the ilium, virtually sets the position of the sacrum, and if the front part of the sacrum is pushed high, the rear part will incline and take with it, to a low level, the set-on of the tail.

The Staffordshire has a tail of medium length. It should extend from its root barely to the point of hock. A tail that is too long or too short detracts from the animal's balance. The long tail spoils a dog's line, and the old-time fighting fraternity believed a dog with too long a tail was a coward. Certainly, such a dog was usually too long all through from neck crest to tail tip, and made 'soft-backed' in this way it is conceivable that he might prove a non-stayer in the pit. To the rough and tough faction of the dog-fight game such a dog would be readily dubbed a coward. The short arrow-head tail, usually coarse at the root, then suddenly coming to a point, makes its owner look cloddy and lack class. The gay tail, set-on too high, is untypical and a stated fault, as is the ugly ring tail. The congenital screw tail, of course, renders a Stafford ineligible for prizes in the show ring because it is a reversionary defect, a reminder of his Bulldog ancestry.

Not many breeds can claim a use for their tails, but the Stafford is one that can. The old Pit Dogs found their strong pump-handle tails useful as rudders in the fight game. A thump down on the floor of the pit with it would help the dog to lever or edge himself into a better position or manœuvre out of an awkward situation.

The Feet. The Staffordshire Bull Terrierr's foot is well

padded, strong, and of medium size. It is well-knit, but not high-knuckled and tight like the cat's or long like the hare's; in fact, a happy medium between the two kinds is most desirable. The Stafford's foot turns out a little at the joint of pastern, and this formation was clearly designed in the old fighting dog to allow him to feint and turn effectively, as well as to maintain his good balance when under stress. The pads contribute substantially to the spring and turn employed in such athletics, being hard-bolstered and generous in design. The fore-foot is made up of four toes and a dew-claw, which is the rudimentary fifth digit equivalent to the human thumb and normally left on the Staffordshire, unlike most breeds which have dew-claws removed by surgery a few days after birth. The hind foot has just four toes, and dew-claws on the rear limbs are rare. Flat and splayed feet caused by slack muscles and tendon are anathema in the Stafford. They lack the elasticity and spring required in such a sporting breed and a dog so hampered would find his movement affected and his stamina curtailed. It is just possible that *if* the Staffordshire Bull Terrier was equipped with a cat-foot, i.e. close-knit and tight-knuckled, round and compact with well-arched toes, such as the Bull Terrier has, the feet, being in straight line with the forelegs, might improve his forward movement. However, as pointed out at the beginning of this chapter, the Stafford was bred to fight, and we must breed as though good fighters, physically and temperamentally, were our aim. So long as we agree this and accept, too, that feet that turn out a little at the pastern are formed to help the fighting dog fight better, we must retain them. It is important to ensure that all ligaments and tendons and muscles playing their parts to bend the toes are firm and tense; the toes will then be bent properly at their joints and be well knitted.

Exercise is important to keep feet in good trim, but it must be on rough ground such as gravel or cinder track. This will bring a dog up on his feet, provided the exercise is with the dog on his leash rather than free running. Grass running and soft ground have a deleterious effect on a dog's feet; so have long nails. These should be maintained always at their minimum length. If normal exercise does not achieve this, then they must be trimmed, otherwise splay feet and poor movement will result.

5
Choosing a Puppy

Most people when embarking upon the purchase of their first puppy do so with some trepidation. Few newcomers to a breed know what to look for so far as breed type, finer points, and conformation are concerned and the prudent buyer will not rely too much on his own judgement, especially if he contemplates exhibition work. However, some folk fancy they have 'an eye for a dog', and this being so it would seem to them worth while to go ahead with a personal choice. The gamble may well pay off, but let it be said now, to pick a show winner from a litter of 'raw' six- or eight-week-old Staffordshire Bull Terrier puppies is very chancy, and many people with years of experience in the breed would hesitate to pronounce too categorically how a puppy will look when it matures.

The breed remains a variable one, even today. Its background is too fluid as far as type and size are concerned. Too often, odd-looking stock turns up in the issue of impeccably planned matings due to the fact that uniformity in the breed is established too near the surface of the breed's ancestry. Because of this, it is not feasible to assess show potential with any degree of certainty, although it is reasonably easy to pick out the best from a litter (as opposed to a show certainty)—not a great deal of knowledge being required to do this.

To make sure of getting at least the best available, it is wise to deal with the most successful breeders. This does not mean necessarily the biggest names. Some of these are has-beens, others merely buy-in to sell, and a few have put themselves on top with achievements that did not include breeding good ones. The breeder you want is one who does breed good ones, exhibits them, and wins first prizes consistently at the premier shows. He should have been doing this for quite a few years, by which time you will find he has usually developed a good bloodline so that his stock is at once recognisable by its hallmark of type. When he breeds Staffords this year they will look like those he bred last year and the year before that, and when you visit his kennel you will find the inmates there all look alike. This is the man you should be able to trust to supply you with a good puppy. Tell him what you want, explain your ambitions in the breed—whether they extend to the show world or the modest requirements of a Stafford for companionship. You will get good and fair treatment, no doubt, with a very good chance of coming away with a likely candidate for show-ring honours, if that is what you seek. Such a breeder knows his stock intimately and will find it reasonably easy to select the best and graduate the show potential of the rest.

Dog or bitch?

If you plan to enter the fascinating field of dog breeding, you will incline naturally towards a bitch, for by virtue of her sex she opens the gate of breeding opportunity for you. Even if, later, you find she has not turned out quite so well as hoped for, there still remains the opportunity of picking one of the finest and most fashionable stud dogs by whom your bitch may produce puppies of greater merit. To progress in type, quality, and show worthiness is the aim of every conscientious breeder. In setting such a target of excellence arises the intense attachment you will develop for this breed. The absorption comes not only from the ownership of a handsome Staffordshire Bull Terrier, but in trying to produce a specimen that will outshine all others.

Apart from an interest in breeding, when, of course, a female becomes the obvious choice, a lot of people seem to prefer a bitch to a dog. The matter is debatable, but it is true that few people who have owned a bitch transfer their affections to a dog when the time comes for buying a new companion. On the other hand, it is not unusual to find a pet owner easily persuaded to buy a bitch when his dog has passed on. It is said, rather crudely perhaps, that a bitch comes into season roughly every six months, whereas a dog remains in season all the time. This is true to some extent, but a bitch certainly seems more home-loving, less inclined to wander, and perhaps more loyal than a dog, although these attributes vary greatly with individuals. A dog, unless he is a particularly good specimen and makes his name in the show world, becoming substantially in demand at stud, often gets unsettled, and yearns for a bitch. This longing is frequently unrequited and frustrated, and he will try to get out of doors on his own to seek one, with no thought for his owner or home-guarding duties. If he is prevented in this, it is conceivable the irritation will upset him to the point of becoming moody or offensive indoors. However, individuals of both sexes do not always conform to what we expect at times, and whichever sex you decide upon you are likely to be well satisfied with your purchase.

The selection

Make up your mind before you start that you will take plenty of time in making a choice. The dog or bitch you buy will probably be your companion for the next twelve years, and the companionship should be harmonious. Get first impressions; these have reasonable importance, and almost certainly you will at once dismiss a few of the puppies put before you as not being to your liking or requirements. Try to put colour preference in the background so that it does not influence your decision overmuch. Dog flesh comes first, colour second, and whereas you may love brindles it would be a mistake to bypass a superior specimen because it was a red or piebald. Always try to make your pick from the litter. It is probably when you have only two to choose between that the best ones have already been sold, but in case not, let the youngsters run free in their pen; later, around your feet, if this can be contrived. Maybe, amid the five or six puppies bounding about you, you will note one that could never appeal to you. You might not know why you feel so disposed, but the instinct is useful when picking livestock, and you are well advised to let yourself be guided by it. In effect, do not buy the dog or dogs you do not take to at first sight. This advice might seem somewhat arbitrary, but its worth in the field of puppy selection has been proved to the author on innumerable occasions. View askance the puppy who skulks in the rear of his kennel or shies furtively away from your outstretched hand. Natural wariness is all right, but these are symptoms of unreliability, a characteristic not common or wanted in the Staffordshire Bull Terrier. Seen from a distance, light eyes can be detected in a young puppy better sometimes than from close up. Although the breed Standard says that eye colour *can* bear some relation to coat colour it is always better for a dog to have a good dark eye. Light eyes frequently go with a dog who is shrewd rather than intelligent and the latter characteristic is to be preferred. Ask the breeder to let his litter run free, preferably on grass for the purpose of inspection, for then the puppies will gambol and reveal their basic limb movements to the full. Some of the youngsters will dash off at once on their own adventures, but a few friendly and curious ones will besiege you. These can be lifted one after the other and examined. Try to find a waist-high kennel or similar platform, putting each puppy on it carefully, reassuring the uncertain ones. Move both hands closely over head and skull, feeling its bulk and blockness. It should handle heavily, the muzzle being very short, very deep and very strong. Never be satisfied with a muzzle that has even a slight tendency for length, for the puppy will almost certainly develop into a long-muzzled adult. The same rule applies to mouth and jaw formation. If the repandus or bent-upward part of the underjaw seems too pugnacious, too determined, there is a good chance you will find the puppy undershot when you open his mouth, or at least with the upper and lower incisors tip-to-tip. Either way, only a miracle will make him level-mouthed at maturity, because few doubtful mouths improve; they always seem to deteriorate. A promising mouth in a small puppy is one where the upper incisors sit freely and positively over and upon the incisors of the lower jaw. If you can slide the thickness of a piece of notepaper between the two rows then your chances of rearing a level-mouthed specimen are good.

Take the puppy's ears and feel them between fingers and thumb. They should be small and calico thin. If they are held well back on the upper part of the neck now, they should promise well for the future. Gristly or leathery tissue supporting the ears at skull level might well mean semi-erect formation later on. Rose ears that fold back like a Bulldog's, exposing part of the inner burr, tuck themselves away better in a fight and are preferable in the show dog. However, ears generally are not easy to foretell in a Stafford; often they seem to change shape and position a dozen times or more while the dog is teething. Sometimes it is wise to wait until the animal is at least seven months old before confirming the worth of his ears. On the other hand, ears are readily transmittable in breeding, and it is a good idea to examine the puppy's parents if you need any guide as to ear potential in your chosen puppy. In any case, always go over the sire and dam if you get the chance. Whereas the mother ought to be near the puppies, it may not be so easy to inspect the sire who could be a stud dog living far afield. In spite of what some people think, the dam casts a good deal of her own likeness on her stock and is probably the more important of the two parents, and her appearance should provide you with a useful indication as to the points, good or bad, she will have passed on to her issue.

The next to assess is body. In one so small, the body from shoulders to tail should be short, deep, and well rounded with rib. It is surprising what great spring will be encountered in the rib-cage of a well-made puppy. Never be deceived by fat; you must feel the bone of the body, and a good Stafford puppy has plenty of substance and resilience in spite of his size. Place a hand between his forelegs so that you can feel the sternum or breastbone. If it projects, giving the puppy a distinct 'pigeon chest' aspect, discard the puppy at once. The sternum should lie as a shapely and firm keel to the body and never project in this way. The forelegs should be placed quite wide apart, the bone being ample and generously turned, rather than round. The hindquarters should be parallel from hip to hock—any suggestion of cow-hocks (when the hock points turn in to each other) should be viewed with suspicion. Turn the puppy over on to his back, examine the belly, groin, and the armpits. Query any spots or rawness you may find there. Sometimes young puppies coming off the kennel floor or dampened by the licking of their kennel mates look a bit red below, but such soreness soon disappears once they fall into private ownership. Look at the genitals, too—a dog should be entire, i.e. with both testicles descended into the scrotum. A cryptorchid (with neither testicle down) or a monorchid (with only one testicle descended) is useless to you if you contemplate breeding later. It is not always possible, however, to see two testicles in a small puppy, although it should not be difficult to feel them, and it is important to satisfy yourself on this point. Keep an eye open for any discharge evident from the penis (or vulva in the case of a bitch puppy), always seeking veterinary advice when in doubt. Lift the tail and examine the anal region to ensure a healthy condition, also that there is no prolapse. With the thumb, turn back the coat hair around the perimeter of the set-on of tail, for if the puppy carries lice some will have collected there. Run finger and thumb down the tail from root to tip—it should be a smooth run with no gristly bumps or turns that indicate the congenital screw-tail, a heritage from Bulldog ancestry. You are now coming to the end of your detailed examination of the puppy, but inspect the feet. They should be neat and well formed with no suggestion of splaying between the digits, or flatness. A slight turn out of the front feet just below the youngster's knee or pastern joint will be observed. This is correct formation and as required by the breed Standard. If the puppy is still equipped with dew-claws, do not worry. Many Staffordshire Bull Terrier breeders, especially the old-timers, prefer to leave them on, this being generally approved by breed pundits. However, if dew-claws are seen on the hind-legs it reflects a little unfavourably on the stock breeding, and in the author's opinion no first-class strain should produce this objectionable feature. The puppy's navel should be looked at in case a slight rupture has occurred. Umbilical hernias, unless big, need not perturb you, although it is better to buy a puppy without one. They are seldom considered an unsoundness, even in professional circles, but they are a little unsightly. The veterinary surgeon can deal with them quite simply when the puppy is a month or two older. Most people can assess condition, and the breeder owes it to you to present his stock for purchase in good coat and health. Run your hand down the puppy from head to tail—the Staffordshire Bull Terrier's coat is a smooth one, short and close to the skin, although in a two-month-old puppy it will seem roomier than one worn by an adult, and this must be taken into consideration. Avoid the puppy with a 'staring' coat or one that is ruffed, especially round and under the neck. He may be 'wormy' or in indifferent health and, like his coat, his eyes will inevitably be found dull, too. Finally, check for pigmentation. Look at his nose—this should be black over the whole nostril area, not off-black or bluish. Sometimes, however, when the puppy has a good deal of white in the muzzle area, his nose may be speckled, i.e. with black segments on the flesh, termed butterfly nose. Provided the dog is generally of sound coat colour, this need not worry, for most of the flesh colour gets blackened over as the dog grows on, and by the time he is four months old it has become totally black. Check the toe nails. The horn should be black. This is desirable but not essential. However, there should be no prejudice against nails that are not so coloured, but it does suggest the dog is possibly poorly endowed with pigmentation. The eye-rims, even the eyes sometimes, reveal colour deficiency, but you should not be taken aback too much if a white-headed dog you examine lacks the black eye-rims required in the Standard. The author has not seen many so-marked specimens that conform even approximately to the rule and it is clear that where Staffords of parti-colour are concerned, the eye can be winked a fraction when considering the feature.

Before deciding on your puppy, try to get him to walk properly and steadily away from you and towards you. This may require the help of another person and a small collar and lead, although if you can possibly get him to move by his own accord it is better. All you can do when assessing a puppy's gait is to make sure that his forelimbs move in parallel as he comes to you, and the same with his hindlimbs as he goes away. Ensure the action is free and purposeful and there is no evidence of steepness in the shoulder joint. In young puppies it is easier to detect this fault by watching them move than it is to feel faulty positioning of the scapula. Also, when in action, a youngster should hold his head up, proud and alert. A head thrust forward and down is untypical, and although some allowance must be made for a puppy's playful disposition and interest in all that surrounds him, he should be seen to move as a Staffordshire Bull Terrier.

Although you may have spent a lot of the breeder's time looking at his puppies, if he is an enthusiast he will not mind this and do his best to help you in your decision. Make sure you look at all the youngsters—even those that prove difficult to catch in the less accessible corners of the place. Ask to see the pedigree and discuss what it tells you with the breeder. Unless you are dealing with an established specialist kennel check that the parents are on the Active Register at the Kennel Club. Lastly, make a point of finding out whether your puppy's dam was a good mother, especially if you have bought a bitch puppy. Bad mothers are a liability to any breeder; worse, they often pass on the tendency to their female offspring.

6
Training and General Management

Training for the home

No one should embark on ownership of a Staffordshire Bull Terrier without due consideration of his responsibilities in training the dog. The real Stafford needs firm handling and control. He carries a good deal of the Bulldog in his mental make-up, stubbornness and a strong individuality being at least two typical characteristics to be contended with in training. Any dog, unless he is a complete imbecile, can be trained to produce a pleasurable companion and make a welcome addition to any family circle. Too many owners are inclined to permit their pets to misbehave, often quite outrageously, to their own and others' discomfort. A badly behaved dog reflects on his owner's training ability, and neither dog nor master enjoys a companionship that could so easily be made pleasant.

The first rule in dog training is to understand your Stafford and make sure that he understands and trusts you. You *can* train a dog by force, but it is not to be recommended, neither is it comparable to natural training methods. The latter system entails studying a dog's habits and instinctive behaviour and employing them to advantage when teaching him. This is not only kinder than training by force, but it is easier for you and the dog and achieves results quicker. You must make a friend of your pupil and it is always simpler to begin serious training with a youngster of say five or six months than with a mature animal. On the other hand, a lot of groundwork can be got in before this, and you should start elementary principles as soon as your new puppy arrives home. Remember, the wild dog learned things from his pack-mates, they from their leader. The domestic Stafford has no leader, so you must be his leader and teach him. He will be gratified at what he learns and will want to please you. Always utilise this tendency to your own advantage, and remember that a dog trains best when he is hungry, and responds well to a moderate tone of voice. Never shout at him, for then he will react unfavourably and may lose confidence in you, which will take time to replace. Keep your words of command to monosyllables or terse orders. Lengthy instruction is usually incomprehensible to a dog and is liable to confuse him, slowing up his progress.

The usual training required for a dog about the house is elementary. First, he must learn the meaning of the word 'No'. He will need to be house-clean, to come, sit, lie down, and keep to heel and, in fact, to be completely under his owner's control. He will need also some encouragement in guarding the home, although many Staffords do this instinctively, but often not until they are in their second year. Make up your mind that you will not lose your temper with the dog and begin with the word 'No'.

Even the youngest puppy should be taught the meaning of this. Prepare a rolled-up newspaper and keep it handy. When the puppy does something he shouldn't, scold him and give him a tap with the newspaper, at the same time saying 'No'. The newspaper will make a bit of a crack but it will not hurt him. Usually, a few such lessons in 'No', with applied newspaper, have good effect and it will not be long before only the word of command is wanted and the newspaper can be thrown away.

House-training

This is another lesson that cannot be given too soon. A lot of people fight shy of dog ownership because they fear for their carpets and floors. However, it is a simple enough procedure to get a small puppy trained, for most dogs are naturally clean in their habits and want to be shown what to do. It is only because they do not know what you want that they offend. The average small puppy sleeps a good deal, just like a baby. As with a baby, when a puppy awakens the first thing he wants to do is to urinate. This is where the owner takes over, for as soon as you note the awakening you pick up your puppy, take him to the garden door or to the dirty-tray, whichever suits, and deposit him where he is to make his puddle. Do this with a good deal of ceremony and the puppy will quickly catch on. You will find that the instant he opens his eyes after a sleep he will wander at once to the garden door or tray and do his duty. When he does this in the early stages pat him and praise him and you will hasten the training. Of course, if you are not there to open the door into the garden for him at any time, do not blame him for making a puddle—that is your fault, not his. Remember, too, that whereas you might have him perfectly trained in your own home, you cannot expect a small puppy living indoors to be house-clean when you take him to visit your friends. The geography of the other home will be quite different and he may not know where their garden is. He will need to be educated to his new surroundings. Likewise, do not expect a small pup to go all through the night without making a mess. Youngsters of a few months are always incontinent, and you should line the floor of the pen or kitchen, wherever you keep him, with newspapers before retiring. It will be easy then in the morning to gather these up and pop the lot into the dustbin. Destructiveness is not a Stafford characteristic, although the best of dogs will gnaw a bit if they are bored. However, it is as well to leave a puppy in a room where he is unlikely to cause damage, when he is left alone. Anyone who goes out and leaves a puppy in the lounge where he can tear up carpets, cushions, and score furniture legs has only himself to blame if damage results.

'Come'

This lesson and the others that follow are for the older puppy, and it is unlikely that proper results can be obtained until the dog is six months of age, although preparatory training can prove useful. Nothing irritates more than a dog that rushes off as soon as released from the leash, not to return in spite of his owner's entreaties. Try such a dog first with a titbit, calling him by name, and enticing him to move towards you with the command 'Come'. The average puppy will be attracted to the morsel, and when he takes it he should be praised. The lesson should be repeated until he approaches you without hesitation and will do so without discouragement if the titbit is not given. On the other hand, a rebel puppy should be kept on a 20 ft light check-cord. When freed from his leash he will dash off as usual. Call 'Come', he will not respond; then, just as the cord is nearing its extent call again 'Come'. Your call will coincide with the cord jerking him to a halt. He will be surprised and not a little shocked. A few such lessons and the command will arrest his progress before the cord does. He can then be cajoled back to the handler.

'Sit'

This is an important lesson. Remember that the pupil should always be on your left side. You might think this relatively unimportant, but it is not. There is an acknowledged and approved way to do most things, and training to the left side is the official, therefore the correct, method and worth emulating even if you have no intention of advanced obedience work. The dog should be moving on a loose lead at your left side. Halt suddenly, giving the command 'Sit', at the same time swinging your body (trunk) round to the left, the feet being set firm. Bring round the right hand which is holding a titbit, across and over the pupil's head. He will look up at it and provided you have synchronised your halt, the turn of the body and the right-hand action, he will at once bring his rear end down on the ground. This formula of synchronisation will usually work, but an awkward dog will have to be persuaded into the sitting position by taking his collar in the right hand and pressing down his back end with the left. Should you find the dog sitting too far away from you, do not move towards him, but lessen the space between you by encouragement with gentle pressure on the lead.

'Down'

This exercise is a natural successor to the 'Sit' lesson. The leash is attached at one end of the dog's collar, then passes under your left foot, the loop being held in your right hand. With the command 'Down', push the dog down with your left hand, at the same time pulling the leash with your right. The word of command should be forceful—this will induce a cringe in the pupil at first, which can be exploited for the purposes of the lesson. The tendency to cringe will disappear as the pupil becomes proficient.

'Stay'

This exercise follows on from 'Down'. It is a useful one, especially now that so many food shops forbid dogs on their premises. The trainer gets the dog into the 'Stay' position by giving the command 'Stay', once the 'Down' has been achieved. He then backs off from the dog, all the time commanding 'Stay'. If the dog moves he is at once got back into 'Down'. It will be found possible gradually to increase the distance between pupil and trainer, eventually to go completely out of sight without the dog stirring from the spot. At this point it is advisable to recommend to Stafford owners that whereas this lesson should be given, it should not be applied overmuch. No Staffordshire Bull Terrier should be left unattended, uncontrolled in any public place. Loose street dogs are likely to interfere with him to his annoyance, and who could blame him if he grabs one? A Stafford should be under owner control always. This is a fighting breed. It might take a good deal to upset or provoke a Stafford these days, but even the best get put out at times and it is usually the Stafford who gets the blame in a dog-fight, often through no fault of his own.

'Heel'

This is an important lesson. When mastered, it forms a useful foundation for more advanced obedience work. The dog should be kept to the left side and should move on a slack lead close by his handler's calf. The leash should be held in the right hand, loose enough to allow a slack loop from dog's collar halfway to the ground. With the command 'Heel', move forward together, the dog needing a slight jerk to get him moving. Reward steady progress with a pat on the head and a titbit. As soon as the dog is good enough to release from his leash, do so. This is the 'Heel Free' exercise and it should be given only occasionally, as no Stafford should be loose for an extended period. Remember always to make the right hand the correcting hand, the left hand being reserved for rewarding.

Training for exhibition

A lot of the training for home will stand your dog in good stead when it comes to giving him a course of instruction in show procedure. He will have become used to obedience by now and will understand command and, more important, he will not mind being handled. In the show ring, a dog is usually put to a lot of indignities. A judge will go over him from muzzle to tail, pressing here, prodding there and shifting him about all the time. Unless a dog is used to this sort of thing it can distract him, make him uneasy, and spoil his show chances. It is important that a dog be trained to stand still and suffer all these things. The expert judge has little time for the exhibit which, because he will not stand still, cannot be assessed. For this reason try always to get friends and breed enthusiasts to treat your dog as a judge might. This means starting at his nose and running the hands right over his body, feeling the contour of his ribs, the depth of his chest, the quality of his bone, the entirety of his private parts (if a male), the positioning of his teeth, and a host of other intrusions upon his form. Get strangers to do this, too, and it will not be long before the dog will accept such handling from anyone without demur.

The puppy must learn to stand firm on all four feet, look natural, comfortable and poised. It is not easy to train a young restless dog to this and a good deal of tolerance and patience will be needed. Initial work on the young Stafford should start when he is about five months old; he should be taken before his evening meal to a quiet place, his handler having a liberal supply of titbits available. Keep him on a thin, comfortable collar and lead and make sure that he has no distractions while training. Place one hand under his chest and between his forelegs, the other under his tail and between his hindlegs. Lift slightly off the ground, replacing him gently with the command 'Stand'. On no account should the front or back limbs be spread out as you do this; all legs should be allowed to come down straight and naturally from the body to the ground. When standing, front legs should stand parallel with the hindlegs. The average pupil will remain at least momentarily where you have put him. Try to maintain his position as long as possible; by this time you will have straightened up and be holding the lead in your left hand. Keep his attention upon you with the titbit in the right hand. The command 'Stand' can be repeated at intervals as long as he stands in position, but do not extend this for too long, otherwise the pupil will become bored. When he shows promise, give him the titbits and praise him, then start again. Do not continue the early lessons for more than ten minutes at a time. As the days go by the time can be increased to half an hour. Some dogs are natural showmen, others will require some patience on your part. It is important that the dog is trained to stand firm and look intelligent. A lot stand well, but look 'dumb', or unhappy. Such outlook militates against good general appearance and will lose points. It can be avoided if the lessons are made interesting, of short duration, and given with kindness and understanding.

Development is the next thing he must learn. This entails clean, positive, typical movement in the ring. No judge will tolerate a scrambler, and good movement is not a strong point in the breed, even today. An exhibit's best effect upon the judge is made usually when it moves at its own *natural* speed. A dog that pulls on the lead throws out its shoulders and elevates its rear; one that drags obscures its front and rear actions and is seldom given a second glance. The ideal gait is an effortless one, the hindlimbs propelling the body, the forelimbs guiding it, the whole proceeding in a relaxed, lithe and athletic fashion, the limbs working in parallel to each other, and the head held erect, the outlook intelligent. It is important that he be exercised up and down a typical ring distance of, say, thirty feet. This will get him used to an about-turn action when he retraces his steps to the judge. So many exhibitors mar the good style of this manœuvre that it is worth cultivating an effective

American Staffordshire Terrier Ch. Indian Doc

Thomas

Ch. Boldmore Black Sabbath

C. M. Cooke

Ch. Langport Spearhead

Ch. Ginnells Black Tuskyanna

C. M. Cooke

Ch. Rapparee Lady Luck

Ch. Curfews White Orchid

C. M. Cooke

Bandits Fawn Dandy

T. Curd

Ch. Indiana Acid Queen

turn, not only to add polish but to gain what might be a deciding point from the judge. Get the dog used to a smart about-turn on a quietly uttered word of command. You can say 'Turn'—the author trained his champion dogs to turn deftly when he clicked his fingers. So long as the dog knows what you want (and does it) you can use any method.

When you feel that the dog looks good standing and is moving briskly and soundly, take him from the quiet surroundings of his training and try him out where there is bustle and noise. Of course, the best place to find dog-show atmosphere is a dog show and one can usually find a small all-breeds show in the locality. Join the society and enter your dog at its next members' event. Do not go with an idea of winning, although if you get a prize it is rather nice. Just enter with the intention of getting your Stafford used to show routine—the exercise might prove useful to you, too. Here he will have to go through all the course of his lessons and learn how to behave with a variety of breeds around him. Later, you can enter him at a show where only Staffordshire Bull Terriers are entered, by which time he should be reasonably proficient and will not disgrace you.

Exercise

The Staffordshire Bull Terrier is an energetic, lusty dog. He needs a good deal of exercise, although he is extremely adaptable and can usually apply himself happily to city life. It is not easy to tire a healthy Stafford, even with free running (which must be conducted well away from the roads). A dog kept alone needs more exercise than one with a companion to play with, as does a kennel-dweller. Road work, which means walking a dog on his leash, preferably on hard ground, even cinder tracks, to strengthen his pasterns and harden his pads, is more important than loose exercise on grass. However, few owners can put in the many miles a day a Stafford thrives on; therefore, ball games in the park become unavoidable. At such times, it is necessary to keep a wary eye open for the intrusion of other dogs and for temptations likely to attract your dog out of the park gates into the road.

Puppies need exercising with care. While in the nest they exercise themselves with the occasional rough-and-tumble. For this reason allow them ample space to indulge their sport. When a puppy goes to his new home, he is usually admired, fondled and played with. It should be remembered that up to two to three months *at least*, most of his time will be spent sleeping. Sleep is vital to his well being, and children in the home must be made to understand this. A small puppy continually snatched from sleep by a child wanting to play with him cannot be expected to develop a happy disposition. Staffords, generally, are marvellous with children. If, by chance, one nips a child, it is usually the latter's fault coupled with the fault of the parents for not keeping the scene properly supervised. However, when the pup is awake he should receive attention and be indulged in a game or two, using a solid rubber ball which cannot be chewed and is too big to swallow. Such a toy will be used only for a short period during puppyhood, and when the youngster's jaws become strong enough to bite it, it should be removed. It is best to forbid very small children to carry a puppy. Tell them the puppy has four feet and these have to be on the ground. Accidents caused by a puppy being squeezed too tightly or becoming bored in a child's arms and precipitating itself to the ground are not uncommon, and a promising show-type puppy can be ruined by such an accident. As the little Stafford grows he can be trained to the lead, which is best done in the home first, for he should not be allowed out of doors for initial road exercise until he has been safely immunised against the various canine diseases. This is done usually at around three months of age, after which time his outdoor walks can be gradually increased, care being taken not to overdo either the distance or the exertion. At this age there should be no question about whether he should be kept on his lead or allowed loose—the former rule should apply. Every outing in the early stages should be treated as a lesson. The youngster should be made to walk easily on a slack lead—no pulling is allowed, for this can develop into a bad habit. Any tendency to lunge towards other dogs and people should be severely discouraged, coupled with a word of command so that he will obey this word at all times. The rolled-up newspaper system, used in house-training, can be employed outside the home too. The puppy who pulls on his lead can be checked by drawing back the lead and tapping him across the muzzle, saying 'Heel'. He will soon learn that it is much more comfortable to walk in the relaxed fashion you insist on. Also, when out you may wish to apply your 'Sit' lesson at the kerb before crossing the road. In fact, any useful lesson (as opposed to tricks that make a good Stafford look ridiculous) is worth while if it contributes to the enjoyment of breed ownership and the dog's welfare and safety. On the other hand, guard against over-training your dog. A dog 'full' of training frequently loses some aspect of his personality, and this must be avoided at all costs.

Punishment

One does not like to dwell on this too much. It is better to punish with words than with hand, but sometimes the latter becomes necessary if the dog is stubborn and fractious. However, when training a dog, better and more lasting results will be achieved with patience, audible and understandable commands, and judicious use of reward and praise. Corporal punishment in the course of a dog's lessons will dampen his interest in the proceedings and shatter his confidence in the trainer.

If a Stafford really needs a 'clump' it should be a modest one. Such a smack probably will not hurt him (they don't appear to feel such things as might a lesser breed of dog) but it will halt him and make him think. Apply it with the word 'NO' and the best and safest place is with the hand around the muscle build-up of the cheeks. Never hit a dog across the loins or tail end; this is dangerous.

Kennels and kennelling

If you keep a number of Staffords it is clear that you will need to maintain them out of doors. Provided the accommodation given is warm, dry and comfortable, completely free from draughts, the dogs will thrive well enough. Obviously, they will need plenty of fresh air and exercise—more of the latter perhaps, than the dog that enjoys the luxuries of the family circle and who can trot around more or less at will. Further, a kennel-kept dog is unlikely to receive much fuss and affection compared with the housedog. An owner is advised to compensate the kennel-dwellers accordingly, to talk to them, and fuss them a little at every opportunity. He will find himself amply repaid with obedience and affectionate response. A kennel dog misses companionship, therefore suffers a little in the development of his intelligence and knowledge of human behaviour. Such dogs sometimes prove failures in the home of a new owner due to their immaturity in these matters.

If a kennel range is to be purchased remember there are some good prefabricated structures available. The models extend from a single dog-kennel to sumptuous ranges fitted out with every conceivable facility. For the small breeder and beginner a range of four kennels is ideal. If possible, have a small equipment cupboard built on the end where brushes, mops, pans, etc., can be stored with wood-wool and sawdust supplies. As far away from the main range as possible install an isolation kennel, suitable for sleeping an 'off-colour' dog or used specifically for whelping bitches. Always ensure that kennels are high enough for you to stand up in, allowing you to work in comfort. The average Stafford requires kennel sleeping space of about 9 sq. ft and a private run of about 10 ft in length from his door, although this can be extended to advantage. No dog should be permitted to sleep on his kennel floor; a raised bench within his house will guard him against killer draughts. This bench should be removed for cleaning and replenishment of bedding. The bedding must be either wood-wool, to be changed daily, or warm blankets which will need frequent attention. Sawdust should be sprinkled on the kennel floor itself, and the entire living room gone over with a mild disinfectant regularly, the same scrupulous cleanliness being applied to the kennel run, although this should be scrubbed with a more powerful agent such as Dettol.

For safety's sake make sure that doors leading into the kennel are contrived in such a way that you can open the exterior door to let yourself into the run. You are then faced with a second door to gain access to the dogs, but you cannot do this until you have closed the exit. Kennel run sides should be at least as high as the kennel; they should be of strong chain-link and, if possible, roofed with the same link. Staffords are determined dogs, and a good one can clamber up 10 ft of chain-link fencing and drop down the other side quite easily.

Never erect kennels under trees. Try to find a well-drained spot for the range and face them to the south or south-west away from the district's prevailing winds if possible. The area should allow free passage of fresh air and a good part of the day's sunshine. Remember that clean, cool water should be available to the dogs at all times, and one last warning—make sure that the link fencing is of small-gauge opening so that neighbouring dogs cannot make contact. The same applies to the partitions between the kennels themselves. The author recalls an incident many years ago when Ch. Fearless Red of Bandits had his kennel mate Major Mont by the lip through a mere aperture of slightly more than one inch between the roof and partition of their adjoining kennels. Major Mont was not particularly 'lippy' either!

Grooming

All Staffords should be groomed daily. The kennel dog may need more attention than the family pet, but regular brushing is important. Use a hound-glove or a medium bristle brush, finishing off with a good polish by chamois leather. While the dog is before you, check his ears; make sure they are clean—no dirt or wax. Look at his teeth and gums; ensure they are healthy. His eyes should be bright and clean too, and his lips free from saliva. Run the thumb round the upper set-on of his tail, peering into the skin beneath the coat as you do it. Any parasites, which so often collect in this area, should be disposed of at once. A few can be picked out, but if a lot congregate then dusting with a suitable proprietary powder is essential. Lift the tail and examine the anus. Sometimes cleaning is necessary; often a soreness will be detected. This is due to the anal glands (one on each side of the anus) being clogged. A veterinary surgeon will attend to the matter for you, but it is easy enough to cope with. Holding the tail up in the left hand, take a flat pad of cotton wool in the right and clamp it over the affected region.

Push in and squeeze at the same time and it will be found that the offending matter will exude and can be disposed of, thus avoiding possible abscesses.

Apart from the foregoing the Stafford needs scant attention. A lot of show exhibitors make a point of trimming below the dog's tail. This entails removing the 'feather' or long hair of the tail's underpart to give a 'whip' or 'rat' tail effect. Officially, it is believed to be frowned upon, but if done, care should be taken to remove none of the side and upper hair and to ensure that the tip of the tail is brought to a fine neat point. No doubt about it, the operation improves a Stafford's appearance and gives him a stylish bearing. Never be persuaded to trim off a Stafford's facial whiskers in the mistaken belief that without them he has a 'cleaner' appearance. Quite apart from the probable inconvenience to the dog, it produces an alien effect.

Bathing

Only bath a Stafford if he has encountered some mess and got it on his coat. Occasionally, after a spell of dirty weather with an important dog show imminent, he will need a bath; other than these factors he can probably go for months before being put in the tub. Excessive or unnecessary bathing will remove the natural oils from a dog's coat, making it dry and probably fluffy. Some Staffords incline towards coat coarseness and these particularly seem to suffer from the results of a bath. A good daily brushing will achieve most that a bath can do without the latter's deleterious effects.

Some Staffords like a swim, although it is not really typical of the breed. In fresh-water lakes and rivers no harm can ensue, but keep your dog out of the sea unless you are in a position to put him under a fresh-water shower to remove the salt, which is liable to 'cake' and dry out the skin. The breed has a propensity to skin dryness anyway and salt water can aggravate the condition and induce a bareness sometimes difficult to repair.

Collars and leads

A Stafford should be equipped with two collars, a narrow strap collar to be worn indoors during the day (taken off at night to avoid ruffing his neckline) and a fancy studded collar for his walks and shows. It is important to keep on the plain strap collar all day for it allows some control should the dog have to be grabbed. The studded collar should not be more than two inches wide; a broader one detracts from the average Staffordshire neckline. How many studs you have in it is a matter of personal taste, but to get the best effect from such a collar, have it liberally studded and with the D-ring (to which the leash is attached) fitted in with the stud design so that it comes on top of the dog's neck when the buckle lies underneath his neck. Thus, when the leash is attached it pulls the D-ring and studded part round for all to see and the buckle slips out of sight.

Dog harness is seldom seen these days, although some American dogs have been pictured with it. It looks a little absurd on the Staffordshire Bull Terrier, and, therefore, is not to be recommended.

The best type of lead to be used for such a strong breed as ours is one made from the strongest bridle leather, ¾ in. to 1 in. wide and thick through. A strong brass buckle should be fitted to one end, and the other sewn into the conventional loop. The buckle fitting is superior to the conventional metal spring clip attachment usually seen and certainly preferable to the scissor release clip, which is liable to open up and free the dog if a careless grab is made at his collar. Chain leads are not popular. They cut into the hands too fiercely, and choke-chains of the kind used in obedience work do not seem to work well on Staffords. This is probably because many dogs of this breed, apparently contemptuous of physical pain, will often allow a chain to cut into the flesh or the neck rather than submit to the training correction such a chain is supposed to give.

Stopping a fight

Staffordshire Bull Terriers, generally, do not look for fights. The average dog is usually quite genial when out and only enters into battle when provoked. The trouble is that so many dogs are allowed out loose and unattended that intruders who irritate the Stafford while out for a walk with his master are common. No one can blame him for protecting himself and owner, but being such a powerful dog and so adept at the fight game, he usually wins. Winning a dog-fight in such a decisive manner makes him an unpopular victor as far as the lookers-on are concerned, certainly the victim dog's owner becomes aggrieved for he, like many a dog owner, will think a dog-fight should be nothing more than a brief tussle coupled with some light-hearted snapping and snarling. Unfortunately, it so often proceeds as a battle to the death.

To be prepared for such an emergency it behoves the owner to know how to deal with a fight. It is unlikely that you will be able to call your dog off a fight. If he is a real Staffordshire Bull Terrier, once he has started he will be beyond audible exhortation. Nevertheless, one well-known figure in the breed claimed he could call his dog off a fight and I saw him do it. The average mongrel dog when seized gives up resistance at once, for the intensity of the attack is too much for him. This means the Stafford has to be broken off his victim. Slipping both hands, knuckles down, under his collar, grab the leather firmly. Then stand astride the dog's loins pressing your knees into his sides. At the same time, begin to twist with your hands relentlessly, pushing your dog's nose deep into the bitten dog's flesh. Apart from the pressure on the Stafford's neck, he will find breathing through the nostrils very difficult and be forced to ease his grip and gasp to get some air through the mouth. Be ready for this to happen, and when it does, pull him away sharply and tie him to a tree or post while you attend to the other dog, assuming that it has not run away. If two Staffords are fighting, the disengagement might not prove so simple, for the bitten dog could put himself into the position of biter as soon as the other dog is broken off. In such cases it is well to tie up the bitten dog before you begin operations, then he cannot come back at his enemy when the breakaway occurs.

Try to avoid panic at such times. It is not always easy when you see what is happening. The worst thing is when the other dog's owner is belabouring your Stafford with his stick. This will have just the opposite effect to that intended. It will inflame the Stafford and drive him to more intense efforts. Buckets of water thrown over the contestants are just as ineffective, although ducking the fighting pair in a water tank has been proved a fair remedy.

After the fight, bathe the wounds, then drip in a fairly strong solution of TCP or similar antiseptic. Do not bandage fight wounds—let the air get to them. If the ears have been torn, clean up inside and attend these at frequent intervals so that the patient becomes used to them being handled. If you leave it too long between dressing the dog will object and make it difficult for you to attend him, thereby prolonging the repair.

Of course, others have their remedies for separating fighting dogs, some quite drastic and, doubtless, efficacious. Whatever the method, the best formula is prevention rather than cure and a Stafford owner should be aware of his responsibility to other dogs, most of them totally unequipped to contest a Staffordshire Bull Terrier. Even if it is the other dog's fault, always try to avoid an incident that will not only cause someone and his dog a deal of distress but give the Staffordshire Bull Terrier breed a bad name.

Games

As soon as a Staffordshire Bull Terrier grows on from the small puppy stage all toys and rubber balls, etc., should be thrown away. By the time he is four months of age his jaw muscles will be quite strong, and with the rigours of teething such playthings will be torn to shreds and constitute a grave danger if he swallows them. Bones are normally forbidden to puppies of a breed descended from the Bulldog, thereby predisposed to the undershot jaw, at least during the term of dentition, for the consistent gnawing might aggravate the tendency should it exist. However, big marrow bones seem innocuous enough, probably due to their circumference preventing the young dog taking the vice-like grip likely to spoil his yet unformed jawline.

A good game, and one that will exercise and strengthen his jaw, neck, and hindquarter muscles, can be made by tying an old tyre to rope and suspending it from a tree branch in the garden. It should hang just high enough from the ground to allow the dog to jump, take hold, then hang, feet swinging free. Staffords have been known to enjoy themselves for hours with such a contrivance which is so beneficial to physical development. Stick games are popular, and any stick unlikely to splinter can be thrown and the dog encouraged to retrieve it. Thrown up a hill or slope, the clambering involved in retrieving it will build up hindquarter muscle very quickly, but avoid stick games when there is more than one Stafford. As soon as two run together you have the nucleus of a pack, and a thrown stick to compete for will soon start trouble. Worse still, the stick in one dog's mouth could gouge out the eye of his companion. Always conduct games with a Staffordshire in such a way that you can call a halt to the excitement at once. A fighting dog, like a fighting man, is a highly bred creature—as far as his sport is concerned, at least. Like a boxer, the good Stafford can quickly become elated and go further than he intended, unless checked. Watch the eyes as you play with your dog. If you get to a stage in the play when they glaze over, stop the game at once. Up to this point you have your Stafford under control no doubt, beyond it you need to bring him back to a more sober mood.

The foregoing advice is given in the light of many years' breed experience. It is hoped that the reader will not henceforth regard the Stafford as neurotic or unreliable. He is far from being either, please be assured. However, all breeds have their idiosyncrasies and it is best to be aware of what lies in the make-up of your chosen variety. The Staffordshire is, and remains, a solid, honest, down-to-earth, reliable dog, wonderful with children and those he trusts.

7

Breeding and Stock Rearing

If you are fortunate enough to own a good Staffordshire Bull Terrier it is easy enough to become interested in the breeding game. Your aim should be to produce stock that is at least as good, preferably better than the one you own, thereby advancing the progress of Staffordshire Bull Terriers generally. Should your Stafford be of indifferent worth, this need not deter you from breeding with him (or her). You are entitled to improve upon this mediocrity, and many an ordinary Stafford has made a worthwhile contribution to his breed. Every new litter created should represent some advance in the Stafford world, and although it is not easy to achieve this ideal it is important to perpetuate the parents' good points in the puppies.

Judging by their successes in the breeding field, most of our leading breeders possess at least some working knowledge of genetics, the scientific study of the principles that govern heredity. The subject is an engaging one, and every serious-minded breeder should acquaint himself with its rudiments. Unfortunately, it is not within the scope of this book to cover its study and readers are recommended to Eleanor Frankling's *Practical Dog Breeding and Genetics*, 3rd edition 1969, and *The Dog Breeder's Introduction to Genetics*, 1966.

There are two important factors in the study of dog breeding. One is pedigree, the other appearance. The first is the animal's genealogical 'tree', and the second how he registers according to the merits and demerits demanded in his breed Standard. The written pedigree is not much good unless it can be interpreted. A jumble of names means nothing, but if you can take each name on the pedigree form and 'see' that dog or bitch in your mind's eye from the information you have collected, then you have a useful foundation for your breeding programme. It is not always easy to obtain specific and reliable descriptions and data about old dogs, most of them dead anyway. Factual information about the champions is readily forthcoming, for most breed people will remember them and furnish you with the salient points of the dossier you seek. However, many pedigrees exist containing the names of Staffordshire Bull Terrier nonentities which will be difficult to track down. Nevertheless, it can prove worth while to investigate their appearance by writing to their owners (assuming the dogs were registered at the Kennel Club, from whom their addresses can be obtained) and requesting details of colour, height, weight, type and, perhaps, a photograph. Of course, you will suffer a few disappointments but sometimes such enquiries can prove rewarding. Once you have all the data you can collect then it requires the formulation of a 'picture', first of the stud dog's ancestry, then of the prospective dam's forbears so that you can 'line up' one with the other. At this point, you begin to read the pedigrees; how cleverly you act upon your findings may well decide whether you will produce a champion from your breeding, or not. Clearly, you must compare the types of both parents. It is not much good mating an ill-assorted pair; their progeny will be made up of some looking like the sire, some like the dam, all the litter being prepotent to both unwanted types when they, in turn, procreate. Make sure that the background is reasonably good—it is not possible to get brilliant pictures from Staffordshire Bull Terrier backgrounds at the present time; the breed is not yet ready to produce uniform and standardised offspring. This attainment is more feasible in breeds longer standardised and purer in the last sixty years at least. Remember then that no dog is worth any more than his pedigree, provided the pedigree is true. Further, no pedigree is worth any more than the dog himself, which means in effect that you can hardly boast a wonderful pedigree for your Stafford if he is a poor one. Similarly, if you have a good-looking dog with shabby breeding behind him, in the breeding field he is unlikely to prove much better than his pedigree. The ideal specimen to own is a good one from good breeding. With such material you can form a nucleus with which to breed and create a successful strain.

If in the course of your planning you contemplate a study of pedigree likely to extend back to the early days when Staffordshire Bull Terriers were first accepted by the Kennel Club for registration—proceed with caution. Before 1935, written pedigrees were virtually unknown in our breed. Admittedly, some existed, and were held by various Black Country breeders, but these were seldom brought out. If a Midlands man owned a good dog he did not intend to divulge to strangers the formula that produced it. This attitude, quite apart from the plain fact that many Staffords were of unknown parentage, meant that a lot of owners 'evolved' pedigrees for their dogs in order to make them eligible for registration. In the somewhat chaotic state of the breed, as it was then, with its divers types and meandering bloodlines, this system, criminal if it were done in dogdom today, did not matter overmuch, one name being as good as another to a dog whose only 'call-sign' was a whistle. Confusion, however, was caused in instances when three different owners, for example, all with Staffords from the same litter, fabricated three different names for the sire of the puppies, according to their individual fancy. With similar treatment meted out to the dam, who also went into official records with varying names, it is small wonder that some pedigrees just prior to the war need taking with the proverbial 'pinch of salt'. However, the years have passed since Staffords were struggling for recognition, and irregularities of nearly forty years ago have since been ironed out. Pedigrees can generally be relied on implicitly by the intending breeder who, having learnt about the individuals on the pedigrees of his chosen mating pair, is now in a position to progress. He will know that in order to perpetuate desirable features in his proposed litter he will need to use a dog and a bitch both possessed of the hereditary factors required. He will further realise that not only is he likely to produce these good points in his puppies, but, also, his chances of endowing them with any prevailing faults is just as likely. Success in fixing desirable characteristics in the puppies becomes more assured if their grandparents, and even earlier ancestors, can be found to own and, therefore, transmit these good points.

The clever breeder makes sure that he keeps in his kennel only Staffords that can be useful to his breeding programme. 'Passengers' are all very well; everyone knows the sentiment of keeping an old companion who has served his or her day in the home and kennel. Such an animal deserves the care you offer, but never retain poor breeding stock for sentimental reasons. These can always be found good homes where they will receive individual attention and maybe learn to appreciate life better than with an owner who has a number to fuss over and care for. Use to advantage the dogs of other breeders but check their antecedents with a fine toothcomb, for an ill-considered choice of stud dog can undo years of your valuable work in developing a strain.

The mating pair

The popular method of breeding is termed 'line breeding'. This entails any of the following crosses: grandsire to grand-daughter; grand-dam to grandson; cousin to cousin. It encompasses also the mating of aunts and nephews, uncles and nieces and half-brothers to sisters. In effect, it is tantamont to 'in breeding', but is normally considered 'safer', and it is at the same time slower in its development of a pure strain.

No one should begin dog-breeding without a complete understanding of the Staffordshire Bull Terrier breed Standard. He must learn to apply the written words of the Standard to the living model—in other words, get to know what his target looks like. Without this knowledge he cannot possibly know where to aim. Not only must he read the Standard, but he should attend as many championship shows for the breed as possible. Here he will see the best dogs and bitches in the breed. He will listen to comment about the winners and the losers and soon learn to form his own conclusions as to the worth of these remarks. He will try to arrange visits to leading Staffordshire Bull Terrier kennels; most exhibitors are amateurs in our breed and he can be assured of a warm welcome and hours of informative chat with most of them. He will obtain a good deal of useful advice and, possibly, some information he can discard. Some breeders are faddists; they are worth listening to, but should not be emulated. Faddists usually produce dogs with exaggerated physical features, completely forgetting to develop the dog as a whole. The physical parts they overlook usually become debilitated in their strains, and eventually unsound. Strains like this affect the breed adversely and must therefore be disregarded by any serious breeder. There is a temptation for some beginners to use a dog from a strain that has developed magnificent heads, but overlooked body and action, the failure in movement being due to faulty limb composition. The breeder may overlook the fact that in using such a dog he will produce stock that will tend to follow the type of the sire only in part, i.e. some of the puppies will have good heads yet unsound bodies, others will resemble the dam whose weaknesses her owner hoped to eradicate. *All* the puppies will carry the ability to pass on to their own progeny in due course a goodly number of unwanted features plus one good feature, a handsome head. The value of what is actually received in the litter of puppies does not warrant the use of such a sire. Stud dogs must be chosen not only for the quality of their get (and this should be investigated and determined by any intending user), but also for their intrinsic soundness, superb breed type (which is created by heredity) and lack of exaggeration. If a stud dog is to prove worth while to Staffordshire Bull Terrier breeders his pedigree should be factual and impeccable. His ancestry should be *sound* throughout. Beauty of pedigree is no good without beauty of type and body. Make sure you have them all before you contemplate the use of a stud dog. He must be purely masculine, hard-muscled; a male too big and too coarse physically to win in show need not deter you. This type often gets the best stock. Never let fantastic show successes tempt you from a good, forceful, proven stud dog to a 'fashionable' sire. The latter might be a beauty, but to be worth while as a stud dog he has to produce super stock, and only by the standard of his get can be he evaluated. Avoid young stud dogs—let others use them and test their abilities to produce winners. You will find a lot of the triers will be disappointed with results. If the young stud looks promising, then step in and use him in a well-designed mating, provided he suits *you*. Never be persuaded to do anything in dogs unless you *feel* it is right for your stock, your kennel, and yourself. Strains take years to build up and perfect. Breeders work on the development of their kennel strain for years, and success is often attributable to a simple instinct —

having 'an eye for a dog'. Always breed according to your instinct; you will seldom go wrong if you are 'doggy'. If you are not, then by all means rely on others, but you will not enjoy the game so much.

If your stud dog is a youngster, try to let him mate a matron bitch. She will show him the 'ropes' and in doing so educate him to facile stud work in incomparable manner. The best time for his first venture is when he is about ten months old, provided he is reasonably sturdy and well grown; then let him rest for the second mating until he is about fifteen months old. By the time he has reached twenty months of age he can have the occasional bitch, coming into regular use as a stud dog from two years onwards. Care must be taken to ensure that a good dog is regulated at stud—a close eye on his condition will soon tell you if he is being overworked. Obviously, a stud dog needs extra sustenance to keep him fit, according to the matings he performs. Young dogs should never be over-taxed; failure to observe this rule will result in too frequent misses when his bitches are due to whelp. The reputation for missing soon gets around in dogdom, and nothing can prove more damaging to a dog's career than reports that his services are unreliable.

The bitch

The bitch contributes in the formation of productive genes equally with the dog. Not enough people realise that the bitch's function in producing good stock is as great as the male's. Too many people concentrate in breeding on 'tail male', which is the sire's sire's sire, known as the 'line'. Tail female is the dam's dam's dam, called in dog parlance 'the family'. This is why you should ensure that your bitch is *good*. A handsome stud dog might well produce fair-grade stock from a mediocre bitch, but from the *good* bitch he would stand a much better chance of getting excellent litters. Discount all bitches that are too small, too weedy, and shelly. They look untypical; not only this, they are physically unsuited to the rigours of puppy-bearing. A good brood bitch needs to have substance; she should be roomy, wide in the pelvis, have plenty of rib and her full quota of femininity. A doggy bitch is a faulty one, although not as repellent as a bitchy dog. Some fanciers incline towards bitches with great heads, heads that are coarse in size and structure. Such an animal is faulty, and the fault should be treated with the same degree of severity as any other fault. Also, her expression should be feminine—a piercing, hard cast of outlook is for the male, not for the bitch. In size she should be at least what the breed Standard demands; a bitch can be allowed some extra length of body compared to the male but this is not essential, and short-backed bitches should be capable of producing young without complications.

Temperamentally, like the stud dog, she should be stable and reasonably equable. Nervous animals are unsuitable for breeding to; a too highly bred Stafford produces unfavourable tendencies. Although an aggressive animal might appeal to some enthusiasts, one over-inclined this way can prove a nuisance and embarrassment. It is as well to keep to *average* features both physically and temperamentally. Make sure that the bitch is well endowed with bone, that she carries her tail correctly, i.e. like an old-fashioned pump handle, and very important, ensure that she comes from a family of bitches noted for their performance as good mothers. The tendency to rear young badly is a transmittable fault. If the bitch has had previous litters, then a few tactful enquiries as to her mothering capacity will satisfy you as to her methods with young. If she is a maiden, then she will reveal her ability with the first litter. Keep a close eye on her attitude to the stud dog when she meets him. Natural matings are always preferable to induced ones, and sometimes they produce extra-good progeny; therefore, if the bitch seems to approve the mate chosen for her it could be significant.

Mating

The best time for the union is early morning, before the pair have been fed. If the stud dog has to be visited, and it is usual to take the bitch to the dog, be sure that all arrangements have been clearly understood by the dog owner and that you keep good time with your visit. The best time to mate a bitch is at her second heat, which is usually around fifteen months of age. The first sign of a heat is when the vulva begins to swell; a clear discharge will appear, followed by a red discharge. This is termed as showing 'colour', and usually twelve days from this symptom is the best time to mate the bitch, for then she is usually ripe to receive the dog. The bitch's oestrum, or heat, or season, has a normal span of twenty-one days. Most bitches become 'ripe' for mating between the tenth and fifteenth day of their term, although some seem to prefer a dog at unconventional times before or after the accepted period. If you have such a bitch, then her inclinations must be studied, and special treatment given to her when the time comes to breed with her. This will entail 'catching' her just at the time when she is ready to receive the stud dog. Sometimes this vital period is no longer than just a few hours on perhaps the ninth day of her heat. Experience will warn you when to have her standing, and it is as well to kennel her near the stud dog of your choice so that he can be introduced at a moment's notice, once she begins to show willing.

Always take your bitch to the stud dog, rather than consign her unaccompanied. Many maiden bitches 'miss', due to their distress at being pushed into a box and railed to some distant address, there to be handled by strangers and worried by a dog. Apart from this, it is best to be present at the mating, for then you can ensure that the dog of your choice was used. A lifetime of planning in the breeding field can be destroyed by the unscrupulous substitution of a dog at mating time.

With the actual mating, try first the 'natural' union. This entails leaving dog and bitch to their own devices for an initial courtship. Sometimes this works out well and the dog mates the bitch without ado. Unfortunately, it is common enough for the pair to fall out and start fighting, especially if the bitch is unreceptive sexually. If the situation looks hopeless, then it is unwise to leave them together running loose and chance damage to valuable stock. The mating must then be manually supervised. This does not mean forced, which is not only cruel, but liable to upset the bitch and affect conception. The best method to adopt is for the bitch's owner to sit at her head. She will see him there and be comforted while he holds her head on either side to prevent her snapping round and grabbing the dog when he mounts. The stud-dog owner should remain at her rear end, supporting her loins with one hand and steadying his dog on to her back with the other. He may find it necessary to guide the dog into the bitch's vulva and this is a useful lesson for any novice stud dog, although an experienced dog will not need such aid.

The Stafford's natural instinct will direct him to effective action. Once he has effected entrance to the bitch he should be held there for a few moments until he has made a 'tie'. At this stage he will have thrust deep into the bitch and his organ will have swollen considerably, the gland halfway down its length having inflated almost to the size of a ping-pong ball, thereby making it impossible for him to withdraw. In this fixed position the pair will remain until copulation is complete. This can take from fifteen to twenty-five minutes, although dogs vary in their time substantially. The natural mating position in canines is tail-to-tail. In the wild state dogs would need to defend themselves from attack when mating and this position allows them to move in a complete circle, the armament of two biting mouths ready to repel intruders. It is best to bring your mating pair into this natural position if they have not acheived it of their own accord. Lift up the dog's right hind leg, at the same time dropping his head and foreparts down beside the bitch on her left side. Keep easing him round towards her rear end, at the same time bringing his hind leg over her body. He can then be brought tail-to-tail with all four feet on the ground. Make sure at this point that the bitch does not begin to drag him backwards, for this might cause damage to the genitals. The two can then be kept in this position until they are ready to disengage. Once parted, the dog's personal comfort should receive attention by ensuring that the sheath has returned to its natural place over the penis. Then both dog and bitch can be watered and, later, fed.

Bear in mind that if the stud used is a novice and unproven dog, it is prudent to use him again within thirty-six hours just in case the first mating lacks effect.

Pre-natal care of bitch

The normal period of gestation is sixty-three days, although this varies according to individuals, maiden bitches often having their litters a little earlier. The bitch's feeding should be improved, where possible, and she should be wormed with a reliable proprietary medicine not more than one week following the termination of her season. Her exercise should be stepped up and every effort should be made to bring her into perfect bloom. By the time four or five weeks have passed since the initial mating it should be apparent if she is in whelp, the teats having become more prominent and the body around and below the loins showing added girth.

It is important, at this stage particularly, to keep her bowels open. A good idea is to dose her with a small teaspoonful of medicinal paraffin daily, starting some ten days or so before the expected whelping date. Just prior to the important day, reduce her food a little and stagger the meals.

A fortnight before she is due to whelp introduce her to a comfortable box where she is to have her puppies. This can be made quite easily, and a suitable size is about 30 in. × 24 in., the sides being high enough to ward off draughts. A 'pig-rail' can be screwed in around the inside. This is a piece of wood measuring about 2 in. × 1 in. affixed to the upright sides about 3 in. to 4 in. above the floor level. It is useful for very small puppies to shelter beneath even when their dam is leaning against the side. Of course, the whelping box can be improved by increasing the height of the sides, adding a platform to the top and a let-down end, the last modification being used to regulate the puppies' movements at weaning time.

It is usual to secure a piece of clean, disinfected sacking to the bottom of the box, making sure that it cannot be scratched up by the bitch in labour. Never use loose bedding or straw in case the whelps become enveloped and sat on. Some breeders use newspaper spread over the base of the box. This has its merits in that it can be easily scooped up and disposed of. However, it seems to lack the essentials of hygiene and should be used only if nothing better is available.

Within a few days of the expected whelping date inform your veterinary surgeon of the event so that he will be prepared to come out in any emergency.

Staffordshire Bull Terriers have a reputation for being good whelpers. It is not often serious difficulties occur to worry the breeder. However, it is always wise to be prepared for anything untoward and the following section will tell you what to have ready for the 'big day'.

Whelping routine

A bitch's normal temperature is 101·4°F. (38·5°C.). An in-whelp bitch about to deliver her puppies mostly shows a drop in body heat to below 100°F. (38°C.), occasionally down to 97·5°F. (36·5°C.), and the tendency is useful to the breeder, warning him that labour is about to start. The bitch is likely to reject her meals at this time and it is not unusual for her to relax into a deep sleep just prior to whelping, her way of preparing for the rigours of the next hour or so. Make sure that she is comfortable in the whelping quarters in a room temperature that should not be less than say 70°F. Strangers, other dogs, and likely distractions should be kept away from her over this vital period.

When about to whelp the bitch will get restless. Even if she is an experienced matron with several litters to her credit, it is a good plan to remain on the scene to supervise matters and give her confidence when she starts. If you are a little nervous, and perhaps inclined to fluster, then it is better to leave this duty to someone else, for your presence will be no help to her. It is prudent to have ready within easy reach of the whelping arena, a number of useful first-aid items; these are:

1. Packet of paper tissues or surgical lint cut into 9 in. squares.
2. Pair of sterilised probe-pointed surgical scissors. Make sure these are sharp.
3. Some lengths of surgical or strong cotton, about 6 in. long.
4. TCP or similar antiseptic and Dettol disinfectant.
5. Vaseline in jar.
6. Some pieces of clean white towelling or face squares.
7. A basin, also covered hot-water bottle, the latter preferably of the old-fashioned stone variety.
8. A feeding bottle.
9. A kettle of water.
10. A little brandy and small teaspoon. Only give the merest two drops if absolutely necessary.

GESTATION CHARTS

Table showing date of service and expected date of whelping based on the sixty-three day period

Served Jan.	*Whelps March*	*Served Feb.*	*Whelps April*	*Served March*	*Whelps May*	*Served April*	*Whelps June*
1	5	1	5	1	3	1	3
2	6	2	6	2	4	2	4
3	7	3	7	3	5	3	5
4	8	4	8	4	6	4	6
5	9	5	9	5	7	5	7
6	10	6	10	6	8	6	8
7	11	7	11	7	9	7	9
8	12	8	12	8	10	8	10
9	13	9	13	9	11	9	11
10	14	10	14	10	12	10	12
11	15	11	15	11	13	11	13
12	16	12	16	12	14	12	14
13	17	13	17	13	15	13	15
14	18	14	18	14	16	14	16
15	19	15	19	15	17	15	17
16	20	16	20	16	18	16	18
17	21	17	21	17	19	17	19
18	22	18	22	18	20	18	20
19	23	19	23	19	21	19	21
20	24	20	24	20	22	20	22
21	25	21	25	21	23	21	23
22	26	22	26	22	24	22	24
23	27	23	27	23	25	23	25
24	28	24	28	24	26	24	26
25	29	25	29	25	27	25	27
26	30	26	30	26	28	26	28
27	31	27	1 May	27	29	27	29
28	1 April	28	2	28	30	28	30
29	2	(29	3)	29	31	29	1 July
30	3			30	1 June	30	2
31	4			31	2		

Table showing date of service and expected date of whelping based on the sixty-three day period

Served May	*Whelps July*	*Served June*	*Whelps Aug.*	*Served July*	*Whelps Sept.*	*Served Aug.*	*Whelps Oct.*
1	3	1	3	1	2	1	3
2	4	2	4	2	3	2	4
3	5	3	5	3	4	3	5
4	6	4	6	4	5	4	6
5	7	5	7	5	6	5	7
6	8	6	8	6	7	6	8
7	9	7	9	7	8	7	9
8	10	8	10	8	9	8	10
9	11	9	11	9	10	9	11
10	12	10	12	10	11	10	12
11	13	11	13	11	12	11	13
12	14	12	14	12	13	12	14
13	15	13	15	13	14	13	15
14	16	14	16	14	15	14	16
15	17	15	17	15	16	15	17
16	18	16	18	16	17	16	18
17	19	17	19	17	18	17	19
18	20	18	20	18	19	18	20
19	21	19	21	19	20	19	21
20	22	20	22	20	21	20	22
21	23	21	23	21	22	21	23
22	24	22	24	22	23	22	24
23	25	23	25	23	24	23	25
24	26	24	26	24	25	24	26
25	27	25	27	25	26	25	27
26	28	26	28	26	27	26	28
27	29	27	29	27	28	27	29
28	30	28	30	28	29	28	30
29	31	29	31	29	30	29	31
30	1 Aug	30	1 Sept	30	1 Oct	30	1 Nov
31	2			31	2	31	2

Table showing date of service and expected date of whelping based on sixty-three day period

Served Sept.	*Whelps Nov.*	*Served Oct.*	*Whelps Dec.*	*Served Nov.*	*Whelps Jan.*	*Served Dec.*	*Whelps Feb.*
1	3	1	3	1	3	1	2
2	4	2	4	2	4	2	3
3	5	3	5	3	5	3	4
4	6	4	6	4	6	4	5
5	7	5	7	5	7	5	6
6	8	6	8	6	8	6	7
7	9	7	9	7	9	7	8
8	10	8	10	8	10	8	9
9	11	9	11	9	11	9	10
10	12	10	12	10	12	10	11
11	13	11	13	11	13	11	12
12	14	12	14	12	14	12	13
13	15	13	15	13	15	13	14
14	16	14	16	14	16	14	15
15	17	15	17	15	17	15	16
16	18	16	18	16	18	16	17
17	19	17	19	17	19	17	18
18	20	18	20	18	20	18	19
19	21	19	21	19	21	19	20
20	22	20	22	20	22	20	21
21	23	21	23	21	23	21	22
22	24	22	24	22	24	22	23
23	25	23	25	23	25	23	24
24	26	24	26	24	26	24	25
25	27	25	27	25	27	25	26
26	28	26	28	26	28	26	27
27	29	27	29	27	29	27	28
28	30	28	30	28	30	28	1 Mar
29	1 Dec	29	31	29	31	29	2
30	2	30	1 Jan	30	1 Feb	30	3
		31	2			31	4

The bitch's subsequent scratching at the floor of her bed will soon give way to distinct signs of labour. She will be seen to strain and reflex her body, the rhythm of the straining becoming more frequent as the first puppy approaches its birth. She might pant; whereupon you could offer her a little warm milk to help matters along, but it is better to let her proceed without interference. Soon, as all goes well, a small water-filled bag about the size of a golf-ball will appear at the vulva's opening. This acts as a cushion or buffer protecting the on-coming puppy against pressure. The bitch's contractions will rend the bag, and the puppy itself should follow soon after in its membraneous sac. If the puppy seems too delayed and the dam is distressed, then it might be wise to call your veterinary surgeon. However, assuming no complications arise, it will arrive and the bitch will break the bag and get her puppy breathing with some vigorous licking. Should she fail to do this the breeder must do it for her by simulating her movements and massaging the tiny body to induce respiration. The puppy will be attached to the placenta (afterbirth) by the umbilical cord. Normally, the bitch will sever the cord close to her puppy's navel with a sharp nip. If she seems disinclined to do this, then it must be done for her. Take one of your ready-cut pieces of surgical thread and tie it *tightly* round the cord about half an inch from the whelp's navel. Cut the cord with your sterilised scissors about one and a half inches above the tie. If the afterbirth has been expelled from the dam it can be disposed of, although no concern need be expended if she has eaten it, this being a natural action. On the other hand, if it still remains in her womb it will have to be withdrawn. Take the hanging cord and pull it gently, gradually bringing out the placenta. Should afterbirth remain in the bitch, it can cause or contribute to a septic womb condition, and for this reason it is most important to ensure that for every puppy born you have noted an afterbirth. A veterinary surgeon with an injection of Pituitrin can expel any retained placenta quite easily, and with the bitch's body comfort attended to she can proceed with the consider-able task of nursing her litter. It is normal for puppies to arrive head first, although occasionally a whelp will arrive feet first, this being known as a breech birth and unlikely to offer any difficulties in delivery. On rare occasions a puppy will be presented 'broadside'. This needs experienced manipulation and is best left to the veterinary surgeon, unless you are personally adept. In any case, the matter needs most urgent attention. Should the mother seem to have lost interest in delivering her puppies but it is apparent that others have yet to come, this might indicate uterine inertia, entailing a Caesarian operation. Again, this is something requiring professional surgery.

Once the bitch starts cleaning up all round and seems calm, it is likely her ordeal is over. Get her out of doors at once to attend to her needs, and as soon as she is absent check over the puppies for any abnormalities, and sex them. Remove all the stained paper or cloth bedding and replace with clean. When the dam returns, she can be left in charge, preferably in a darkened, certainly a quiet, room, following a meal of warm milk and water to which has been added a teaspoonful of glucose or a dessertspoonful of honey.

Post-whelping procedure

Some bitches get very nervous soon after their litter arrives. This is symptomised by panting and continually moving the puppies from place to place. The condition is caused usually by deficiency of calcium and phosphorus with Vitamin D. The veterinary surgeon may decide to inject her with Collo-Cal-D preparation, which will help to replace the temporary shortage and calm her. Once she is back to normal serenity and engaged with her litter, begin trying to arrange the whelps at feeding time, for some puppies are stronger than others and hog the dam's milk. The best flow comes from the inguinal teats down in the groin area. In the early feeding stages try to position the various puppies on these teats, in turn, so that they all get a fair share. Later, when their eyes open, at about ten days, they will fend better for themselves, but it is always wise to keep an eye on the weak litter member to ensure that he gets an adequate chance to build up. At this point the bitch should be getting plenty of liquid intake to encourage a plenteous supply of milk. She will need extra feeding, too, in order that her body is compensated for the goodness being taken out of it by the puppies. Make a rule that she (and the puppies) are inspected individually twice a day, in the initial stages, to ensure health and condition is being maintained.

Dew-claws

Four days after whelping the puppies will need to have their dew-claws removed, although this is a matter of choice since some of the old Stafford breeders elect to leave these rudimentary digits untouched. However, if dew-claws appear on the hind-legs they *must* be removed as they are then objectionable and indicative of some quirk in the breeding. It is unlikely that the dog will suffer any disadvantage by having his dew-claws remain, although there is a tendency for them to get caught up with obstructions in later life. The old fighting dogs found them useful tearing weapons and in the show dog they seem to add to substance in the foreparts, thereby improving general appearance.

Any qualified person can do the job, using a sharp pair of snub-nosed scissors, but if you are in doubt ask your veterinary surgeon to remove them. The bleeding can be stemmed with Friars' Balsam, but the wounds should be examined twice a day until completely healed.

Emergency measures

Hand-rearing

If you are unfortunate enough to lose your bitch either during whelping or later while she is in course of nursing her puppies, you will have to obtain a foster-mother for the youngsters, or hand-feed them. It is fairly easy to get a foster-mother from one of the suppliers who advertise in the canine Press. Collies are often used because of their ready milk supply and there is usually little difficulty in introducing the whelps to them. However, hand-feeding is a different matter. This entails a lot of patience, loss of sleep, and a certain amount of dedication. If the bitch died while whelping, the pups will never have known the benefit of her milk, and accordingly lost the immunising effect of the colostrum, which impregnates the initial flow of milk. This means that the antibodies in the colostrum, which help to stave off various viral diseases, will have to be artificially simulated. Your veterinary surgeon will know what to do, probably injecting each puppy with a preparation such as gamma globulin.

Lactol is a useful substitute for bitch's milk in the circumstances. The makers offer clear instructions for hand-rearing, and these should be followed. It is important to maintain the feed temperature, to watch the quantity does not vary with each meal, and to ensure strict regularity of meal times. The best way to ensure an even temperature is to keep the dish of Lactol standing in a bowl of hot water so that when the final puppy is fed, his meal will be just as warm as that of the first feeder. Note, too, that every meal must be freshly made; the puppies will never thrive on heated residue of previous feeds.

As soon as a youngster has been fed, his nose and face should be gently wiped over with a soft tissue or cloth to remove milk, which will have dried and become tacky. It is vital that the puppies urinate and pass motions regularly, too. If their dam was alive she would, with constant licking around their parts, induce this following every meal. In her absence this will have to be simulated by taking a pad of cotton wool dampened with warm water and stroking the genitals and anal region of every puppy with it. This will cause almost immediate defecation and urination, following which the parts should be smeared with a little Vaseline. If there is any hold-up in a puppy's main motion, gently slip a well-greased veterinary thermometer a fractional distance into its rectum, and this will induce a motion. It is important to ensure that no blockage takes place in the intestines, for this can prove fatal.

If you have an infra-red lamp it can be used to great advantage, for it helps maintain an even temperature so essential to the puppies' well-being. The first few days it should be set to give between 75°F. (23·9°C.) and 80°F. (26·7°C.), then by elevating the lamp the temperature can be gradually reduced to 60°F. (16°C.). Such lamps, besides being invaluable in any hand-rearing exercise, are useful requisites to the breeder who produces a number of litters annually. Always use dull-emitter bulbs, for these are harmless to the bitch's eyes; remember to protect the reflector with a wire cage as the bulb might work loose and fall on the puppies.

Lack of milk (aglactia)

It is not uncommon for a bitch, once her puppies have arrived, suddenly to acquire a high temperature, completely shutting off her milk supply for as long as two days, this at a vital time when the whelps need not only sustenance to thrive but also the protective colostrum in the dam's milk. The latter acts as a gentle laxative, expelling the impurities youngsters may have assimilated while in the womb. Sometimes the milk flow can be encouraged by continually placing the puppies to the dam's teats, but if this method fails and the state persists for more than six hours, the veterinary surgeon should be called in. He will inject the bitch to reduce her temperature, and once she reverts to normal body heat the milk will flow evenly and the puppies will feed contentedly.

Weaning

The weaning process should begin when the puppies are about 3½ weeks old, and the care you give to this and the goodness put into them will stand them in good stead so far as their future health is concerned. If by chance they have not thrived so well as you hoped, possibly due to the dam's milk flow being insufficient or of poor quality, then you might have to start weaning a day or so earlier. This decision will have to be yours, or you may prefer to seek expert opinion. Lactol is invaluable for puppy weaning, making an excellent substitute for bitch's milk. It is a powdered form of concentrated milk and instructions for feeding puppies according to their age will be found with the preparation. It should be fed at blood heat, and the cup of Lactol must be stood in a pan of hot water to ensure that every puppy in the litter is fed at the same temperature. The puppies should be encouraged to lap by taking each one and smearing a few drops of the food under its lips. Each puppy will take in the mixture and start to lap, slowly at first, but soon with enthusiasm.

Once the puppies are ready to be fed communally, it is wise to keep them off their dam for an hour or so before you put down the meal. This will encourage an appetite and prepare them for regular mealtimes. After three days of one Lactol meal a day, you can step up to two meals a day, following which cow's milk can be introduced to the mixture, bringing it to a thin cream-like consistency. By this time the pups will be eager feeders. It is a good plan to raise their feeding trough about two inches off the ground to ensure that they do not fall into the food, and to induce a better head posture. The raised feeding bowl system should be continued right into maturity as an aid to improvement in general bearing. During weaning time, keep an eye on the bitch. She is likely to disgorge some of her partly digested food, the puppies falling upon this with relish. Do not be appalled by this, it is a natural function, but make sure that the food you give her in this period is minced or of a consistency the pups can assimilate. Give the bitch another meal, too, or she will be hungry. It is the time to be building her up with plenty of high-protein food—raw meat, eggs, cheese, biscuits, etc., but keep fluids down to a bare minimum in order to help the natural falling-off of her milk supply. The puppies will bother her less and less as they become satisfied with the more solid food, but they should be examined regularly for cleanliness in the anal regions as their dam will no longer be attending to them. A cotton-wool pad dampened in warm water—add a few drops of antiseptic to it if you like—should be wiped round under each tail and the puppy inspected thoroughly at intervals.

Once the puppies have been on two Lactol meals for three days they can be introduced to a little fresh, raw butcher's meat. This should be finely shredded or minced and only a very small quantity given at first, until they get the taste for it. The diet can include minced boiled tripe, poached egg, and very light milk puddings, but meat should represent half their intake. Quantity can be stepped up gradually, but to avoid overeating at one sitting, the daily amount for each puppy should be divided into at least four portions and spread over about twelve hours. This will mean two meat meals and two milky meals every day, the meat meals alternating with the milk meals. By the time the youngsters are six weeks old they should have been away from their dam for a week and be entirely self-supporting, although some people like to let in the dam on occasions even up to this age. It is a mistake to do so, for puppies pulling at her teats will encourage milk flow rather than induce its dispersement. Quite apart from this, most bitches have had enough of their puppies by the time they are six weeks old, when the average Staffordshire Bull Terrier puppy is ready to start his own life in a new home. However, before he is sold he must be wormed. Few puppies are free from worm infestation. The round-worm is a parasite that looks rather like vermicelli, and is a creamy-yellow in colour. An upset stomach with diarrhoea of a jelly-like quality is the usual symptom; often the puppy noses round to his rear-end or squats suddenly as though in brief discomfort. Oddly enough, the appetite may either increase or fall away completely, but the youngster will not thrive well until the worm pest has been expelled. There are many proprietary vermifuges and vermicides on the market today, most of them excellent, and a puppy can be dosed when quite young, with no ill-effects. Most breeders prefer to see the job through themselves, but for those who don't, the veterinary surgeon is always available. The worms will come out in a tight, writhing ball, and you may be surprised at the number emitted. Burn them immediately and disinfect the area.

Another worm, even less pleasant, is the tapeworm. It is not so frequently encountered, but when present in a dog it can be detected by the grain-like segments adhering to his anus or in the motions. A dog with tapeworm is usually listless and very much out of sorts, the breath and body odour being offensive. The worm seems to be contracted either from the flea or through eating rabbit. It is best to consult your veterinary surgeon, and he will arrange to expel this parasite, which is often several feet in length.

Make sure that any puppy in course of being wormed is kept warm and dry. Always worm at least three days before a puppy is due to go to his new home. It is not fair to the purchaser to supply a youngster ill-affected in his motions by medicine, and any puppy showing such signs should be put on to warm bread and milk feeds, raw meat being withdrawn temporarily until the motions are firm. Motions should always be firm—view with suspicion any that are not.

Feeding

Good food and plenty of it is essential to the well-being of a strong and energetic breed like the Staffordshire Bull Terrier. No one should begrudge the extra shillings spent on superior food, for it will be found a good investment and likely to insure against sickness and subsequent veterinary fees. The dog's menu needs to be good and varied, although based largely on fresh raw meat. The wise breeder, however, ensures that his dog will eat anything: raw meat, cooked meat, fish, proprietary dog foods (many of which are excellent), eggs, and so on. By so doing he will never rear a fastidious dog, which can prove more than a nuisance when the food of his choice is not available. A good eater is known as a good do-er, which is the best kind of dog to own, for by his good appetite and intake he will develop and keep himself in good condition. All meat should be as for human consumption, pet food meat usually being inferior. Some people like to feed their dogs paunches and various offal. This is cheap, possibly good, but, just the same, fresh raw meat is better. If animal feeding meats have to be used, then boil them. When feeding puppies, a sound guide as to quantity at each meat meal is to lightly compress in the hand enough meat to represent the size of the youngster's head. Always keep an eye on animals when they are feeding. It will be found that when a dog has had his fill he will halt at least momentarily in his attack on the meal. This should guide you as to how much food he needs at this stage. Meat should be minced while the puppies are very small, say up to nearly five weeks of age, but after this it should be chopped into manageable size, for then the dog will gain from it the most nutriment.

Here are a few suggested menus for Staffordshire Bull Terriers from puppyhood to maturity:

Puppies from start of weaning, i.e. about 3½ weeks of age up to 2 months
At least four meals a day:

8 *a.m.* Milk meal, e.g. bread and milk, porridge, cereal and milk, Farex, etc.

Noon. Meat meal, minced raw butcher's meat. Add Saval No. 1 for roughage, also vegetable juices in moderation.

Alternative: steamed or boiled white fish, fresh herrings.

C. M. Cooke

Ch. Jolihem Dreadnought

Ch. Duke of Ducks Hill

Gibbs

Constones Yer Man

Ch. Eastaff Guardian

Ch. Wallace the Wizard

Above: A rare photograph of Harry Mellings' Lioness, dam of Tough Guy

Left: Ch. Fearless Red of Bandits

Constones Tuscaloosa Sam

Keith Yull

Australian Ch. Eastaff Bruiser

Ch. Maljue Cutters Boy

4 p.m. Repeat the 8 a.m. meal.

Alternative: soup or gravy poured over rusks.

8 p.m. Repeat the noon meal. A 'nightcap' of warm milk can be given before the house retires. This will help the puppy to sleep through the night.

Puppies from 2 to 4 months
As above, but larger quantities, with the 4 p.m. meal omitted.

Puppies from 4 to 12 months
8 a.m. Milk meal as above, or rusks and Terrier Meal soaked in gravy.

Noon. Few dog biscuits (dry).

8 p.m. At *least* ½ lb raw meat with ample roughage, according to size up to 1 lb.

Adult dog or bitch
One big meal a day, preferably in the evening after exercise. Quantity *at least* 1 lb chopped raw butcher's meat, plus a little roughage.

Stud dog
As for adult, but 1¼ lb raw meat, teaspoonful of cod liver oil, pinch of salt and Vetzymes. Liver once a week. Raw egg broken over meal.

In-whelp or nursing bitch
As for adult stud dog. Take care not to overfeed.

Fresh cool water should be available to the dog at all times.

Coarse cod-liver oil (about 1 teaspoonful for adults, half quantity for puppies) can be given every evening. Malt extract is particularly good as a body builder in winter months, pure olive oil being better in the summer.

Avoid game and poultry, the bones being dangerous to dogs. Fish must be boned carefully, and given only when absolutely fresh.

Vetzymes (Phillips Yeast product) are excellent and should be given according to recommended dosage.

Abidec in liquid or capsule form is invaluable for administering Vitamins A, B, C, D, and E.

Calsimil and Collo-Cal-D both contain a balanced form of calcium for dogs, also phosphorus and Vitamin-D.

Lines and families

Early livestock breeders would contend that the way to produce good winning stock was to use the best stud dog available, regardless of the bitch's worth to the union. Of course, a few 'sports' or chance good ones appeared from matings arranged to this formula, but these dogs actually held scant value when the time came to breed from them. This was because a dog so produced, while having some of the physical and latent points of his handsome sire, also possessed some features inherited from his third-rate dam, and the aptitude to reproduce them. Had the dam been a beauty like the sire, and the youngster owned two good parents instead of one, then as a producer he might have proved useful.

When Bruce Lowe's researches into the breeding of racehorses were edited and published many years ago, they opened up an entirely new aspect to the female's worth and contribution in the breeding field. The 'Figure System' now termed the 'Line and Family' breeding method is today considered a certain way of producing good livestock, provided the animals used are healthy, sound, and bred from an established 'Line' and an accepted 'Family'. To explain these terms simply, take an ordinary pedigree form as shown in the diagram below. The important line of paternity or 'Line' is that followed by the sire's sire's sire, etc. The important family of maternity or 'Family' is that followed by the dam's dam's dam, etc. Thus if you examine the diagram, which shows the 'Line' of Ch. Fearless Red of Bandits and the 'Family' of Dee's Pegg, his dam, you will follow how 'Tail-Male' and 'Tail-Female' are evolved to make 'Line' and 'Family'.

Sire's Sire's Sire, etc. — Perry's Tiger *MLine*

Brindle Mick

Ch. Gentleman Jim

Ch. Fearless Red of Bandits *MLine*

Dee's Pegg

Fearless Floss

Dam's Dam's Dam, etc. — Game Smut *Family* 2

Some breeders are already proving the value of the system of planning their breeding with top-line sires and bottom-line dams, treating these as more important than the individuals appearing in the middle part of the pedigrees under review. The main thing is that when you consider Line and Family in your breeding, make sure that both are established and productive of superior stock. Never experiment with the unknown quantity. To breed good dogs you must place your trust in proven stock with quality background.

When the breed was 'recognised' in 1935, a certain pattern evolved from the limited number of stud dogs then representing the breed. Mr H. N. Beilby, a disciple of the Rev. Rosslyn Bruce, DD (OXON), FLS, Fox Terrier expert and advocate of the 'Line and Family' method, went to work to establish Lines and Families in Staffords. In those days, of course, this was a reasonably easy task to complete. The breed was virtually in its infancy so far as planned breeding was concerned. Mr Beilby found six main Lines of varying importance, these being identified according to their founder's name, i.e. the stud dog of the Line in question, and responsible for furthering it from the start. Thus, we got:

'J' Line	'J' for Fearless *J*oe
'M' Line	'M' for Brindle *M*ick
'L' Line	'L' for Game *L*ad
'B' Line	'B' for Rum *B*ottle
'R' Line	'R' for *R*ibchester Max
'C' Line	'C' for *C*inderbank Beauty

the order shown above being the relative order of importance in the middle 'thirties up to the subsequent eight years. Today the position has changed. The 'M' Line has forged ahead by leaps and bounds, due probably to the work put in at stud by Ch. Gentleman Jim and his various champion sons, notably Ch. Widneyland Kim. The former dog, a piebald, was bred by Mr Jack Dunn out of Triton Judy but owned by Mr Joe Mallen, a colourful personality, with a pub in the Black Country, who did much to emblazon the breed in the Midlands and beyond. Just as Jim excelled his sire Brindle Mick in stud achievements, so did Brindle Bill, another of Mick's sons, contribute greatly to the Line. Beilby reports that this dog was smallish, sturdy mahogany brindle, short in muzzle with a tendency to being 'dished', a feature some of his progeny inherited. This dog's leading son was Ch. Brigands Bo'sun whose fame as a stud dog is already well established in breed annals.

In current times most of the leading stud dogs are from the 'M' Line. this is the way the breed has shaped itself, and no doubt the 'M' Line will continue in its pre-eminence. In the following pages will be found the pedigrees of six important sires since 1940.

CH. BRINSTOCK GLENAGOW

K.C.S.B. 745 AQ

Colour: Black brindle and white — Born: 26 Jan 56
Owner: Mr W. A. Boylan
Breeder: Mrs G. W. R. Burge Smith — M-Line

Parents	*Grand-parents*	*G.G.-parents*	*G.G.G.-parents*
Sire Ch. Delveth's Pride	*Sire* Ch. Pal of Aveth, C.D. Ex.	*Sire* Ch. Quiz of Wyncroft	*Sire* Jolly Roger
			Dam Gamesters Hot Black
		Dam Elegant Girl	*Sire* Tenacious Pete
			Dam Blandona Black Queen
	Dam Dellfrey's Pride	*Sire* Ch. Godfrey's Pride	*Sire* Ch. Widney-land Kim
			Dam The Empress Theodora
		Dam Ch. Della of Impkin	*Sire* Ch. Widney-land Kim
			Dam Christie of Wyncroft
Dam Ch. Brinstock Welsh Maid	*Sire* Timothy of Dugarde	*Sire* Jake's Jest of Dugarde	*Sire* Ch. Brigands Bo'sun
			Dam Ch. Perfect Lady
		Dam Princess Pat of Alum Rock	*Sire* Brindle Bill
			Dam Fredancer
	Dam Queen of Barry	*Sire* Pendower Invincible	*Sire* Int. Ch. Head Lad of Villmar
			Dam Nightshade of Pendower
		Dam Pendower Biddy	*Sire* Brinstock Pimpernel
			Dam Brinstock Charmaine

CH. BANDITS BRINTIGA

K.C.S.B. 63 AV

Colour: Dark brindle — Born: 1 Oct 59

Owner: Mr T. Field

Breeder: Mr F. Southall — R-Line

Parents	*Grand-parents*	*G.G.-parents*	*G.G.G.-parents*
Sire Georgecroft Mandumas	*Sire* Int. Ch. Head Lad of Villmar	*Sire* Vindictive Monty of Wyncroft	*Sire* Ribchester Max
			Dam Spitfire Freda of Wyncroft
		Dam Fred's Fancy	*Sire* Brindle Jim
			Dam Golden Dawn
	Dam Georgecroft Gem	*Sire* Cheiron's Black Mike	*Sire* Foxhill Monarch of Wychbury
			Dam Cherion's Dumb Blonde
		Dam Georgecroft Lady	*Sire* Young Ripley of Georgecroft
			Dam Sally Grise
Dam Satan's Mistress	*Sire* Ch. Bellerophon Billy Boy	*Sire* Ch. Quiz of Wyncroft	*Sire* Jolly Roger
			Dam Gamesters Hot Black
		Dam Honest Martha Le Loup	*Sire* Le Loup Pride
			Dam Rita Loup
	Dam Tickey of Butternab	*Sire* Squib of Senlin	*Sire* Ch. Goldwyn's Leading Lad
			Dam Bumblebee of Senlin
		Dam Foldegate Cadette	*Sire* Brigands Bo'sun's Beau
			Dam Lady Pat of Killyglen

CH. EASTAFF DANOM

K.C.S.B. 1331AP

Colour: Red-fawn and white — Born: 7 Aug 55
Owner: Mr J. McNeill
Breeder: Miss J. Brightmore — M-Line

Parents	*Grand-parents*	*G.G.-parents*	*G.G.G.-parents*
Sire Ch. Goldwyn's Leading Lad	*Sire* Wheatley Lad	*Sire* Brindle Bill	*Sire* Brindle Mick
			Dam Sunny Lady
		Dam Goldwin	*Sire* Monty's Double
			Dam Gainas Lady
	Dam Brindle Diana	*Sire* Sunny Bill	*Sire* Brindle Mick
			Dam Sunny Lady
		Dam Goldwin	*Sire* Monty's Double
			Dam Gainas Lady
Dam Ch. Linda of Killyglen	*Sire* Brigand's Bo'sun's Beau	*Sire* Wychbury Trouble	*Sire* Clarkstead Pete
			Dam Lady Benita
		Dam Scamper's Judy	*Sire* Scamper
			Dam Nellie Dene
	Dam Colleen of Killyglen	*Sire* Pat the Boy	*Sire* Jolly Roger
			Dam Tooby
		Dam Ch. Eastbury Lass	*Sire* Ch. Gentleman Jim
			Dam Invincible Belle

CH. GAME FLASH

K.C.S.B. 457AW

Colour: Black brindle and white — Born: 15 July 61
Owner: Mr A. Baxter
Breeder: Mr A. Baxter — M-Line

Parents	*Grand-parents*	*G.G.-parents*	*G.G.G.-parents*
Sire Hydiamond King	*Sire* Black King	*Sire* Somerville Black Bomber	*Sire* Prince Rajah
			Dam Bonnie Red Lady
		Dam Its A Pal	*Sire* Son o' Roger
			Dam Miss Patch
	Dam Ch. Little Diamond Tiara	*Sire* Ch. Wychbury Red Riband	*Sire* Ch. Wychbury Kimbo
			Dam Regnant Show Lady
		Dam Queenie's Dynamite	*Sire* Ch. Wychbury Diamond King
			Dam Ch. Little Brindle Queen
Dam Midnight Mischief	*Sire* Ch. Major in Command of Wychbury	*Sire* Ch. Wychbury Diamond King	*Sire* Diamond Bill
			Dam Granby Lass
		Dam Ch. Little Brindle Queen	*Sire* Ch. Widney-land Little Gent of Pynedale
			Dam Bonnie Briar
	Dam Tiptonian Peggy	*Sire* Ch. Toro	*Sire* Ch. Wychbury Diamond King
			Dam Lady Lesette
		Dam Lady Suzette	*Sire* The Major of Uddffa
			Dam Vickie of Uddffa

CH. MAJOR IN COMMAND OF WYCHBURY

K.C.S.B. 348AN

Colour: Brindle and white — Born: 7 Jan 54

Owner: Mr G. A. Dudley

Breeder: Mrs D. Hoggarth — J-Line

Parents	*Grand-parents*	*G.G.-parents*	*G.G.G.-parents*
Sire Ch. Wychbury Diamond king	*Sire* Diamond Bill	*Sire* Faithful Pal	*Sire* Bomber Command
			Dam Pride of the West
		Dam Lovely Sue	*Sire* Draycott Lad
			Dam Birdy
	Dam Granby Lass	*Sire* Pete	*Sire* The Great Bomber
			Dam Lady Maureen of Fordbrook
		Dam Snowdonia Queen	*Sire* Brindle Boy
			Dam Bull Ant
Dam Ch. Little Brindle Queen	*Sire* Ch. Widney-land Little Gent of Pynedale	*Sire* Ch. Wychbury Kimbo	*Sire* Ch. Widney-land Kim
			Dam Wychbury Peggy
		Dam Pal o' Derek	*Sire* Son o' Roger
			Dam Lady o' Lin
	Dam Bonnie Briar	*Sire* Bo'sun Again	*Sire* Ch. Brigands Bo'sun
			Dam Coldbath Chippy
		Dam Handsome Nell	*Sire* Ch. Brigands Bo'sun
			Dam African Queen

CH. RELLIM A'BOY
K.C.S.B. 1645AR

Colour: Pied — Born: 1 Sept 57
Owner: Mrs T. Miller
Breeder: Mrs T. Miller — M-Line

Parents	*Grand-parents*	*G.G.-parents*	*G.G.G.-parents*
Sire Ch. Wychbury Red Riband	*Sire* Ch. Wychbury Kimbo	*Sire* Ch. Widney-land Kim	*Sire* Ch. Gentleman Jim
			Dam Game Judy
		Dam Wychbury Peggy	*Sire* Ch. Brigands Bo'sun
			Dam Newhall Bess
	Dam Regnant Show Lady	*Sire* Nuneatonion Boy	*Sire* Brindle Bill
			Dam Little Gem's Pride
		Dam Brindle Trix	*Sire* Leader of Wyncroft
			Dam H'pool Drifter
Dam Ch. Wychbury Midly Girl	*Sire* Ch.Widney-land Kim	*Sire* Ch. Gentleman Jim	*Sire* Brindle Mick
			Dam Triton Judy
		Dam Game Judy	*Sire* Game Bill
			Dam Reddall Bess
	Dam Regnant Show Lady	*Sire* Nuneatonion Boy	*Sire* Brindle Bill
			Dam Little Gem's Pride
		Dam Brindle Trix	*Sire* Leader of Wyncroft
			Dam H'pool Drifter

8
Shows and Showing

Most owners on finding they have acquired a good specimen become enthusiastic about the breed and evince a desire to exhibit in competition with other Staffordshire Bull Terriers. Dog-showing can prove a most interesting hobby and one that, in spite of its rivalry, offers many opportunities for making friends. It is as well, before exhibiting, to get an expert's opinion on whether or not your Stafford is worth showing, or, if he is a puppy, ready to show. On the other hand, you can take the plunge just by entering a show and finding out on the spot.

The first thing you must do is register your puppy with a name at the Kennel Club. It is possible that the breeder or dealer who sold him to you will already have done this, in which event you must then apply to the Kennel Club to transfer him to your ownership. If he has not been registered, then you will need Salmon Form 2, and when filled in the application must be lodged before the date of the show you wish to attend. No dog can be exhibited at a regulation dog show unless this has been done. Dog shows are advertised in the canine Press, *Dog World* and *Our Dogs* being the two prominent weekly journals in Britain. From the lists you will be able to select either a local show, where all breeds are eligible to compete (and these are useful events at which to get yourself and your dog used to dog-show routine), or a specialist breed show where only Staffords will be on view, such shows being held usually in a major town or city. A telephone call or written application to the society's secretary will quickly obtain the show schedule and entry form; also the rules by which you must abide if you enter your dog. Assuming he is a puppy and not growing on too unevenly you may consider entering him in the Special Puppy Class (6–9 months) or Puppy Class (6–13 months) provided. It is wise never to show a puppy in the former class until he is 8 months old, or in the latter until he is at least 10 months old.

It is a waste of time to show a puppy that is too immature, and at six months of age most Stafford youngsters are too 'raw' to make any impact, even in a Special Puppy Class. In fact, if a Staffordshire Bull Terrier puppy looks like an adult it is a fair sign that he will be too big and coarse by the time he enters the yearling stage. Slow furnishers usually last longer than those who develop too quickly: consequently, the former are preferable for those who look forward to a few years of exhibiting although the latter may well win more puppy classes. It should be realised that the Stafford is strongly akin to the Bulldog and, like this progenitor, rather slow to mature. For this reason discretion should be used as to the best and most effective time to show your puppy. In the puppy stages a Stafford changes extraordinarily; from a wriggling, slender youngster of six months he can develop into a sturdy, well-ribbed and tank-like canine by the time he is a year old. In this interim period he will change a dozen times, one week for the good, the next apparently for the worse. More than one champion dog well known today was discarded by an original owner during puppyhood because he looked worthless, so deceiving is this breed in its adolescence.

Quite apart from the foregoing, when you exhibit your dog, especially if against other Staffordshire Bull Terriers, you should try for a win. Nothing is more demoralising in dogdom than a series of 'also-ran' positions, and many a potential show-goer has given up the game prematurely after several such disappointments. Another thing: you must not let your dog get known as an 'all-time loser' either. Rightly or wrongly, such an exhibit gets branded and needs to make good with an awful lot of winning subsequently in order to vindicate himself with the show crowd.

Assuming that you have prepared your dog for his first show by training him to pose alertly, suffer physical handling, and to move effectively (*see* 'Training for Show'), you should attend the event in plenty of time and settle down to make preparation for your class. You should not have fed him prior to starting off and he should have had ample time to relieve himself before arriving at the show venue. Have your dog on a taut lead when you enter the hall to present your exhibitor's pass, which will have come to you in advance of the show date; other dogs with their owners will usually linger near the entrance and you will not wish to begin your day with a dog-fight as your exhibits and theirs come nose to nose. If the show is a benched one (all championship and some open shows are), your pass will have a number that corresponds with a similar number affixed to the bench where your dog will be penned. At such shows you must bring a bench chain (obtainable at any pet shop) and secure your dog with it from his collar to a ring at the rear of the bench. Make sure the length of chain is such that the Stafford can lie down and move with reasonable comfort, yet insufficient to allow his nose to protrude beyond the walls and floor of the pen. Put down a rug or coverlet for him to rest on, and you can tuck away your personal possessions such as bag, hat, catalogue behind him. If the show is an all-day event, you can take your own sandwiches or use the bar which is always in evidence at such affairs. Be sure that you have a water bowl, a pocket first-aid kit, and some sustenance for the dog, but do not feed him until he has completed his class otherwise you are likely to have a sluggish dog on the lead when you enter the ring. Ensure that you have an adequate supply of titbits in your pocket to reward him for good behaviour.

However, most shows are unbenched, which are less formal than the benched events. All you need do is find yourself a quiet corner somewhere in the hall, keep your dog under control and watch for other dogs poking in their noses too closely. When your class is announced, step into the ring with all the confidence you can muster, determined to do well for yourself and the dog. The ring stewards will tell you where to stand in the ring, and soon the judge will call you over towards him. He will indicate where he wants you to pose the dog; this will be on floor level. Staffords are never hoisted on to tables like Toy breeds, unless the judge has a bad back or some other ailment. At this point you will remember (and let us hope your Stafford does too) the home training for show. Try to keep him alert—this is important, for a floppy dog looks bad and is seldom known to bring home the prizes. The judge will examine him, assess him, maybe ask you a question or two, then instruct you to move him. You will turn away from the judge and walk the best part of a ring's length away, during which time the judge will be eyeing the exhibit's hind action and ring behaviour, always watchful for any signs indicating unsoundness. You will then turn about face, retracing your steps to where the judge waits observing the dog's front, balance, and forward movement. Halt just ahead of him and wait for him to have another brief look or to tell you that he has finished with you for the moment, whereupon you can return to your place. Never make the mistake of slackening your vigil on the dog at this time; you must concentrate on this showing job all the time you are in the ring. Concentrate on making the dog look good but at the same time keep an overt eye on what is going on in the ring around you. Guard against the neighbouring exhibitor who tries to edge you out of the judge's vision by moving almost imperceptibly in front of you. It is a common enough trick by some rivals when the competition is 'hot'. Watch, too, for the noisy and perhaps ill-trained dog, kept on a slack lead deliberately, so that it may attempt to engage your dog. It is all very unfair of course, but done 'with a smile' and, unless the provocation is obvious, no one can say much about it.

Remember that the standard of dog-handling today leaves plenty of room for improvement. This applies just as much to Staffords as any breed and, generally speaking, if you can cultivate an effective and stylish manner of handling you will acquire a big advantage over many exhibitors, some perhaps with better dogs than yours. It is important that the exhibit should be *presented*, and even a little flamboyance will not come amiss at times in a ring when mere points will force a decision. Many a judge has been induced to favour the better-handled dog of a well-matched competing pair, and if you can train your exhibit to look alert while moving freely and naturally on an 'easy' lead it is better than all the fussing and overhandling that sometimes goes on. Some handlers make quite a ritual out of it—down on their knees, and holding up the dog's head with one hand, his tail with the other. In dog parlance this is termed 'topping and tailing', and although some breeds are inclined to wink an eye at it, it is not good procedure and should not be employed with Staffordshire Bull Terriers. If a Stafford cannot hold up his head unassisted and his tail needs to be dragged out from beneath him to make him look good, then he is a doubtful Stafford and cannot be worth a prize.

If you are fortunate enough to have a dog good enough to

win a prize, no matter what its worth—First (red), Second (blue), Third (yellow), Reserve (green), or even one of the commendation cards—be pleased, and try to accept it rationally. Too many first-time exhibitors get elated with initial success, only to bewail when they lose next time out. Often, when this happens, the judge gets blamed. The fact is overlooked that not only do judges' opinions vary but competition alters in its strength from show to show, quite apart from the condition of dogs, which tends to improve or deteriorate from week to week. Over a given number of shows even a super dog will win at some, lose at others. However, if he *is* a good specimen and he is shown regularly, he must make his mark eventually, maybe get to the top if he is of really good class material. The average dog, because he is average, will seldom achieve the heights of fame, unless he is fortunate in that he has an owner who is an expert in campaigning a dog to stardom. Such instances are rare, which is just as well for the breed, but the novice with a good dog should rest content that with persistence, coupled with dedication, his dog will eventually be recognised, just as the poor one will fall by the wayside and finally be left at home.

There are many clubs specialising in the Staffordshire Bull Terrier. A list of these with their secretaries will be found in Appendix B. Join the ones nearest to you; many of our leading exhibitors of Staffordshires belong to them all. Here you will find breed enthusiasm in plenty where you can get all the advice and encouragement you need to further your interest in this remarkable dog.

Kennel Club matters

The Kennel Club was founded in 1873 by S. E. Shirley, and with a committee of twelve well-known fanciers had offices in Westminster, London. The club's current offices are at 1–4 Clarges Street, Piccadilly, London W1Y 8AB (Telephone: 01 493 6651), and enquiries should be addressed to the Secretary there. A list of the fees applicable is given here.

The Kennel Club registration fees
as from 1 October 1985

	Fees (inclusive of VAT) £
Litter Recording/Registration by Breeder:	
(The total number of puppies in the litter must be declared)	
Litter Recording Fee (payable in every case)	5.00
Plus per puppy in litter registered (named)	(each) 5.00
Plus per puppy in litter not registered (unnamed)	(each) 1.00
e.g. A litter of five puppies of which two are registered (named) and three are unnamed will cost £5.00 plus £10.00 plus £3.00. Total £18.00.	
Dog Naming by Owner:	
Registration (Salmon Form 2)	5.00
Registration in Obedience Register (Buff Form 1A)	5.00
Change of Name. Affix holders only (Pink Form 8)	5.00
Transfers:	
Transfer by new owner	5.00
Other:	
Re-registration	5.00
Loan or Use of Bitch	5.00
Pedigrees:	
Export Pedigrees	20.00
Three Generation Pedigree	3.00
Affixes:	
Registration of an affix by qualification only, see regulations	35.00
Affix Maintenance Fee (Annual)	10.00

NOTE

Affix. This term has supplanted the word prefix. It is a name granted by the Kennel Club committee to a breeder allowing him the sole right to use such affix as part of a name when registering or changing the name of a dog. Where the grantee of a registered affix wishes to use it when naming a dog bred by him or which was bred from parents which were bred by him, then the affix must be used as a *prefix*, i.e. as the first word of the dog's name. Otherwise it must be used as a *suffix*, i.e. as the last word of the dog's name.

9
The Final Stages

The amateur breeder can obtain considerable satisfaction and no doubt a sense of some achievement as he watches the litter of home-bred Staffords romping in his pen. The fact that he planned the union of their parents, saw the dam through her ordeal, and built up the puppies through their weaning period into the ready-for-going-away stage is a matter for some pride. However, whereas it is not hard to sell well-bred stock, finding suitable homes for the youngsters may prove difficult. A lot will have to depend on your personal judgement of prospective buyers. Staffords are good with children, but sometimes children are not so good with Staffords. In fact, some families with a number of very small children are quite unsuitable as owners of a dog. The parents might well be dog-lovers, but they cannot forever be watching for and controlling the often unintentional cruelties of their young to a puppy in the family circle. Very old people, too, will be ill-advised in buying a Stafford. The breed is too strong, too lusty for the frail to handle, and the dog will not get the exercise he needs to thrive. Homes where the owners are business-folk and out all day are no good either, for a small puppy needs four meals a day, quite apart from the fact that he needs companionship and some training at this early stage of his life. Husband and wife buyers, when it is obvious the latter especially lacks keenness, seldom adapt to puppy ownership because the woman often becomes responsible for its feeding and training, which either she does with resentment or not at all. Never sell a puppy that is to be given to someone else for whom it is to be a 'surprise', unless, of course the person concerned can assure you the dog is really wanted. Most people wanting a dog, however, go out and buy one, and an unexpected gift of a small puppy needing special attention, while appreciated at the time, soon loses its novelty, often to the puppy's disadvantage. It is usually worth putting a subtle form of questionnaire to intending buyers. This can be done in a respectful manner—most people will be sensible enough to realise you have their interests at heart, as well as the puppy's. Finally, make sure they want the dog because they have chosen it to join them in their family circle and because they are dog-lovers. A dog bought merely to guard the property from an outside shed or kennel has no worthwhile life and becomes miserable.

If you are a one-bitch owner and therefore but an occasional breeder, you will not worry overmuch about the commercial side of dog-breeding. Your odd litter or two will not be difficult to sell, provided they do not arrive and become ready for selling at an unfavourable time—just before or during the peak holiday period between June and August, or coinciding with some national emergency. The best months for having your Staffords ready to go are January and February, followed by September to mid-December, then March to May, in that order. Of course, winter puppies are better raised in a warm, airy room in the house rather than in a kennel or shed where the temperature is liable to fluctuate and produce less than perfect coats on the youngsters.

Apart from any puppy or puppies you intend to retain for your own use, the litter should be off your hands by the time it reaches eight weeks of age. Once puppies exceed this age they begin to be a liability from an expense point of view. If kept up to the age of three months with no buyers in sight they can prove an embarrassment, and every day will add something to the cost of their keep, apart from the time given to cleaning them up and settling their squabbles. Worse, the older they get, the more apparent become their faults and their chances of selling lessened. People like to buy a Staffordshire Bull Terrier puppy that, although a little 'buccaneer' in its manner, is solid, blocky and snug. In effect, when a Stafford puppy has gone beyond the three-months stage it is rather too big to appeal to the average buyer. Many first-time breeders, daunted by the thought of seeing their puppies go, have run on the entire litter up to three months only to find they have what is virtually a hornets' nest on their hands. The tragedy can be that with no one to offer overgrown puppies new homes, the litter has to be put down. Fortunately, this result is rare, but not unknown.

Advertise early

By the time the puppies have entered their fifth week of life you should prepare to advertise. You have a choice of using the canine Press, *Dog World* and *Our Dogs* being excellent weekly papers and appealing to people who really want dogs, also *Exchange and Mart*, which has a dog section, or the national Press. If you decide on the big evening papers as a medium, Friday-night issues seem to have the best effect, either the livestock or personal columns being good. Avoid the use of box numbers; puppies are usually wanted at once, and few buyers have the patience to wait for information. This is why you should include a telephone number in your advertisement, if possible. For your part, as the seller, it is better if you are contacted in advance of a visit so that you can quote a price for a specific puppy and, if an interest is shown, this is the youngster that can be introduced to the prospective buyer when he calls. Many buyers prefer this (although they might not admit it) to the responsibility of selecting from a litter of puppies. Most have little or no knowledge of the breed's finer points, but many have a keen enough eye for health and condition. A puppy *must* be sound, healthy, and in generally good bloom when you offer it. It is your responsibility to see to this, not only for the client's sake but in fairness to the puppy itself. Never worry too much if you cannot assess a Stafford puppy's show potential. Few people, even breeders with many years of experience in the game can do this, although some like to think they can. Admittedly, the man who has bred and developed a distinct strain on established bloodlines for several generations might have a fair idea as to the show future of certain of his puppies, but even he cannot be infallible, for there are too many hazards involved in this breed. Apart from type, which varies in Staffords too much, the mouth is probably still the breeder's biggest worry. The Staffordshire Bull Terrier has the Bulldog as a progenitor, and the latter is a congenitally undershot breed. It is not therefore surprising that some Staffords, in spite of selective breeding to obviate and correct this fault, develop an undershot jaw. If you are selling your puppies merely as pedigree Staffordshire Bull Terriers for pets and companionship, this does not matter overmuch to the average buyer.

However, if you claim show-winning potential for the stock, then you must be reasonably sure that the puppy you sell will maintain a level mouth. The truth is that you cannot do this, because of the many formation changes that occur in a Stafford puppy between the ages of two and eight months. That is why buyers interested in show material should have this risk made quite clear to them at the time of purchase. Even parental stock with level mouths, and level mouths in its immediate ancestry, is quite capable of presenting the breeder with half his litter predisposed to an undershot mouth. So never be truly assured about any puppy until he has had his permanent teeth in level form up to the age of eight months. Even after this age jaw formation *can* deteriorate, but it is unlikely. If you breed and sell to the exhibitors' market take care in your phrasing when drafting an advertisement. Whereas 'show puppies' is misleading, 'bred from show winners' and similar phrases are not, provided the sire and dam have indeed won in shows.

Keep to realistic selling prices too; never sell too cheaply since this debases the breed, apart from the fact that if you want to retrieve some of your financial outgoings (and in correct pedigree dog breeding there are many) you just cannot afford to cut your prices. A fair guide to selling prices is to take your stud fee and multiply it by four. Some people charge more, but when puppies are sold individually it should not be less. If you have a useful 'trade' outlet such as a noted Staffordshire Bull Terrier kennel seeking to fill an overflow of orders for which they have no stock of their own, or a reputable dealer for example, then you should accept a lower price, on the understanding that the entire litter must be taken up at, say, seven weeks of age. A lot of well-known breeders find that to sell their whole litter in this way is better financially and makes less work. You will discover, too, if you are anxious as to the ultimate whereabouts of your puppies, that most breed-associated buyers will allow you to know where they have gone so that you can follow up their progress later. But bear in mind that you should negotiate such enquiries with tact since some new owners object to being interrogated about their possessions.

Local papers seldom prove fruitful to Staffordshire Bull Terrier advertisers. Not a great deal is known or understood about the breed, many lay people being wary of it and not realising its steadiness with children and its effect on intruders. Such papers seem better media for those who have such breeds as the Poodle, Dachshund, and small better-known Terrier breeds to offer.

Selling

A telephone number will often help to speed up selling your litter but, whatever method you employ, always make it clear to would-be buyers that your offer is made 'subject to being unsold'. Some people hesitate to say that a price is too high for them and often promise to call and buy. By the time they arrive you may have refused half a dozen genuine purchasers, only to find yourself with a puppy on your hands—unsold. If you book an order by post, get a deposit before you agree to hold the puppy— a few pounds is enough. Not many people will bother to remit even a nominal sum unless their interest is genuine and they have every intention of buying. When the time draws near for the puppy to be despatched or handed over to his new owner, make sure of the balance of remittance before parting with the dog. Livestock is notoriously a bad credit risk and you need have no qualms about insisting on payment before delivery.

Sending by rail

Railway freight charges for livestock are today quite expensive. Generally speaking, the railways do a good job, but very often the senders themselves cause confusion by poor labelling, inadequate crating, and by being too casual in making arrangements with the consignee. Always try to send livestock away from a main-line station allowing direct rail connection with the new owner's station. It is better to mark your labels

'For Collection at . . . . station by Mr . . . .' than to consign the puppy to the buyer's private address. This brings to a minimum the puppy's time in transit, and no purchaser should mind collecting his new pal. The best receptacle for freighting a puppy is an ordinary tea-chest. It is strong yet light enough to incur minimum rail charges. Further, unlike a conventional travel kennel, it costs so little that the recipient need not return it. Always travel these boxes open end up; if you can get the original lids too, these can be affixed diagonally across the top to allow ventilation. Failing the lids, put battens across or staple-in small-mesh wire netting. You can drill a few large holes in the upper side of the box for added ventilation and put labels and livestock stickers on the top and all sides. Make it quite clear to the railway staff as to the live contents and that it is not just a box on top of which anything can be piled. If you have not already mailed the puppy's pedigree to his new owner in advance of despatch day, this should be inserted with other relevant documents, feeding instructions, etc., in a strong envelope, marked 'Documents', and affixed to the box in a conspicuous position. Be at the railway parcels despatch office at least half an hour before the departure of the train that is to take your puppy. There you will have to complete a form and pay the freight. If you can persuade the porter to let you go round to the platform and see the valuable cargo loaded into the guard's van you will feel easier in your mind, no doubt. If the routing entails a transfer somewhere along the line, a word in the guard's ear is sometimes worth while, although not strictly necessary. Be quite sure that your client knows the time of the despatch train, the time of arrival his end, and details of any train changes en route. If you are on the telephone get him to ring or cable you as to the youngster's safety on receipt, also to tell you whether he is satisfied with his purchase. On this issue, it is a good plan to supply puppies, bought unseen by distant customers, on an approval basis. This is a perfectly simple system, and fair to both sides. On the condition that you have full purchase price in hand before consigning, the puppy is sent to the buyer 'On Approval On Receipt'. This puts the far-flung client in the same happy position as the local man who can call upon you and satisfy himself as to a puppy before paying. Your customer then has the opportunity to take his new puppy home, assure himself as to its value, and advise you accordingly *immediately*. In practice, a vendor should allow his customer about forty-eight hours to confirm, although most owners make up their mind in moments as soon as they see their new Stafford puppy. Never be persuaded to grant extended terms of approval, with a small puppy at least. However, if an adult is involved in changing its home, this is different, seven to ten days' approval being normal in such instances.

Sending by air

This is work for the specialist livestock agent of which there are many around today, most of them very experienced and useful to know. Most countries abroad allow import by air, but a few do not, insisting on boat or surface travel. Your agent will inform you of the various foreign rules to be followed, the injections involved, and so on. In fact, he will advise and do the work for you. All you need do is to deliver the puppy at the appointed hour; he might even collect it for you. Of course, there will be his agent's fee over and above the normal air freight for the puppy and his kennel, but this is often ridiculously small. Be sure when you consign a puppy abroad that you register him first at the Kennel Club, transfer him to his new owner, and obtain an Export Pedigree. The last document costs £20.00 and it should be charged to the new owner, but it will help him to clear his puppy quickly through Customs with minimal charges when it arrives. The Kennel Club will not issue an Export Pedigree on a male puppy unless you supply with your application an Entirety Certificate, which confirms by any veterinary surgeon or practitioner that the puppy is entire, i.e. with both his testicles descended into the scrotum. Documentation of this kind must be effected before the puppy leaves his home shores as it cannot be done afterwards.

In conclusion, never feed a small puppy just prior to despatching or he will be sick and start his big adventure feeling miserable. If there is a long enough interval before he leaves in the morning give him a light milky meal about two to three hours earlier, making sure that he has an opportunity of clearing himself before entering his box or kennel.

10

Minor Ailments

It is hardly within the scope of this book to cover and discuss the many and varied forms of disease and complaints that beset the dog. The vast majority of these are for the veterinary surgeon to deal with and no owner of a Stafford should be reluctant in seeking professional advice, for the animal's sake. Of course, it is useful to have some working knowledge of first-aid for dogs, for prompt home action in an emergency has saved many a dog's life; certainly it will allay his pain until qualified help arrives.

The Staffordshire Bull Terrier is not only very strong physically, but hardily constituted too. One seldom encounters him in major sickness, and the preventive vaccinations readily available today to ward off virus and bacterial infections keep him reasonably free from these one-time killers. No one should buy a Stafford unless he is prepared to have it immunised against the threat of these diseases and to maintain protection with periodical booster doses.

The serious diseases include distemper, with its off-shoot hard pad, canine virus hepatitis (Rubarth's disease), leptospiral jaundice and parvovirus. Apart from the last-named disease (see separate section on parvovirus following), these can be competently dealt with by a single dose injection. Leptospiral jaundice is a scourge arising from contact with the urine of contaminated rats. Leptospiral canicola is a less virulent type of bacteria which attacks the dog's kidneys, giving him a fever that he seems soon to get over. However, its effect is believed to contribute to nephritis in later life. All treatment by vaccines should be followed by booster doses at recommended intervals.

The average Stafford owner with just one or two dogs should ensure that kennels and living quarters are kept scrupulously clean and that his dog or dogs are well swabbed round with cotton wool dabbed in a mild solution of TCP or similar antiseptic about their eyes, ears, lips, feet, and anus following attendance at any show or after contact with an unhealthy-looking dog. Draughts are killers, too; sleeping benches and beds should be raised above floor level and holes and cracks likely to admit draughts must be plugged.

A few of the minor complaints likely to be met with are listed below:

Abscess. A localised collection of pus under a hard swollen area of skin. It can appear on any part of the body and is best brought to a head, like a boil, with hot fomentations until it bursts, and the poison within squeezed away, pressing from the lowest point to expel it entirely. Dress with a solution of antiseptic, keeping an eye on the wound until healed. If the abscess is stubborn and does not burst, the veterinary surgeon will lance it.

Appetite (Perverted). Puppies especially are sometimes seen eating their own stools or crunching up coke and coal. Mostly the habit is grown out of, but it is worth while changing the dog's diet and giving more raw meat.

Asthma. Usually found in veteran dogs and those carrying too much weight. Reduce food intake to essential meals only and confine to raw meat.

Balanitis. A discharge from the penis, although seldom encountered in a dog engaged in stud work. It can be bathed or syringed away using a TCP solution of 1 in 5 of tepid water.

Bites. If the bites are deep, a TCP solution can be dripped into them with a dropper and bathed with warm water. If serious, consult the veterinary surgeon. Keep the dog warm during treatment.

Cancer. This is common in older dogs. It is insidious and is usually well-established before treatment can be given. The advisability of operating should be left to a qualified opinion.

Canker (of Ear). This takes a number of forms, the commonest being a hard, waxy and smelly substance that blocks the ear channel. It is best to consult your veterinary surgeon and treat with the remedy supplied, although there are a number of effective proprietary medicines available.

Concussion. This is the result of accidents and blows on the head. Keep patient warm until veterinary surgeon arrives, meanwhile applying ice-pack to the patient's head.

Constipation. Often due to a faulty diet or too much biscuit. Give the dog more exercise and change his diet to include more raw meat; also, a dessertspoonful of olive oil for a short period will be found useful. If the conditions persists, seek veterinary advice in case of an obstruction in the bowel.

Coughing. This is often infectious among dogs, and if more than one is kept the affected one should be isolated. The dog usually goes off his food and should be fed with milky meals with egg and honey or glucose until better.

Cysts. Staffords often get cysts between the toes, occasionally on the back. Those on the toes frequently become inflamed as the dog licks them, and relief can be given by dipping the feet in a jar of warm water containing a mild antiseptic. A complete change of diet has been found successful in dispersing cysts and avoiding surgery, which is sometimes necessary in stubborn cases.

Diarrhoea. This signifies an internal upset, as it is the body's way of expelling toxic matter such as might be caused by impure food. Remove meat from the dog's diet and give warm bread and milk or egg-and-milk feeds for two days, when the condition should disappear. However, if persistent, consult your veterinary surgeon, as diarrhoea is part of the pattern of virus disease, especially when accompanied by a high temperature. Always isolate the patient until diagnosis has been confirmed.

Eyes (Watery). If it is simple conjunctivitis the matter can be dealt with simply and effectively with an application of Golden Eye ointment or similar, after swabbing round the eyes with damp cotton wool. If chronic, get the veterinary surgeon to examine, for it may be something more serious, like malformation of the eyelids or abnormal eyelash growth.

Fleas, Lice, etc. Even the cleanest Stafford can pick up a few of these from time to time. They often congregate around and under the set-on of tail, and are reasonably easy to pick out. However, a good dusting with dog flea-powder or a warm water bath containing Jeyes will deal with a mild infestation. Make sure that the dog's bedding is either burned or washed and, if a kennel dog, spray a safe insecticide into every nook and cranny.

Hernia. The commonly observed umbilical hernia, usually caused at birth when the dam bites roughly at the cord that joins at its navel, is of small consequence, and as the dog grows it becomes inconspicuous. If it is a large one, however, it can be treated easily by the veterinary surgeon at around six months of age. It is not considered a fault, although the inguinal hernia (in the groin) and the perinial hernia (side of the bowel) are much more serious, and need surgery.

Hip Dysplasia (HD). A genetic problem which involves the degeneration of the *acetatabulum* (hip socket) into which the femoral head (knuckle bone) should easily slide. In an affected dog, this connection is retrograde and is eventually revealed in a dog's hind action. The disease has been evident in humans for centuries but recognised in dogs for a comparatively short time. Many breeds are affected and the Stafford is no stranger to the condition. Corrective treatment is available under a joint scheme managed by the BVA (British Veterinary Association) and the Kennel Club.

Indigestion. Often due to overeating or taking in unsuitable food. All food and drink should be withheld, and the dog given a Milk of Magnesia tablet every two hours. In small puppies the cause is often due to worms, in which case a suitable worm eradicator should be used without delay.

Mange. There are two main varieties of mange, both with a somewhat mousey smell. The least persistent is Sarcoptic Mange, which is nothing more than Scabies and is transmittable to humans. The parasites burrow into the skin and cause intense irritation. Modern veterinary medicine can deal with it fairly easily. The other form is Follicular or Demodectic Mange, which appears especially in young dogs during the term of dentition. It is rather difficult to treat as the parasite exists in the hair follicles well below the surface of the skin. Irritation is rather less than with Sarcoptic Mange, and it is less contagious. In the old days, whole litters would be destroyed as it was almost impossible to cure. However, a number of cures have been made, although the mange seems to vary in its defence and response to treatment. The Staffordshire Bull Terrier, in common with some of the other so-called Bull breeds, seems fairly prone to a patchy skin trouble which besets him mainly during puppyhood between the ages of three and seven months. This is the time when he is making his permanent teeth and, like a baby, at such a time his resistance is low. Occasionally, patches will appear on the side of the face, on the shoulders, the forelegs, and front. It may be an inheritance from the Old English Bulldog, who is said to have suffered from it. Whether this is true or not, if the patches get big and seem persistent, thyroid glandular treatment has been known to restore the coat. However, if only small patches appear, the coat is best left alone, when it usually mends without treatment. Never attempt a cure without qualified advice. Always dispose of an affected dog's bedding before and after treatment.

Parvovirus. This virus was discovered in or around 1978 and because it does not appear to be a manifestation of another disease in the same way as hard pad is of distemper, it can be termed new as far as canine medicine is concerned. Antibodies, which are the markers of infection, are not to be found in samples of dog blood stocked prior to 1978. It is the smallest of those viruses which attack the dog, being less than one-millionth of an inch in diameter, as its name indicates by the Latin word *parvo* meaning small.

The virus, smaller to one found in cats and certain other mammals, is a powerful and formidable one and is often fatal to dogs, especially puppies. The symptoms are severe gastro-enteritis usually accompanied by sub-normal temperatures, by vomiting and watery blood-stained faeces of a dirty greyish putty colour. The disease is communicated orally and has an incubation period of 5+ days which is the time from the start of the infection to the commencement of the clinical illness.

Although the vaccination of dogs against parvovirus still engenders controversy in the veterinary world, early and urgent attention must be given to the patient. Effective vaccination should entail a course involving treatment at 8, 12 and 16–18 weeks with a fourth shot at 20–22 weeks as recommended by Dr H. Thompson, BMVS PhD of the University of Glasgow Veterinary School, whose literature and data on the subject have been kindly sent to me by Dr A. S. Bryden, PhD FIMLS.

Not every dog which contracts the illness dies or becomes critically ill. Puppies of 8–12 weeks are more prone to develop a severe condition than adults, which are less commonly affected. There is a heavy fluid loss resulting in intense dehydration, which is symptomatic of the disease, and effort must be made to counter this immediately if the dog is not to deteriorate and succumb. In small puppies the virus attacks the heart muscle and it is not unusual for heart failure to result. Following the course of vaccination mentioned above, an annual booster is advisable.

Sprains and Strains. Probably, these are the commonest occupational hazards of an athletic Staffordshire Bull Terrier. Keep the dog warm and reduce his exercise to a minimum. Massage the affected limb with olive oil several times daily. Embrocation can be used if its smell is weak; strong purulent lotions tend to upset a dog. A course of tablets strong in calcium, phosphorus, and Vitamin D will aid recovery.

Stings. Wasps are the main offenders during summer months; their stings can be dealt with satisfactorily by soaking a wad of cotton wool in a strong solution of bicarbonate of soda and water, and compressing on the spot. Strong TCP solution is just as effective, but mouth, eye and bare-flesh stings are better referred to the veterinary surgeon without delay.

Toxocara Canis Infection. All owners should be aware of this disease which is a dangerous one and can extend to children. As recently as 1987 the British Medical Association and the British Veterinary Association issued a joint statement which recommended that dogs should be excluded from children's play areas in parks.

The disease arises from the larvae of the common roundworm found in breeding bitches and whelps. The worms' eggs are passed out of the puppy via its faeces and can be found adhering to the puppies' box and bedding, also to the anal regions. A child handling the puppy may well get some on his or her skin and the resulting larvae could enter the child's body through the skin, which would first have to be pierced. A very remote chance exists that the larvae could travel behind the child's eyes and damage its sight.

The danger period in this unpleasant malady ranges from two months of age to a year by which the time the worm is believed to be ineffective. Owners will realise however, how important it is to worm their puppies for roundworm. Worm at six, ten and twelve weeks, then at nine months. A brood bitch assumed in whelp following a successful mating should be wormed seven days after mating.

APPENDIX A

KENNEL CLUB REGISTRATION TOTALS

1935	174	1953	1319	1971	2017
1936	179	1954	1118	1972	2118
1937	264	1955	1017	1973	2193
1938	343	1956	920	1974	2103
1939	310	1957	960	1975	1903
1940	150	1958	1000	1976	895[1]
1941	135	1959	1000	1977	666[1]
1942	360	1960	888	1978	2013
1943	541	1961	1119	1979	2792
1944	841	1962	1166	1980	3094
1945	1097	1963	1259	1981	3374
1946	1762	1964	1330	1982	3968
1947	2206	1965	1315	1983	4709
1948	2211	1966	1228	1984	4809
1949	2357	1967	1466	1985	6419
1950	2171	1968	1611	1986	6473
1951	1870	1969	1919	1987	6233
1952	1408	1970	1824		

[1] As recorded in the Active Register. No figures recorded for the Basic Register.

APPENDIX B

STAFFORDSHIRE BULL TERRIER ASSOCIATIONS, CLUBS AND SOCIETIES IN GREAT BRITAIN AND ABROAD

The associations listed concern themselves solely with the Staffordshire Bull Terrier's welfare and development. They hold shows, discussion groups, and issue breed information to members. Every Stafford owner should join a breed club. There is usually one to be found within reasonable distance, and application to the secretary will elicit the required information. It should be noted that the names and addresses given are of the current secretaries. These change, and should you be unable to contact the person named, you are advised to write to The Secretary, The Kennel Club, 1–4 Clarges Street, Piccadilly, London W1Y 8AB asking to be put in touch with the secretary of the club that interests you.

Alyn & Deeside Staffordshire Bull Terrier Club: Mrs M. Byrne, 20 Beeston Road, Higher Kinneton, Clwyd. (0244) 660758

East Anglian Staffordshire Bull Terrier Club: Mrs J. Shorrocks, Weston Hall, Beccles, Suffolk. (0502) 713472

East Midlands Staffordshire Bull Terrier Club: Mr John Monks, 88 Briar Meads, Oadby, Leicester. (0533) 713122

Irish Staffordshire Fanciers Club: Mr T. Cleary, Granitefields, 21 Johnston Road, Dun Laoghaire, Co. Dublin, Eire.

Israel, Staffordshire Bull Terrier Club of: Mr M. Friedman, 21/2 Arava Street, P.O. Box 135, Arad, Israel 80700. (010 972) 57951 364

Mashonaland, Staffordshire Bull Terrier Club of: Mr V. Haines, 187 Glenside Drive, Strathaven, Salisbury, Zimbabwe

Merseyside Staffordshire Bull Terrier Club: Mr K. Swift, 1 Littler Road, Haydock Street, St Helens, Merseyside. (0744) 584220

Morecambe Bay & Cumbria Staffordshire Bull Terrier Club: Mrs C. Sumner, 10 Windermere Avenue, Farringdon, Leyland, Lancashire. (0772) 439203

North Eastern Staffordshire Bull Terrier Club: Mr G. Purvis, 1 Lyons Cottage, Hutton-le-Hole, Tyne & Wear. (091) 526 7817

Northern Counties Staffordshire Bull Terrier Club: Mrs Clare Lee, Orchard House, Hazelheads Lane, Knaresborough, Yorkshire. (0423) 863829

Northern Ireland Staffordshire Bull Terrier Club: Mr W. McKnight, 9 Mountcole Gardens, Belfast. (0232) 711608

North of Scotland Staffordshire Bull Terrier Club: Mrs K. Carmichael, 97 Malcolm Road, Peterculter, Aberdeen. (0224) 734441

North West Staffordshire Bull Terrier Club: Mrs C. Atherton, Cross Cottage, Shaw Brow, Whittle-le-Woods, Chorley, Lancashire. (02572) 60273

Notts & Derby Staffordshire Bull Terrier Club: Mr B. Grattridge, 3 Angela Avenue, Kirkby-in-Ashfield, Notts. (0623) 75234

Potteries Staffordshire Bull Terrier Club: Mr Lionel Hemstock, 56 Cherry Avenue, Kirkby-in-Ashfield, Notts. (0623) 753084

Scottish Staffordshire Bull Terrier Club: Mr Abe Harkness, Senkrah Villas, Chapel Street, Carluke, Lanarkshire. (0555) 70564

Southern Counties Staffordshire Bull Terrier Society: Mr R. Cox, 356 Garth Road, Morden, Surrey SM4 4NW. (01) 330 5971

Staffordshire Bull Terrier Club: Mr F. Gough, 1 Bury Hill Road, Oldbury, West Midlands. (021) 544 5869

Southern Cross Staffordshire Bull Terrier Society: Mr J. Goodfellow, P.O. Box 5109, Green Meadows, Napier, New Zealand.

Staffordshire Bull Terrier Breed Council of Great Britain and Northern Ireland: Mr John Monks, 88 Briar Meads, Oadby, Leicestershire. (0533) 713122

Staffordshire Bull Terrier Club of Australia and New South Wales: Mrs A. Bailey, 8 Marigold Avenue, Blacktown, New South Wales, Australia 2148.

Staffordshire Bull Terrier Club of Canada: Mr & Mrs I. Trott, 36–3175 Kirwin Avenue, Mississauga, Ontario, Canada.

Staffordshire Bull Terrier Club of Finland: Mrs Heidi Sjoblom, Sukikuja–1A, 01280 Vantaa, Finland (9) 0–306744

Staffordshire Bull Terrier Club of the Netherlands: Mr A. van Herpen, 'Melmars', Handum Huizen, 9200 Friesland, Netherlands.

Staffordshire Bull Terrier Club of Queensland: Dr Lois Davidson, 40 Exeter Street, Ashgrove, Brisbane, Queensland, Australia.

Staffordshire Bull Terrier Club of South Wales: Mr J. Holle, 22 Heol-y-Gors, Townhill, Swansea, Glamorgan. (0792) 582597

Staffordshire Bull Terrier Club of the Transvaal: Mrs S. Knowles, Box 3297, Johannesburg 200, R.S.A.

**Staffordshire Bull Terrier Club of the United States of America*: Mr and Mrs

M. Crowe, 13022 Paloma Way, Santa Ana, California 92705, U.S.A.

**Staffordshire Bull Terrier Club, U.S.A.*: Mrs Irma Rosenfield, 2315 N. 56th Street, Omaha, Nebraska 68104, U.S.A.

Western Staffordshire Bull Terrier Society: Mr B. Cadogan, Dogan Heights, Ponthir, Newport, Gwent. (0633) 420457

Western Australia, Staffordshire Bull Terrier Club of: Mrs J. Francis, 7 Salandra Way, Forrestfield 6058, Western Australia.

In the case of overseas names and addresses in the foregoing list, intending correspondents are advised to request mailing authorities to return their letters should deliveries be aborted due to removal of the secretary or discontinuance of the club or society.

* These two clubs have no connection with each other.

The Staffordshire Bull Terrier Rescue Service This highly commended service was conceived by Mr Vic Pounds, well-known veteran of the Southern Counties Staffordshire Bull Terrier Society. It aims to rescue any Stafford in distress and rehabilitate the dog in a genuinely good home. Full details of the service are available from the hon. secretary Mrs A. Gatenby (073088) 402 or from Mr and Mrs V. Pounds (0323) 843955. Mr A. W. A. Cairns is chairman.

Several other breed societies run a similar service for their particular breed.

APPENDIX C

COMPLETE LIST OF STAFFORDSHIRE BULL TERRIER CHAMPIONS, 1939–December 1988

The following is a list to date of Staffordshire Bull Terrier champions, dogs and bitches since the breed was first granted challenge certificates in 1939.

To Mr A. K. Hill ('Kinderlee') and Mrs Joyce Shorrock ('Eastaff') acknowledgement is given for their research and work in compiling much of this data. Also to Mr Alf Tittle ('Alpaka') who kindly supplied the 1983 to 1988 data.

Name of Champion	*Sex*	*Sire*	*Dam*	*Owner*	*Breeder*	*Date of Birth*
1939:						
Ch. Gentleman Jim	D	Brindle Mick	Triton Judy	J. Mallen	Jack Dunn	27.5.37
Ch. Game Laddie	D	Game Lad	Mad Molly	W. A. Boylan	W. A. Boylan	2.1.36
Ch. Lady Eve	B	Barney	Gipsy	Joseph Dunn	J. Evans	10.6.35
Ch. Midnight Gift	B	Game Bill	Blue Bell Bess	Mrs M. Beare	G. Ashman	22.7.37
Ch. Madcap Mischief	B	Ch. Game Laddie	Timyke Mustard	Miss A. Harrison	W. A. Boylan	8.7.37
1947:						
Ch. Head Lad of Villmar	D	Vindictive Monty of Wyncroft	Fred's Fancy	R. Servat	Mr & Mrs Martin	2.3.45
Ch. Widneyland Kim	D	Ch. Gentleman Jim	Game Judy	G. A. Dudley	H. Harris	8.3.44

Ch. Widneyland Model	B	Togo	White Bess	Mrs D. M. Payton-Smith	W. R. Marsh	4.1.44
Ch. Wychbury Red Cap	B	Ch. Brigands Bo'sun	Rita's Pride	G. A. Dudley	J. Bloomer	20.9.46
1948:						
Ch. Fearless Red of Bandits	D	Ch. Gentleman Jim	Dee's Pegg	Mrs J. F. Gordon	H. Priest	22.7.44
Ch. Wychbury Kimbo	D	Ch. Widneyland Kim	Wychbury Peggy	G. A. Dudley	G. A. Dudley	19.7.46
Ch. Sandra's Boy	D	Bomber Command	Crossguns Sandra	C. Blackwell	C. Blackwell	10.11.44
Ch. Wychbury Oak Beauty	B	Prince St John	Vindictive Flirt	G. A. Dudley	J. Birch	25.10.44
Ch. Widneyland Ritver Ringleader	B	Ch. Brigands Bo'sun	Uta of Roxana	A. P. Smith	Miss R. Vernon	17.6.46
Ch. Perfect Lady	B	Furnace Jake	Plucky Queen	A. Tryhorn	T. W. Cooper	14.3.44
1949:						
Ch. Monty the Monarch	D	Black Bottle	Willowmay	J. Hudson	T. J. Machin	8.10.44
Ch. Brigands Red Rogerson	D	Jolly Roger	Lady Juror	Mrs J. F. Gordon	A. Brazenhall	1.9.45
Ch. Brindle Mac	D	Boy Dan	Our Cissy	H. Ashton	N. Lever	10.1.45
Ch. Brigands Bo'sun	D	Brindle Bill	Fredancer	A. P. Smith	J. Hall	14.6.43
Ch. Jim's Double of Wychbury	D	Ch. Gentleman Jim	Brindle Trix	G. A. Dudley	R. C. Washington	21.12.45

Name of Champion	*Sex*	*Sire*	*Dam*	*Owner*	*Breeder*	*Date of Birth*
Ch. Quiz of Wyncroft	D	Jolly Roger	Gamesters Hot Black	L. Cowgill	A. Bradley	11.5.46
Ch. Brindle Crescendo of Wychbury	D	Walters Gift	Brins Best	G. A. Dudley	Mr & Mrs Attwood	14.8.47
Ch. Thornhill Pride	D	Ch. Brigands Bo'sun	Clipper of Bodenham	Jack Dunn	F. Heydon	9.5.48
Ch. Brinstock Sandy Bridget	B	Ch. Game Laddie	Brinstock Bridget	W. A. Boylan	W. A. Boylan	23.4.47
Ch. Our Queeni	B	Tiger's the Boy	Bombshell Judy	Mrs N. Dunsmuir	F. J. Holloway	15.7.44
Ch. Wychbury Pied Wonder	B	Ch. Widneyland Kim	Quicksilver	G. A. Dudley	R. Willets	30.9.47
Ch. Lucky Star of Bandits	B	Bucks Mick	Lucy's Luce	E. R. Davis & Mrs J. F. Gordon	P. K. Boxley	24.6.47
Ch. Eastbury Lass	B	Ch. Gentleman Jim	Invincible Belle	J. McNeill	Mrs A. T. Boyes	14.8.44
1950:						
Ch. Wychbury Kimson	D	Ch. Widneyland Kim	Cradley Janet of Wychbury	G. A. Dudley	G. A. Dudley	23.5.47
Ch. Constones Cadet	D	Ch. Godfrey's Pride	Constant Coquette	A. W. A. Cairns	A. W. A. Cairns	2.12.48
Ch. Peter the Bomber	D	Bomber Command	Pat's the Girl	Mrs E. D. G. Jolly	H. Hatton	31.8.47
Ch. Godfrey's Pride	D	Ch. Widneyland Kim	The Empress Theodora	Ford & Dady	D. F. W. Ford	23.5.47

Ch. Nuneato Dinah	B	Nuneatonion Boy	Lady Shân	Mrs D. H. Williams	Mr Clements	5.1.48
Ch. Tawny of Dugarde	B	Ch. Sandra's Boy	Jezebel of Dugarde	A. Tryhorn	A. Tryhorn	4.11.48
Ch. Brinstock Red Radiance	B	Ch. Game Laddie	Red Sadie	W. A. Boylan	R. Wilkinson	10.2.46
Ch. Della of Impkin	B	Ch. Widneyland Kim	Christie of Wyncroft	Ford & Dady	Mrs D'Arcy Robins	17.10.47
1951:						
Ch.Goldwyns Leading Lad	D	Wheatley Lad	Brindle Diana	J. A. Altoft	J. A. Altoft	12.1.48
Ch. Red Atom Bomber	D	Bomber Command	Blackies Girl	F. W. Holden	E. Bradley	26.6.47
Ch. Widneyland Little Gent of Pynedale	D	Ch. Wychbury Kimbo	Pal O'Derek	A. P. Smith	S. Postin	24.10.48
Ch. Gillcroft Guardson	D	Milkern Guardsman	Lady Patikin	F. Gill	F. Gill	16.9.49
Ch. Emden Corsican	D	Jolly Roger	Emden Clipper	G. C. Henderson	R. Timmins	2.9.45
Ch. Tearaway Rover	D	Son O'Chall	Troublesome Lass	J. Barnard	H. Fowler	25.5.49
Ch. Widneyland Panda	B	Widneyland Little Patch	Brindle Daisy	E. J. Marchant	A. P. Smith	3.4.48
Ch. Nita's Choice	B	Tenacious Pete	Blandona Black Queen	Salisbury & Guest	G. Guest	24.5.47
C. Tessa's Gem	B	Ch. Wychbury Kimbo	Tess of Burnttree	R. V. Tranter	R. V. Tranter	14.9.48

Name of Champion	*Sex*	*Sire*	*Dam*	*Owner*	*Breeder*	*Date of Birth*
1952:						
Ch. Pal of Aveth, C.D.Ex.	D	Ch. Quiz of Wyncroft	Elegant Girl	E. H. Payne	G. Guest	23.11.48
Ch. Chestonion Annoyance	D	Brigands Benbrook Pirate	Beautiful Black Jane	J. Barnard	Mr Willetts	4.7.49
Ch. Freden Fireworks	D	Sans Cooper	Perfect Nance	R. M. Stevenson	F. W. Holden	1.9.49
Ch. Wychbury Diamond King	D	Diamond Bill	Granby Lass	G. A. Dudley	Mr Cherry	13.8.51
Ch. Constones Ballyhill Bruce	D	Idol Bruce	Idol Jill	A. W. A. Cairns	A. W. Cooper	14.12.49
Ch. Gwornall Eve	B	Rambling Knight	Gwornall Britannia	H. Bennett	Mrs R. Cartwright	3.5.50
Ch. Linda of Killyglen	B	Brigands Bo'sun Beau	Colleen of Killyglen	J. McNeill	J. McNeill	5.9.50
Ch. Fancy Fay of Summermuir	B	True Briton	Ch. Our Queeni	D. E. A. Meredith	Mrs N. Dunsmuir	18.3.49
Ch. Freden Blonde Bombshell	B	Sans Cooper	Perfect Nance	F. W. Holden	F. W. Holden	9.5.51
Ch. Lady Cherie of Uddffa	B	Allan's Dynamo	Felicitas of Nunholme	G. W. Bass	G. W. Bass	3.1.49
1953:						
Ch. Wardonian Corniche	D	Ch. Chestonian Annoyance	Wardonian Cintra	J. T. Ward	J. T. Ward	28.9.51

Ch. Hillside Toby	D	Wishbone Willie	Bourhill Lass	A. J. Wingfield	C. A. Heap	30.9.50
Ch. Mahogany Democrat	D	Brinstock Democrat	Destructive Meg	A. Fox	W. Kingham	10.1.50
Ch. Little Brindle Queen	B	Ch. Widneyland Little Gent of Pynedale	Bonnie Briar	Mrs D. Hoggarth	Mrs D. Hoggarth	17.5.50
Ch. Red Biddy of Zendiks	B	Brian's Choice	October Lady	Dr J. Silveira	Mr Morley	29.12.50
Ch. Brinstock Welsh Maid	B	Timothy of Dugarde	Queen of Barry	W. A. Boylan	D. Morgan	17.11.50
Ch. Wychbury Midly Girl	B	Ch. Widneyland Kim	Regnant Show Lady	G. A. Dudley	G. A. Dudley	1.11.51
1954:						
Ch. Godella's Pride	D	Ch. Godfrey's Pride	Ch. Della of Impkin	Ford & Dady	Ford & Dady	6.4.49
Ch. Corsair of Wyncole	D	Jolly Roger	Game Lady of Wyncroft	Miss J. D. Peebles	Miss J. D. Peebles	11.5.50
Ch. Chestonian Satan's Fireworks	D	Ch. Freden Fireworks	Barrs Road Pride	J. & T. W. Barnard	F. W. Holden	1.9.52
Ch. Wychbury Red Riband	D	Ch. Wychbury Kimbo	Regnant Show Lady	G. A. Dudley	G. A. Dudley	24.9.52
Ch. Gentleman Bruce	D	Crippsian Brindle	Gentle Lady	W. Cutler	Miss Blunday	21.11.51
Ch. Wychbury Sportsman	D	Ch. Widneyland Kim	Primrose Nance	Miss J. M. Cart	R. Heath	1.9.50
Ch. Wyngate Lady	B	Corinthian Rick	Red Demon Lass	R. Walker	G. Miller	25.4.52
Ch. Gwornall Judith	B	Rambling Knight	Gwornall Britannia	V. A. Johnson	Mrs R. Cartwright	3.5.50

Name of Champion	*Sex*	*Sire*	*Dam*	*Owner*	*Breeder*	*Date of Birth*
Ch. Emden Cuttysark	B	Ch. Godella's Pride	Emden Charanda	Servat & Timmins	Dr P. Lambah	27.8.52
1955:						
Ch. Bellerophon Billy Boy	D	Ch. Quiz of Wyncroft	Honest Martha Le Loup	Alan Greenwood	Arnold Greenwood	4.10.53
Ch. Major in Command of Wychbury	D	Ch. Wychbury Diamond King	Ch. Little Brindle Queen	G. A. Dudley	Mrs D. Hoggarth	7.1.54
Ch. Subtle Difference	D	Ch. Widneyland Kim	Model Miss	S. Worrall	S. Worrall	12.12.50
Ch. Troglodyte	D	Ch. Constones Cadet	Monkswood Menace	B. Yates	Mrs Handley	29.9.52
Ch. Challenger of Dugarde	D	Bo'sun of Dugarde	Peggy of Dugarde	A. Tryhorn	A. Tryhorn	1.2.52
Ch. Williamwood Golden Lass	B	Ch. Wychbury Kimbo	Williamwood Wonder Girl	E. R. Judge	E. R. Judge	16.1.52
Ch. Tawn Diamond of Dugarde	B	Ch. Wychbury Diamond King	Ch. Tawney of Dugarde	Mrs D. Hoggarth	A. Tryhorn	18.3.53
Ch. Fredanseuse	B	Fredante	Apache Princess	F. Baddeley	W. Price	3.3.54
Ch. Linksbury Derry	B	Ch. Godfrey's Pride	Ch. Nuneato Dinah	Mrs D. H. Williams	Mrs D. H. Williams	17.2.51
Ch. Goldwyns Gracious Lady	B	Wheatley Lad	Brindle Diana	J. Altoft	J. Altoft	2.12.52
Ch. Lady of Barnfield	B	Ch. Thornhill Pride	Fred's Lass of Summermuir	Mrs J. Horsfall	L. Aspin	16.5.51

Ch. Eastaff Nicola	B	Ch. Wychbury Kimbo	Ch. Linda of Killyglen	J.McNeill	Miss J. Brightmore	7.12.53
1956:						
Ch. Golden Boy of Essira	D	Ch. Goldwyns Leading Lad	Titian of Dugarde	Mrs N. Weller	Mr N. Weller	20.10.53
Ch. Aphonic True Pal	D	Ch. Hillside Toby	Firey Lass	Dean & Roylance	E. Bullough	12.4.53
Ch. Weycombe Cherry	B	Gentleman Jackson	Weycombe Judy	G. R. Down	G. R. Down	10.3.54
Ch. Wychbury Sporting Girl	B	Ch. Wychbury Sportsman	Saucy Dinah	Mrs J. Horsfall	D. Palmer	25.9.53
Ch. Andra of Towans	B	Ch. Wychbury Sportsman	Tina of Towans	G. H. Smith	G. H. Smith	16.3.54
Ch. Smallthorn Brindle Peggy	B	Cheirons Black Mike	Lovely Cottage	S. T. Mansfield	R. Stredwick	27.3.51
Ch. Chestonian Elegance	B	Ch. Chestonian Annoyance	Ch. Freden Blonde Bombshell	J. & T. W. Barnard	J. & T. W. Barnard	25.1.54
Ch. Eastaff Danom	D	Ch. Goldwyns Leading Lad	Ch. Linda of Killyglen	J. McNeill	Miss J. Brightmore	7.8.55
Ch. Peter's Boy	D	Ch. Peter the Bomber	Brinstock Game 'Un	Mr & Mrs H. R. Wilson	Mrs Doncaster	28.2.52
Ch. Son of Billy Boy	D	Ch. Bellerophon Billy Boy	Little Kip	C. E. Hipwood	C. E. Hipwood	20.8.55
Ch. Dellveth's Pride	D	Ch. Pal of Aveth, C.D.Ex	Dellfrey's Pride	Ford & Dady	Ford & Dady	10.7.53
Ch. Constones Eastaff This'll do	D	Ch. Troglodyte	Jill of Prested	A. W. A. Cairns	Miss J. Brightmore	7.9.54

Name of Champion	Sex	Sire	Dam	Owner	Breeder	Date of Birth
1957:						
Ch. Little Diamond Tiara	B	Ch.Wychbury Red Riband	Queenie's Dynamite	Mrs D. Hoggarth	Mrs D. Hoggarth	5.6.55
Ch. Linksbury Amanda	B	Linksbury Victor	Ch. Linksbury Derry	Mrs D. H. Williams	Mrs D. H. Williams	3.2.53
Ch. Williamwood Fawn Lass	B	Ch. Wychbury Red Riband	Ch. Williamwood Golden Lass	E. R. Judge	E. R. Judge	23.6.55
Ch. Bankhead Beauty	B	Southfield Rufus	Sally Pride of Mayeswood	Mrs E. M. Wylie	Mrs E. M. Wylie	1.10.55
Ch. Trenton Tiger Lily	B	Ch. Goldwyns Leading Lad	Deceptive Dora	Mrs H. B. Owen	Mrs H. B. Owen	31.10.52
1958:						
Ch. Toro	D	Ch. Wychbury Diamond Kim	Lady Lesette	L. C. Brown	L. C. Brown	6.6.54
Ch. The Red Brickmaker	D	Ch. Wychbury Red Riband	Bilvick Fawn Vixen	T. Batham	T. Batham	4.11.55
Ch. Harwyns Choice	D	Kim the Duke	Bill's Baby	T. Roscoe	H. D. Peele	29.7.54
Ch. Brinstock Glenagow	D	Ch. Dellveth's Pride	Ch. Brinstock Welsh Maid	W. A. Boylan	Mrs G. W. R. Burge-Smith	26.1.56
Ch. Fiona Beauty	B	Crown Major	Ch. Cwornall Judith	J. Craig	V. A. Johnson	18.6.55
Ch. Wawocan Benita	B	Ch. Peter's Boy	Wawocan Little Choice	Latham & Bywater	Latham & Bywater	17.5.56

Ch. Dennybeck Graftwood Tanya	B	Jupiter of Graftwood	Graftwood Melissande	Mrs J. Horsfall	W. E. Butter	13.1.56
Ch. Townas Merry Maid	B	Ch. Wychbury Red Riband	Tina of Towans	G. H. Smith	G. H. Smith	18.3.55
1959:						
Ch. Iron Bill of Phylmajar	D	Ch. Peter's Boy	Tinkerbelle Susan	A. D. Thomas	Mr & Mrs H. R. Wilson	12.2.56
Ch. Weycombe Dandy	D	Ch. Golden Boy of Essira	Ch. Weycombe Cherry	Nicolls & Underwood	G. R. Down	30.6.56
Ch. Buster Bill	D	Ch. Bellerophon Billy Boy	Bowbrooke Bess	T. Ward	T. Ward	26.9.56
Ch. Goldwyns Lucky Lad	D	Ch. Goldwyns Leading Lad	Ch. Goldwyns Gracious Lady	J. Altoft	J. Altoft	12.1.55
Ch. Rellim A'Boy	D	Ch. Wychbury Red Riband	Ch. Wychbury Midly Girl	Mrs T. Miller	Mrs T. Miller	1.9.57
Ch. Moira Meg	B	Ch. Constones Cadet	Nancie's Pride	Mrs E. M. Wylie	C. H. Townsend	10.7.56
Ch. Weycombe Julie	B	Ch. Golden Boy of Essira	Ch. Weycombe Cherry	A. W. Harkness	G. R. Down	30.6.56
Ch. Pitbul Lindy Lou	B	Ch. Eastaff Danom	Pitbul Amber Queen	Mrs M. K. Fensom	Mrs M. K. Fensom	9.9.56
Ch. Mandy of Mandalay	B	Ch. Godella's Pride	Hayward's Flash	G. Stormont	K. Jones	16.1.56
1960:						
Ch. Sahib of Senkrah	D	Ch. Eastaff Danom	Ch. Weycombe Julie	A. W. Harkness	A. W. Harkness	22.4.58
Ch. Stretfordian Little Gem	B	Stretfordian Lad	Stretfordian Weycombe Trudy	Mrs J. Horsfall	J. Davies	28.4.57

Name of Champion	*Sex*	*Sire*	*Dam*	*Owner*	*Breeder*	*Date of Birth*
Ch. Fredanita of Wychbury	B	Ch. Major in Command of Wychbury	Fredansante	Mrs E. M.Myles	E. W. Holden	14.3.58
Ch. Weycombe Melody of Senkrah	B	Ch. Golden Boy of Essira	Ch. Weycombe Cherry	A. W. Harkness	G. R. Down	30.6.56
Ch. Judy of Brunaburgh	B	Ch. Bellerophon Billy Boy	Bellerophon Brindle Sue	Dr A. Nugent	Alan Greenwood	16.10.57
1961:						
Ch. Top Hat	D	Ch. Bellerophon Billy Boy	Ruf-E-Nuf of Fulstone	Mr & Mrs A. Eastwood	Mr & Mrs A. Eastwood	12.6.57
Ch. Chestonion Campaign	D	Ch. Son of Billy Boy	Maid of Kinderlee	Miss R. J. A. Swindells	H. Simpson	1.7.57
Ch. The Prince of Diamonds	D	Ch. Major in Command of Wychbury	Lady Flossie of Uddffa	Mrs V. Johnson	G. W. Bass	12.11.58
Ch. Brindle Ballerina	B	Ch. Major in Command of Wychbury	Lady Black Beauty	Mrs E. E. Hill	L. Harris	13.4.56
Ch. Yasmin of Beredhar	B	Ch. Peter's Boy	Rivaz of Beredhar	Mrs C. Mercer	Mr Cross	26.5.59
Ch. Gay Moment	B	Ch. Major in Command of Wychbury	Spring Fury	G. Shaw	W. Beasley	5.9.58
Ch. Fiery Goddess	B	Georgecroft Golden Boy	Satan's Mistress	F. Southall	F. Southall	24.4.58

1962:						
Ch. Rellim Ferryvale Victor	D	Ch. Rellim A'Boy	Chestonion Chimes	Mrs T. Miller	Mr Ramshaw	8.10.60
Ch. Wynchal Buckeroo	D	Ch. Son of Billy Boy	Stanwell Cheeky Charlotte	C. E. Hipwood	C. E. Hipwood	27.6.59
Ch. Jolihem Forclip Christy Bella	B	Ch. Goldwyns Lucky Lad	Forclip Poor Mary	L. F. Hemstock	D. C. Briggs	15.7.59
Ch. Marjorie's Choice	B	Ch. Bellerophon Billy Boy	Dorothy's Choice	K. Whiteley	W. Barnsley	21.10.57
Ch. Game Penny	B	Weycombe Shan	Glendover Brindle Beverley	A. G. Robbins	A. G. Robbins	17.12.59
Ch. Fredenzella	B	Ch. Major in Command of Wychbury	Fredansante	F. W. Holden	F. W. Holden	1.1.60
Ch. Vesper Andromeda	B	Rambuster	Vesper Countess	J. Sykes	J. Sykes	16.11.60
1963:						
Ch. The Black Monarch	D	Black King	Atoms Choice	M. Boam	Barker & Aherne	10.5.59
Ch. Jolihem Fine and Dandy	D	Jolihem Adonis	Black Fury	Hemstock & Bottomore	C. Bottomore	23.2.61
Ch. Weycombe Benny	D	Weycombe Timothy	Weycombe Beauty	L. H. Lunn	G. R. Down	14.12.57
Ch. Bandits Brintiga	D	Georgecroft Mandumas	Satan's Mistress	T. Field	F. Southall	1.10.59
Ch. Bandits Red Armour	D	Weycombe Gerard	Jill of Bovinger	M. R. Tranter	C. Lowery	1.9.60

Name of Champion	*Sex*	*Sire*	*Dam*	*Owner*	*Breeder*	*Date of Birth*
Ch. Senkrah Saffron	B	Ch. Weycombe Dandy	Senkrah Sabelle	S. W. Craik	A. W. Harkness	26.12.60
Ch. Stonnards Nell	B	Ch. Eastaff Danom	Stonnards Imogen	Mrs B. Cassels	Mrs B. Cassels	10.1.61
Ch. Senkrah Sapphire	B	Ch. Weycombe Dandy	Senkrah Sabelle	A. W. Harkness	A. W. Harkness	26.12.60
Ch. Bandits Brindemara	B	Trenton Colonel	Linksbury Dillyness	P. D. Perry	Mrs D. H. Williams	14.11.61
1964:						
Ch. Hoplite Red Devil	D	Ainwyn's Redike	Bellerophon Belle Star	T. Rowe	A. Mitchell	9.10.61
Ch. Game Flash	D	Hydiamond King	Midnight Mischief	A. Baxter	A. Baxter	15.7.61
Ch. Jolihem El Toro	D	Bankhead Bullet	Ch. Mandy of Mandalay	L. F. Hemstock	G. J. Stormont	2.3.62
Ch. Freden Dominate	D	Ch. The Black Monarch	Ch. Fredenzella	F. W. Holden	F. W. Holden	10.6.61
Ch. Hyndland Cardinal	D	Hyndland Akela	Williamwood Snow Queen	C. Albrecht	J. Gillespie	16.9.59
Ch. The Red Battler	D	The Red Avenger	Kentucky Sue	G. Rogers	E. S. Ward	17.2.61
Ch. Pitbul Sally Ann	B	Winterfold Danny	Widneyland Pitbul Lassie	K. Fensom	K. Fensom	31.8.60
Ch. Wychcombe Rob's Pride	B	Ch. Weycombe Benny	Ch. Game Penny	A. G. Robbins	A. G. Robbins	5.5.61

Ch. Regency Gal	B	Rumbuster	Clear Brew	F. Randall	R. E. Salisbury	1.6.62
Ch. Wirswall Betsy	B	Admiral Albert	Rhod. Ch. Stanestreet Glenbriar	Mrs E. M. Myles	Mrs E. M. Myles	16.1.60
Ch. Monkhill Candy	B	Rumbuster	Wynchal Bluebell	F. Randall	F. Randall	13.11.62
Ch. Senkrah Sabutae	B	Ch. Weycombe Dandy	Senkrah Sabelle	Mrs T. Miller	A. W. Harkness	23.9.62
1965:						
Ch. Walstaff Domino	D	Black King	Walstaff Midnight Tina	G. W. Walton	G. W. Walton	10.5.60
Ch. William the Conqueror	D	Winterfold Danny	Gentle Tamsie	Miss J. Crew	T. Hanks	10.10.61
Ch. Camdonian Contender	D	Ch. Rellim Ferryvale Victor	Ch. Game Penny	Misses K. G. & M. E. Morris	A. G. Robbins	23.12.62
Ch. Hyndland Jaunty Jock	D	Ch. Eastaff Danom	Hyndland Cherry	M. Gillespie & G. Stevenson	F. & G. Gillespie	3.2.63
Ch. Senkrah Sabeau	B	Ch. Weycombe Dandy	Senkrah Sabelle	R. McEvoy	A. W. Harkness	26.12.60
Ch. Dennybeck Dani of Belsivore	B	Ch. Eastaff Danom	Dennybeck Dinkum	Mesdames P. M. & D. M. Holmes	Mrs J. Horsfall	18.8.63
Ch. Rapparee Ashfield Star	B	Boy Pat	Padarn Rosebud	Mr & Mrs J. Bolton	E. Brown	18.8.62
Ch. Dyrex Duskie Belle	B	Hydiamond King	Dyrex Fair Jayne	D. J. Wilkes	D. J. Wilkes	28.10.62
Ch. Sanville Wild Puma	B	Saracen of Senkrah	Sanville Wild Maid	W. Watson	W. Watson	16.12.62

						Birth
Ch. Kinderlee Cavalcade	B	Ch. Son of Billy Boy	Ch. Brindle Ballerina	Mrs G. Gallimore	Mrs E. E. Hill	15.9.61
1966:						
Ch. Knight Templar	D	Ch. Rellim Ferryvale Victor	Ch. Marjorie's Choice	K. Whiteley	K. Whiteley	5.2.63
Ch. Buninyong Caesar	D	Ch. Weycombe Dandy	Frolicking Flip	H. Folkes	Mr & Mrs B. Wiltshire	7.8.64
Ch. Jolihem Dreadnought	D	Ch. Eastaff Danom	Jolihem Nuncargate Josie	L. F. Hemstock	L. F. Hemstock	14.6.64
Ch. Famous Lad of Wirswall	D	Ch. The Black Monarch	Wirswall Duchess	Mrs E. M. Myles & C. Townsend	Mrs E. M. Myles	9.6.63
Ch. Pitbul Colleen	B	Ch. Eastaff Danom	Pitbul Amber Princess	Mr & Mrs K. Fensom	Mrs M. K. Fensom	9.9.61
Ch. Freden Bothered	B	Ch. The Black Monarch	Ch. Fredenzella	N. Edwards	F. W. Holden	15.6.63
Ch. Jolihem Black Beauty	B	Ch. Jolihem El Toro	Jolihem Isabella	L. F. Hemstock	L. F. Hemstock	25.4.64
Ch. Lydes Cygnet	B	Ch. Rellim Ferryvale Victor	Linksbury Derry Dhu	Mrs M. C. Hughes	Mrs M. C. Hughes	18.10.63
Ch. Constones Compact	B	Bankhead Benjamin	Constones Comette	Mr & Mrs A. M. Lee	A. W. A. Cairns	5.9.63
Ch. Curfews White Orchid	B	Ch. Eastaff Danom	Ch. Orchid Beauty	F. J. Clark	V. Pounds	7.3.65
1967:						
Ch. Rapparee Renegade	D	Ch. Game Flash	Walstaff Tigre Tigrato	Mr & Mrs J. Bolton	S. Bennett	7.10.64

Ch. Gwynford Drumbeat	D	Ch. Game Flash	Gwynford Winter Witch	F. Burford	F. Burford	13.7.63
Ch. Rellim Warpaint	D	Ch. Rellim Ferryvale Victor	Ch. Senkrah Sabutae	G. Downs	T. Miller	21.10.65
Ch. Rossisle Rivorich Maxmillion	D	Ch. Chestonian Campaign	Freden Beguiled	Miss R. J. A. Swindells & C. A. Smith	J. Talbot	9.6.64
Ch. Jasper of Witts	D	Ch. Eastaff Danom	Lass of Nutgrove	S. Bartlett	S. Bartlett	12.10.64
Ch. Badgerlea Biddy	B	Ch. Eastaff Danom	Ch. Senkrah Saffron	S. W. Craik	S. W. Craik	20.12.63
Ch. Kinderlee Cashelle	B	Ir.Ch. Thoroak Sorrel Sam	Int.Ch. Senkrah Sabeau	Mrs E. E. Hill	R. McEvoy	4.5.65
Ch. Brindis Kim	B	Brindis Jaguar	Brindis Juno	M. Hoban	Mr & Mrs W. Atkinson	30.11.63
Ch. Sanville Wild Clover	B	Weycombe Shan	Senkrah Wild Maid	W. E. Burrows	W. Watson	21.8.64
Ch. Orchid Beauty	B	Ch. Brinstock Glenagow	Black Orchid	V. H. Pounds	V. H. Pounds	21.12.62
1968:						
Ch. Topcroft Toreador	D	Ch. Bandits Brintiga	Topcroft Tar Baby	H. Latham	H. Latham	27.11.65
Ch. Rossisle Hobson	D	Ch. Chestonion Campaign	Rossisle Fredenina	Miss R. J. A. Swindells & C. A. Smith	Miss R. J. A. Swindells & C. A. Smith	30.3.63
Ch. Linksbury Augustus	D	Trenton Colonel	Linksbury Mairi	Mrs J. Fisher	Mrs J. Fisher	27.8.63
Ch. Lydes Winston Defiant	D	Ch. Jolihem El Toro	Freden De Lovely	Mrs S. M. Fox	Mrs M. C. Hughes	30.11.64
Ch. Badgerlea Rascal	D	Ch. Eastaff Danom	Ch. Senkrah Saffron	Craik & Howarth	S. W. Craik	28.8.65

Name of Champion	*Sex*	*Sire*	*Dam*	*Owner*	*Breeder*	*Date of Birth*
Ch. Wirswall Jet the Monarch	D	Ch. The Black Monarch	Georgeous Gusie of Wirswall	Mrs E. M . Myles & M. Boam	Mrs E. M. Myles	19.12.65
Ch. Sanville Wild Cheetah	B	Saracen of Senkrah	Senkrah Wild Maid	W. Watson	W. Watson	16.12.62
Ch. Dennybeck Brindis Liqueur	B	Dennybeck Diamond King	Dennybeck Delight	Mrs P. Brooks	Mr & Mrs W. Atkinson	8.12.63
Ch. Topcroft Temptress	B	Ch. Bandits Brintiga	Topcroft Tar Baby	Mr & Mrs E. J. Bywater	H. Latham	27.11.65
1969:						
Ch. Rapparee Threap-wood Handyman	D	Ch. Rapparee Renegade	Betchgreen Blacklass	Mr & Mrs J. Bolton & H. W. Clamp	Mrs A. Banks	4.9.67
Ch. Red Zarni	D	Rebel Man	Miss Penny Packer	Mrs D. M. Woodward	P. Parkes	20.7.66
Ch. Red Kim	D	Bantam Boy	Dennybeck Drum Girl	Mrs E. P. Stark	A. Thackray	14.8.64
Ch. Langport Spearhead	D	Ch. Freden Dominate	Rossisle Marquita	K. C. Langdon	H. V. Langdon	2.3.67
Ch. Christopher of Geneva	D	Admiral Robert	Sisao Lubby Lou	Mrs R. Williams	Mrs M. Earwaker	25.12.63
Ch. Wystaff Warfare	D	Kinderlee Commando	Wystaff Rossisle Rosina	Mr & Mrs R. Armitage	Mrs G. Gallimore	20.1.66
Ch. Jubilant of Jolihem	D	Ch. Jolihem El Toro	Jolihem Isabella	G. Goddard	L. F. Hemstock	27.4.63

Ch. Benext Beau	D	Ulsterville Major	Ch. Benext Beauty Be	Mr & Mrs K. Bailey	Mr & Mrs K. Bailey	20.1.67
Ch. Durward Demon	B	Ir. Ch. Raynan Dandy	Ir. Ch. Weycombe Vanessa	Harkness & Dunn	R. McEvoy	2.1.65
Ch. Dennybeck Eliza Doolittle	B	Dennybeck Hard Diamond	Dennybeck Drum Girl	Mrs P. Brooks	Mrs J. Horsfall	12.11.66
Ch. Battlers Pop-Along-A-Bit	B	Ch. The Red Battler	Nuzwig Kanga	A. G. Phillips	H. M. Tynesley	6.3.64
Ch. Benext Beauty Be	B	Gwen's Danny Boy	Benext Pamarandy Christabella	Mr K. & Mrs G. B. Bailey	Mr K. & Mrs G. B. Bailey	27.7.64
Ch. Jolihem Gallant Bess	B	Ch. Jolihem Dreadnought	Hillstaffs Lucky Gem	L. F. Hemstock	Mrs J. Pellington	4.2.68
Ch. Sanville Red Dawn	B	The Young Pretender	Ch. Sanville Wild Cheetah	W. Watson	W. Watson	12.11.67
Ch. Kinderlee Critique	B	Ch. Topcroft Toreador	Kinderlee Cambrian	H. Latham & Mrs E. E. Hill	Mr & Mrs A. K. Hill	1.7.68
1970:						
Ch. Hambrea Super Flash	D	Ch. Game Flash	Fulfin Firefly	H. J. Wall	Mr & Mrs A. Hammersley	8.9.65
Ch. Rossisle Alverthorpe Dark Judy	B	Red Fury	Dark Eyed Kim	Miss R. J. A. Swindells	T. Cunnane	19.9.64
Ch. Rapparee Roulette	B	Ch. Jolihem Dreadnought	Ch. Rapparee Ashfield Star	Mr & Mrs J. Bolton	Mr & Mrs J. Bolton	1.9.65
Ch. Gamestock Bonnie of Burns	B	Jack of Spades	Dark Castle Lass	P. Jepson	Mr B. Bradley	14.5.67

Name of Champion	*Sex*	*Sire*	*Dam*	*Owner*	*Breeder*	*Date of Birth*
Ch. Jumping Bean of Grenoside	B	Ch. Topcroft Toreador	Grenoside Honey Bee	C. H. Senior	W. W. Greaves	27.8.67
Ch. Rainsbrook Renegade	D	Mountainash Xmas Titian	Rainsbrook Trial Edition	J. Bamber	Mrs D. Parker	15.6.67
1971:						
Ch. Ashstock Artful Bess	B	Ch. Camdonian Contender	Barrington Wild Rose	Mr & Mrs A. A. Waters	Mr & Mrs A. A. Waters	18.4.68
Ch. Blakens Dark Prospect	B	Ch. Wystaff Warfare	Blaken's Battlers Brew	A. G. Phillips	A. G. Phillips	7.1.69
Ch. Brocliffe Brindis U Like	B	Dennybeck Hard Diamond	Dennybeck Delight	Mrs J. Horsfall	Mr & Mrs Atkinson	2.10.68
Ch. Buccaneer Shoemaker	D	Ch. Topcroft Toreador	Bridgehouse Sandpiper	A. Johnson	W. Sheeny	20.3.69
Ch. Jolihem Ringmaster	D	Ch. Jolihem Dreadnought	Hillstaff's Lucky Gem	L. F. Hemstock	Mrs J. Pellington	4.2.68
Ch. Rapparee Rothersyke Vow	D	Ch. Rapparee Threapwood Handyman	Rothersyke Gem	Mr & Mrs J. Bolton	Dr I. W. Davidson	6.6.69
Ch. Rapparee Look Lively	D	Hydiamond King	Rapparee Lady Luck	L. Barnett	Mr & Mrs J. Bolton	20.4.67
Ch. Sanville Red Rhapsody	B	Senkrah Sabre	Ch. Sanville Wild Cheetah	G. A. Dudley	W. Watson	18.11.68

Ch. Satan's Master	D	Ch. Topcroft Toreador	Kinderlee Conchita	K. J. Boyham	Mrs B. Topping	19.5.69
Ch. Staffshaven Artificer	D	Ch. Topcroft Toreador	Badgerlea Kate	Mrs J. R. Bennett	Mrs J. R. Bennett	8.9.68
Ch. Torosay Black Fern	B	Ch. Bandits Brintiga	Torosay Masterpiece	D. Gilmour	Dr C. MacLean	8.9.67
Ch. Wawocan Jezebel	B	Wawocan Buccaneer	Ch. Popcroft Temptress	Mr & Mrs E. J. Bywaters	Mr & Mrs E. J. Bywaters	16.1.68
Ch. Yennips Sarabelle	B	Mountainash Xmas Atlas	Countrymans Coppice	Mr & Mrs W. Todd	R. P. Henshaw	4.11.66
Ch. Hoplite Fearless Devil	D	Hoplite Horniman	Hoplite Hot Tamale	W. McKnight	A. Mitchell	1.2.67
1972:						
Ch. Rockmere Rip-it-up	D	Sanville Red Ranger	Rockmere Vernport Shina	Mr & Mrs J. R. McKellar	Mr & Mrs J. R. McKellar	4.7.69
Ch. Rellim Saratoga Siddy	B	Ch. Rellim Ferryvale Victor	Rellim Fenella	Mrs T. Miller	Mrs T. Miller	22.10.68
Ch. Langport Avenger	D	Ch. Gwynford Drumbeat	Langport Solitaire Queen	H. V. Langdon	H. V. Langdon	2.4.70
Ch. Ruadh of Hawkslee	B	Sanville Wild Beaver	Lass of Senkrah	D. R. Grant	D. Weston	1.9.67
Ch. Gadet's Last Chance	B	Ch. Rapparee Look	Buccaneer Penny	T. Fury	A. Johnson	11.3.71
Ch. Rapparee Grand Slam	B	Larujan Leader	Rapparee Razzle Dazzle	Mr & Mrs J. Bolton	Mr & Mrs. J. Bolton	26.1.70
Ch. Highland Squire	D	Sanville Red Warrior	Cheshire Brandy	Mr J. Stirling	Mr D. T. Reid	14.2.69

Name of Champion	*Sex*	*Sire*	*Dam*	*Owner*	*Breeder*	*Date of Birth*
Ch. Rothersyke Maid	B	Larujou Leader	Calderbrig Carmen	Dr & Mrs I. W. Davidson	Dr & Mrs I. W. Davidson	5.10.67
Ch. Ginnels Moonlight Madonna	B	Chestonian Arrogant	Liam's Gire	W. E. Jones	W. E. Jones	3.2.69
1973:						
Ch. Durwood Deodante	D	Rellin Billy Bow	Flora of Stockwell	Mr & Mrs I. Dunn	Mrs Campbell	2.2.71
Ch. Rapparee The Gladiator	D	Larujan Leader	Rapparee Razzle Dazzle	Mr & Mrs A. Sparks	Mr & Mrs J. Bolton	26.1.70
Ch. Moi Daredevil	D	Ch. Rapparee Rothersyke Vow	Moi Carousel	Mr J. J. Dibling	Mr K. Layland	21.10.70
Ch. Wawocan Kinsman	D	Ch. Topcroft Toreador	Ch. Topcroft Temptress	Mrs M. Graham	Mr & Mrs E. J. Bywater	2.3.69
Ch. Quite Contrary of Rapparee	B	Ch. Rapparee Rothersyke Vow	Dusky Maid	Mr & Mrs J. Bolton	Mr R. Martin	17.2.72
Ch. Reetuns Lord Jim	D	Ch. Rapparee Threapwood Handyman	Elvinór Miranda	Messrs Wood & Holmes	Mr A. Wood	20.4.72
Ch. Barrington Golden Toga	B	Ch. Buninyong Caesar	Barrington Rellim Regina	Miss P. Machaglan	Maj. & Mrs Rowley & Miss Anderson	16.2.67
Ch. Meaduns Polly Flinders	B	Ch. Rapparee Rothersyke Vow	Somerset Sheila	Mr H. A. Dunn	Mr J. Evans	1.11.70

Ch. Elegance of Sanville	B	Print of Wyncole	Sanville Red Enchantree	J. Prentice & Mrs Watson	W. Watson	14.9.69
Ch. Mill Lass of Judael	B	Matt of Stainlaw	Janine of Judael	Searle & Earle	M. Searle	18.8.69
Ch. Sanville Red Ember	B	Senkrah Sabra	Ch. Sanville Wild Cheetah	J. G. Porteous	W. Watson	18.11.68
Ch. Constones Grim Girl	B	Ch. Freden Dominate	Ch. Constones Compact	Mr & Mrs W. Alexander	Mr & Mrs A. W. Lee	16.5.69
1974:						
Ch. Redeal Mik	D	Ch. Satan's Master	Mistress Sheba	J. Leader	J. Leader	13.5.70
Ch. Ashstock Max the Miller	D	Dennybeck Hard Diamond	Ch. Ashstock Artful Bess	Mr & Mrs A. Waters	Mr & Mrs A. Waters	13.1.71
Ch. Lunar Flash	D	Ch. Rapparee Look Lively	Perky Ellen	Mr & Mrs Fern	A. W. Skett	10.7.69
Ch. Pitbul Jeff's Pal	D	Ch. Jolihem Dreadnought	Pitbul Christabelle	Mr & Mrs W. Jones	Mr & Mrs K. Fenson	1.2.69
Ch. Cardinal Sin of Beaconmoor	D	Verles Victory	Asbury Mulla	Mr & Mrs M. Mitchell	Mrs G. Ormonde	20.2.72
Ch. Cradbury Flash	B	Ch. Rapparee Rothersyke Vow	Cradbury Lady Flash	F. A. Phillips	F. A. Phillips	27.5.72
Ch. Betchgreen Sheena	B	Ch. Rapparee The Gladiator	Betchgreen Flashless	W. Hodgkinson	W. Hodgkinson	24.5.71
Ch. Yennips Golden Wonder	B	Mountain Ash Xmas Titan	Towans Mia Petite Ami	Mr & Mrs F. Ward	Mr & Mrs W. Todd	6.4.70

Name of Champion	*Sex*	*Sire*	*Dam*	*Owner*	*Breeder*	*Date of Birth*
Ch. Spotty Lady	B	Ch. Rapparee Look Lively	Buccaneer Penny Black	C. Whitworth	A. Johnston	11.3.71
Ch. Ashtock Black Maria	B	Ch. Rapparee Rothersyke Vow	Ch. Ashstock Artful Bess	Mr & Mrs A. Waters	Mr & Mrs A. Waters	11.4.72
Ch. Red Rapture of Hamason	B	Ch. Rockmere Rip-it-up	Sanville Red Rhapsody	Mr & Mrs Robinson	Gerald Dudley	7.5.72
Ch. Westpoint Warrior	D	Ch. Topcroft Toreador	Owd Bett	A. McDermott	W. Whitehurst	8.9.69
Ch. Brocliffe Best Bet	D	Kinderlee Cobra	Ch. Dennybeck Eliza Doolittle	Mrs P. Brookes	Mrs P. Brookes	24.4.71
Ch. Dark Rose of Topcroft	B	Ch. Westpoint Warrior	Topcroft Caprice	Mr & Mrs W. Bennett	Messrs Latham & Rickard	31.7.71
1975:						
Ch. Ashtock Brinchester	D	Dennybeck Hard Diamond	Ch. Ashstock Artful Bess	Mr & Mrs E. Skeets	Mr & Mrs A. Waters	13.1.71
Ch. Jokartan Royal Tan	D	Ch. Jolihem Ring-master	Brocliffe Bountiful	J. Argile	J. Argile	30.6.73
Ch. Midnight Riot	D	Ch. Rothersyke Vow	Rapparee Riot Belle	Mrs P. Carless	B. Corbett	12.2.72
Ch. St Simon's Argonaut	D	Ch. Westpoint Warrior	Sanbryn Comedy	Mrs P. Hayes	G. M. Grosvenor	9.2.72
Ch. Tom Crib of Sparpit	D	Livstaff Black Knight	Dusky Maid	Mr & Mrs A. Sparks	A. Burrows	29.4.73

Ch. Cradbury Lord Vow	D	Ch. Rapparee Rothersyke Vow	Lady of Verona	R. D. H. Gittins	M. Gwilt	14.7.73
Ch. Staffs McMichael	D	Burntwoods Red Devil	Dark-eyed Sandra	L. Berry	J. Larkin	27.11.71
Ch. Reetuns Aristocrat	D	Ch. Westpoint Warrior	Elinor Miranda	Mrs T. Ward	A. Wood	26.9.73
Ch. Rossisle Trump Card	B	Satchmo Goodliness	Ch. Rossile Alverthorpe Dark Judy	Mrs R. J. A. Swindells	Mrs R. J. A. Swindells	18.7.72
Ch. Kerrisdale Orchids Fancy	B	Trebblo Little Fella	Kerrisdale Little Miss Cinders	V. H. Pounds	Mrs A. Gatenby	4.1.73
Ch. Ashmoss Billy's Girl of Valgo	B	Son of Templar	Black Orchid of Touchstone	Mr & Mrs G. Golding	J. Acton	28.10.72
Ch. Lida of Tinkinswood	B	Brombill Chief Stoker	Bonny Queen	T. Fletcher	P. E. Lewis	22.11.71
Ch. Kerrisdale Tufnut of Raan	B	Trebblo Little Fella	Kerrisdale Little Miss Cinders	Mr & Mrs R. Blackmore	Mrs A. Gatenby	2.1.73
Ch. Durward Dorlesa	B	Kimbrook of Suffolk	Danville Red Sparkler	M. Currie	I. Dunn	22.2.72
Ch. Vencristo Ambience	B	Brindis Ultimate	Elvinor Westwards Bess	N. Entwistle	N. Entwistle	19.4.72
1976: Ch. Bronco Morning Light	B	Ch. Rapparee The Gladiator	Sparpit Sea Sprite	Mr & Mrs J. Webley	Mr & Mrs J. Webley	16.1.74

Name of Champion	*Sex*	*Sire*	*Dam*	*Owner*	*Breeder*	*Date of Birth*
Ch. Hurricane of Judael	D	Sheila's Little Skipper	Crisp of Judael	Mr & Mrs J. E. Pringle	Mr Searle & G. Earle	27.6.74
Ch. Swinfen Sky Scraper	D	Brindis Ultimate	Dennybeck Diehard	Mr & Mrs H. Gudgeon	S. Saul	6.3.71
Ch. Anjemag Aussie	D	Bertjen Jordanhill Rebel	Senkrah Sanell	Mr & Mrs A. Humphreys & A. Harkness	Mr & Mrs A. Humphreys	15.9.73
Ch. Ashstock Red Buttons	B	Ashstock Thornhill Prince	Ashstock Iron Peg	Mr & Mrs W. G. Dew	Mr & Mrs A. Waters	6.7.73
Ch. Moekems Cyclone	D	Dunbriton Baldie Thompson	Swinfen Sunflower	J. Dunn	Mr & Mrs K. Brown	1.7.74
Ch. Hamasen Red Rambler	D	Sanville Red Ranger	Dark Demon Lass of Hamasen	Mr & Mrs H. Robins	Mr & Mrs H. Robins	11.10.74
Ch. Thorndyke White Miracle	D	Janesen Boy	Thorndyke Jane	E. Dyke	E. Dyke	2.8.74
Ch. Ashstock Lucky Jim	D	Ch. Rapparee Rothersyke Vow	Ch. Ashstock Artful Bess	Mr & Mrs A. Devlin	Mr & Mrs A. Waters	11.4.72
Ch. Boggarts Black Pearl	B	Ruffhill Brindle Basher	Keencluff Carousel	L. B. Walker	L. Barnett	13.2.73
Ch. Sparpit Lavender Liz	B	Livstaff Black Knight	Pit Rose	Mr & Mrs A. Sparks	Mr & Mrs A. Sparks	10.10.74

1977:

Ch. Pitbul Red Regent	D	Irish Ch. Ban Ri of Cuileog	Pitbul Bulwip Ebony Princess	Mr & Mrs K. Fenson	Mr & Mrs K. Fenson	10.11.75
Ch. Pitfighta Dark Duke	D	Ch. Langport Avenger	Ch. Constones Grims Girl	Mr & Mrs W. Alexander	Mr & Mrs W. Alexander	10.3.75
Ch. Tenax Trampas	D	Dennybeck Devilmaycare	Tenax Thumblina	J. Gibson	J. Gibson	29.11.74
Ch. Eilesteve Bella	B	Comanche Thunderflash	Steveleen's Judy	Mr & Mrs A. Rowe	Mr & Mrs S. Kelly	9.10.72
Ch. Kinderdijk Petite Cherie	B	Ch. Pitbul Jeff's Pal	Hot Chocolate	Mr & Mrs R. Astley	Mr & Mrs Sadler	22.9.74
Ch. Glenrhondda Sombre Bell of Dogan	B	Ch. Westpoint Warrior	Isengard Patsy	B. Cadogan & A. Thomas	Mrs Thomas	2.9.74
Ch. Rumbows Black Bess	B	Ch. Rappareethe Gladiator	Wiley Dark Rose	A. E. Jones	J. Till	7.2.74
Ch. Moekems Whirlwind	B	Ch. Dunbriton Baldie Thompson	Swinfen Sunflower	Mr & Mrs K. Brown	Mr & Mrs K. Brown	1.7.74
Ch. Copcoch Whiplash	D	Fighting Mike	Copcoch Tuti Fruite	K. W. Harwood	Mr Oakley	3.3.75
Ch. Rocketeer Nancy Girl	B	Ch. Redeal Mik	Vrand Geg Flash	Mr & Mrs B. Noon	Mr & Mrs G. Parry	18.8.74
Ch. Gamestock Love Bug of Cubik	B	Buckhill Black Bomber	Buckhill Hostess	Mrs J. Ashburner	Mr Peter Jepson	8.11.71
Ch. Carndearg Ne'erday	B	Dumbriton Baldie Thompson	Durward Dusky Dinah	Mr & Mrs I. MacEachern	Mr & Mrs I. MacEachern	1.1.74

Name of Champion	*Sex*	*Sire*	*Dam*	*Owner*	*Breeder*	*Date of Birth*
Ch. Delastar of Durward	B	Ch. Tom Crib of Sparpit	Maromen Attar of Minx	Mr & Mrs I. Dunn	Mr & Mrs H. Kennedy	22.2.75
Ch. Hamason Red Radiance	B	Ch. Hamason Red Rambler	Ch. Red Rapture of Hamason	Mr & Mrs H. Robinson	Mr & Mrs H. Robinson	28.8.75
Ch. Touch and Go of Beaconmoor	B	Verles Viceroy	Tyrunnus Belle	Mrs F. MacMillan	Miss A. Rogers	28.8.73
1978:						
Ch. Rendorm Deadly Nighshade	B	Ch. Hurricane of Judael	Rendorm Rapid Reprisal	Mr & Mrs N. Berry	Mr & Mrs N. Berry	6.9.76
Ch. Cotfol Princess of Tridwr	B	Irish Ch. Carivale Conquestor	Fawn Fury	T. Fletcher	Cotter & Foley	1.6.76
Ch. Eastern Star of Zilabra	B	Zilabra Son of Squire	Zilabra Miss	Mesdames Dewar & McKinnon	Mrs M. Graham	23.11.72
Ch. Alpaka Lola's Dream	B	Royal Duke of Scarthwaite	Alpaka Bob's Fancy	Mr & Mrs A. S. Tittle	Mr & Mrs A. S. Tittle	17.3.73
Ch. Acid Queen	B	Ch. Hurricane of Judael	Jimmy Arenskaya	M. J. Green	Mrs J. Plowes	6.1.76
Ch. Black Tusker	D	Black King	Lady Bella Madonna	B. Bates & M. Boam	G. Cowdell	8.10.75
Ch. Frolbeca Fireraiser	D	Ch. Jolihem Ring-master	Iron Porsche	Mr & Mrs C. H. Green	F. Sweeney	22.9.72
Ch. Scarthwaite - Coachman	D	Royal Duke of Scarthwaite	Eshbee Beauty of Scarthwaite	L. Aspin	L. Aspin	16.8.75

1979:

Ch. Bobom Amber Gambler	B	Ch. Moekems Cyclone	Moekems Onyx	Mr & Mrs A. Bloomfield	Mr & Mrs A. Bloomfield	26.6.76
Ch. Montbell Barbarossa	D	Ch. Pitbul Red Regent	Ch. Ashstock Red Buttons	Mr & Mrs J. G. Bird	Mr & Mrs W. G. Dew	12.2.77
Ch. Angelstaff Blue Max	D	Benext Begin of Angelstaff	Kerrisdale Debbie Bess	Mr & Mrs A. Carilini	Mr & Mrs A. Carilini	4.6.77
Ch. Kandony Brindle Ben	D	Ruffhill The Midlander	Nethertonian Saucy Girl	Mr & Mrs P. Lloyd	Mr & Mrs L. Westood	28.9.77
Ch. Sundow Swashbuckler	D	Brijon Battlehymn	Kelba of Kinderlee	Mr & Mrs G. Pearson	Mr & Mrs G. Pearson	25.1.77
Ch. Kaluki Duke	D	Warlock of Rotherskye	Cradbury Flash Gem	Mr & Mrs G. Dickins	R. & P. Benson	22.10.75
Ch. Macschiehallion	D	Ch. Hurricane of Judael	Red Kate	Mrs J. Short	Mrs M. Kinsley	5.7.76
Ch. Shepstaff Black Pearl	B	Raphaels Black Ace	Westbourn Brindle Plague	Mrs B. H. Buxton	Mr & Mrs D. W. Shepherd	11.1.75
Ch. Little Miss Kek	B	Ch. Hurricane of Judael	Black Velvet	Mr & Mrs C. Green	Mr & Mrs C. Green	2.11.76
Ch. Meadums Emma Hamilton	B	Ruffhill Show Bow	Ch. Meadums Polly Flinders	H. A. Dunn	H. A. Dunn	26.5.76
Ch. Tafstaff Samantha of Chalfont	B	Torcrest Ambassador	Tafstaff Beauty	Mrs P. A. Painter	R. G. Bradshaw	14.9.73

Name of Champion	Sex	Sire	Dam	Owner	Breeder	Date of Birth
1980:						
Ch. Rendorn No Retreat	B	Brewmaster Spartacus	Rendorn Regal Flash	N. Berry	Owner	20.10.77
Ch. Goldwyn Leading Star	B	Ch. Red Rum	Star Prize	P. Wall	Owner	27.4.78
Ch. Scarthwaite Temptress	B	Royal Duke of Scarthwaite	Eshbee Beauty of Scarthwaite	L. Aspin	Owner	16.8.75
Ch. Durward Dark Dancer	B	Ch. Durward Deodante	Ch. Delaster of Durward	I. Dunn	Owner	2.6.78
Ch. Briglen Arcturus	B	Ch. Scarthwaite Coachman	Briglen Adversary	B. Whitehouse	Owner	15.2.78
Ch. Bracken of Judael	B	Highmoor Dandy of Judael	Gold Pride of Judael	J. Preston	Searle & Earle	29.7.78
Ch. Meaduns Cleopatra	B	Ruffhill Showboy	Meaduns Marie Antoinette	H. Dunn	Owner	26.2.76
Ch. Red Rum	D	Vencristo Domino	Vencristo Amber	T. Ruddie	D. Birchall	20.7.76
Ch. Martonger Rip Rap	D	Gypsy Daniels of Sparpit	Martonger Bess's Girl	G. Byrne	Owner	31.10.75
Ch. Skean Dhu	D	Ch. Black Tusker	Constones Paragon	G. Carter	Mrs Grotrain	24.4.78
Ch. Brocliffe Benjamin	D	Carivale Double Century	Ch. Brocliffe Best Bet	Mr Donnley	Mrs Brooks	16.11.76

1981:

Ch. Duchess of Aubrey	B	Ch. Rapparee Rotherskye Vow	Honey End Bess	M. Burke	Mrs Bishop	10.8.78
Ch. Evaredee Sergeant Pepper	B	Sir Sous Nox	The Foundling	Mr & Mrs Homan	J. Peters	7.7.76
Ch. Ginnels Black Tuskyanna	D	Ch. Black Tusker	Ginnels Madonnas Moon Maid	Mr & Mrs Shoulder	W. Jones	10.12.78
Ch. Jolaine Wild Gypsy	B	Livstaff Black Knight	Mosscroft Kimbella	Mrs Eva	Mr & Mrs Cooper	28.10.77
Ch. Karjobri Black Pepper	D	Ch. Black Tusker	Karjobri Precious Lass	Mr & Mrs Grattidge	Owners	17.11.77
Ch. Lawbury Cadiz Kid	D	Ch. Pitfighta Dark Duke	Hazelberry Go Go	Mr & Mrs Lawlor	Owners	2.6.78
Ch. Nethertonion Tweedle Dee Dee	B	Betchgreen Dubber	Ruffhill Queenie	Mr & Mrs Westwood	W. Beasley	19.10.77
Ch. Pegs Bolton Trip	D	Ch. Hurricane of Judael	Sharnford Black Diamond	J. Pringle	R. Henry	5.12.78
Ch. Pitmax the Matador	D	Ch. Swinfen Skyscraper	Lady Red Samba	R. Harper	P. Shelley	30.8.77
Ch. Red Prince of Hamason	D	Hamason Red Rajah	Powerstown Susie	J. Ratcliffe	J. Ford	23.9.77
Ch. Whitebury Crown	D	Brijon Battle Hymn	Ch. Boggarts Black Pearl	H. Ward	P. Walker	24.6.77
Ch. Worden Queen	B	Benjamin Worden Lad	Ch. Acid Queen	Mrs Gilfoyle	M. Green	10.10.78

Name of Champion	*Sex*	*Sire*	*Dam*	*Owner*	*Breeder*	*Date of Birth*
1982:						
Ch. Bodger of Kenstaff	D	Mercian Turque	Miriam of Mercia	F. Gough	M. Henderson	10.2.77
Ch. Pitmax Pasidion of Dumbriton	D	Ch. Red Rum	Lady Red Samba	D. Gilmour	P. Shelley	8.11.80
Ch. Bens Renegade of Baracane	D	Baracane Midnight Marauder	Jephson Jane	B. Munro	V. White	22.9.80
Ch. Maradin Master Mariner	D	Betchgreen Dubber	Bethane Bitter Sweet	E. Bradford	Owner	28.10.79
Ch. Earlsdon Viceroy of Benfirth	D	Ch. Black Tusker	Earlsdon Spitfire	D. Bentley	Mr & Mrs Booth	14.5.81
Ch. Baroness of Bettandy	B	Ch. Hurricane of Judael	Pitmax Hot Ember	F. Saunders	Mr & Mrs Whelan	31.5.80
Ch. Rocellio Miss Supreme	B	Goldwyn Golden Lad	Rocellio Belle Starr	R. Pugh	Owner	7.9.80
Ch. Sze Lyng Uno Who	B	Ruffhill the Midlander	Sze Lyng Harry's Choice	S. Goode	Owner	25.1.80
Ch. Solo Gypsy Fiddler	B	Ch. Karjobri Black Pepper	Prudy Prima Donna	R. Wint	Owner	24.8.80
Ch. Rendorn Devils Timpani	B	Ch. Black Tusker	Ch. Rendorn No Retreat	N. Berry	Owner	19.11.80
Ch. Gardell Salusian	B	Ch. Pitbul Red Regent	Gardell Do Well	M. Edwards	Owner	12.6.79

Ch. Redstaff King	D	Ch. Jokartan Royal Tan	Pitmax Brazen Lady	H. Doughty	J. Pearson	27.7.79
1983:						
Ch. Nethertonion Stormtrooper	D	Ch. Kaluki Duke	Ch. Nethertonion Tweedle Dee	Mr & Mrs Westwood	Mr & Mrs Westwood	7.5.80
Ch. Wardrum Dixie	B	Wardrum Geronimo	Wardrum Black Benita	D. W. Smart	D. W. Smart	17.7.78
Ch. Bobstaff Grand King of Durward	D	Ch. Black Tusker	Ch. Briglen Bellona	Mr & Mrs Dunn	Mr McMunn	14.8.80
Ch. Cradbury Flash Danny Boy	D	Ch. Cradbury Flash Earl	Cradbury Flash Beauty	F. Phillips	F. Phillips	13.5.79
Ch. Whitehaven Charlie Boy	D	Ch. Kandony Brindle Ben	Gypsy Girl	F. Cadd	Messrs Gwilt & Westwood	21.1.79
Ch. Goldwyn Lucky Star	B	Ch. The Malaser Mauler	Ch. Goldwyn Leading Star	Mr & Mrs P. Wall	Mr & Mrs P. Wall	13.6.81
Ch. Judy of Jolihem	B	Goldwyn Lucky Lad	Emma of Gal	L. Hemstock	J. Tomlinson	18.4.81
Ch. Marples Black Opal	D	Ch. Kaluki Duke	Dellaga Lady	P. White	P. White	8.10.80
Ch. Kendris Gay Abandon	B	Kendris Runamok	Scarssyks Whisky Bell	Mr & Mrs Turnbull	Mr & Mrs Lovelady	7.11.80
Ch. Brindle King of Jeystone	D	Ch. Staff McMichael	Princess Kathy's Lass	S. Rumble	Mr & Mrs Bowles	11.11.77
Ch. Rendorn Delta Dawn	B	Ch. Hurricane of Judael	Rendorn Georgie Girl	N. Berry	N. Berry	12.11.80

Name of Champion	*Sex*	*Sire*	*Dam*	*Owner*	*Breeder*	*Date of Birth*
Ch. Lydes Cleopatra	B	Ch. Black Tusker	Constones Posie	Messrs Bates & Boam	Mrs M. Hughes	24.1.81
Ch. Yankeestaff Bolivar	D	Kerrisdale Thieving Demon	Astaff Clares Cassandra	Mr & Mrs Malec	Mr & Mrs Malec	4.1.81
Ch. Rowenda Devils Disciple	D	Ch. Black Tusker	Rowenda Midnight Venture	N. Patey & J. Rowe	J. Rowe	30.8.81
Ch. Stalest Delilah Dear of Jensbeck	B	Bethane Don Juan of Gamestock	Gamestock Sparklin Sal	B. Aubrey	J. Round	9.6.81
Ch. Spadille Spare the Rod	B	Ch. Skean Dhu Black	Black Magic of Spadille	Mr & Mrs W. Hunter	Mr & Mrs W. Hunter	18.8.81
Ch. Serrel White Lightning	D	Ch. Pitmax the Matador	Amanda Arabella Lear	Mr & Mrs Young	S. Stockfis	4.10.81
Ch. Briglen Bellona	B	Ch. Sundow Swashbuckler	Briglen Dreadnought	R. McMunn	Mr & Mrs Whitehouse	26.2.79
1984:						
Ch. Yankeestaff Serendipity	B	Ch. Yankeestaff Bolivar	Ainsair Fancy Lass	Mr & Mrs Malec	Mr & Mrs Malec	24.4.82
Ch. The Malaser Mauler	D	Ch. Jokartan Royal Tan	Pitmax Brazen Lady	Thomson & Shelley	W. J. Pearson	27.7.79
Ch. Carndearg Jake The Rake	D	Ch. Bobstaff Grand King of Durward	Carndearg Southern Star	Mr & Mrs MacEachern	Owners	27.1.82
Ch. Ben Hur	D	Ch. Moekems Cyclone	Spartans Glory	Mr & Mrs Austin	Watson	26.10.80

Ch. Carstaff Dancing Queen	B	Goldwyn Golden Lad	Sunrise Black Rose	Mr & Mrs Cunningham	Owners	31.3.81
Ch. Tridwr Dicey Riley	D	Ch. Pitbul Red Regent	Ch. Cotfoll Princess of Tridwr	T. Fletcher	T. Fletcher	25.5.79
Ch. Scarthwaite Rema	B	Ch. Moekems Cyclone	Ch. Scarthwaite Temptress	Mr & Mrs Wolliscroft	L. Aspin	31.7.78
Ch. Allandale King	D	Ch. Skean Dhu	Briglen Tamarisk	E. Britton	Mr & Mrs Small	22.4.82
Ch. Jolihem Wildfire	B	Ch. Jokartan Royal Tan	Boadicea of Jolihem	L. Hemstock	L. Hemstock	19.4.82
Ch. Lydes Hermione	B	Ch. Black Tusker	Constones Posie	Mrs M. Hughes	Mrs Hughes	17.9.79
Ch. Belnite Belladonna	B	Bronchonian Wellbread	Belnite Bellestar	W. McKnight	W. McKnight	15.2.81
Ch. Teutonic Warrior	D	Ashstock Wild Colonial Boy	Regal Princess	Rivenberg/Shorrocks	Rivenberg	29.7.81
Ch. Belle Hurricane Duchess	B	Ch. Skean Dhu	Piper Knowle Gipsy	Mr Francis	D. Eddy	15.3.82
Ch. Ainsair Fancy Lass	B	Wardrum Geronimo	Astaff Fashion Girl	Mr & Mrs Malec	Mrs Ainslie	5.6.80
Ch. Ecstaff Tuxedo Warrior	D	Rendorn The Mighty Quinn	Ecstaff Fiery Angel	Mr Cooke	Mr & Mrs Dooston	1.12.81
1985:						
Ch. Spadille Midnight Lace	B	Ch. Nethertonion Stormtrooper	Black Magic of Spadille	Mrs Nelson	Mr & Mrs Hunter	6.2.82
Ch. Karjobri Pure Silk	B	Ch. Pegs Bolton Trip	Karjobri Penny Black	Mr & Mrs Grattidge	Owners	6.2.83

Name of Champion	*Sex*	*Sire*	*Dam*	*Owner*	*Breeder*	*Date of Birth*
Ch. Elvinor Contessa	B	Whitstaff the Red Rebel of Elvinor	Elvinor Ruby Royale	Mr & Mrs Emmett	Mrs Newton	20.6.83
Ch. Belnite Blitzkreig	D	Bronchonian Wellbread	Belnite Bellestar	Mr W. McKnight	Owner	15.2.83
Ch. Eastaff Guardian	D	Ch. Black Tusker	Eastaff Yoshka	Mesdames Shorrock	Mrs Shorrock	4.3.84
Ch. Tondoo Miss Moonshine	B	Ch. Ginnels Black Tuskyanna	Ladies And Gentlemen	Mr T. Jones	Mr T. Jones	18.6.83
Ch. Hoplite Another Ace	D	Rowenda Roman Warrior	Hilly Jean of Hoplite	A. Mitchell	A. Mitchell	16.2.83
Ch. Mud Guts	B	Red Avenger	Pitdale Boadicea	Meakin & Leyland	Mr Bell	12.4.83
Ch. Cradbury Flash Boyo	D	Kenstaff Flash Flyboy	Cradbury Flash Showgirl	H. Phillips	F. A. Phillips	25.9.83
Ch. Rendorn Drummer Boy of Kazemick	D	Rendorn The Mighty Quin	Ch. Rendorn Devils Timpani	Worthington	N. Berry	4.6.83
Ch. Topcroft Trailblazer	B	Ch. Black Tusker	Solitaire of Topcroft	T. Norton	H. Latham	19.3.83
Ch. Boldmore Black Sabbath	D	Ch. Marples Black Opal	Boldmore Shady Lady	Mr & Mrs Clarke	Owners	12.11.83
1986:						
Ch. International Champion River-Mount Black Beauty	B	Caliphs Jester (IKC)	Rivermount Beauty (IKC)	Mr & Mrs Kelly	A. Boland	6.8.79

Ch. Caravella Queen	B	Dark Dandy of Aubrey of Betchgreen	Emma's Pride and Joy	C. A. Brindley	A. Wetton	28.9.82
Ch. Wallace the Wizard	D	Ch. Teutonic Warrior	Ragside Afficionado	Wood & Hedges	Squires	20.4.83
Ch. Fulfin Black Eagle	D	Ch. Black Tusker	Fulfin Good Time Girl	Bates & Boam	Bates & Boam	4.10.83
Ch. Max Max of Hazledean	D	Ch. Teutonic Warrior	Marojo Sundae Girl	Mr Dowling	Mrs Cunningham	24.5.83
Ch. Spartan Victor	D	Ch. Skean Dhu	Attaho Pride of Padingo	Mr & Mrs Drummond	Mrs Molyneaux	10.12.82
Ch. Rendorn Right Marker	B	Constones Tuscaloosa Sam	Ch. Rendorn No Retreat	N. Berry	N. Berry	21.5.84
Ch. Devil's Trill	B	Ch. Black Tusker	Ch. Solo Gipsy Fiddler	Mr Wint	Mr Wint	4.6.83
Ch. Lawbury Cracklin Rose	B	Ch. Lawbury Spiker Joe	Maid Cadiz of Lawberry	Mr & Mrs Lawlor	Mr & Mrs Lawlor	10.11.84
Ch. Jacmartyn Jacks Jewel	B	Ch. Nethertonion Stormtrooper	Lucky Wishbone of Jacmartyn	Messrs Johnson	Messrs Johnson	26.8.83
Ch. Jennabeck Gwenllian	B	Ch. Maradin Master Mariner	Ch. Stalest Delilah Dear of Jennabeck	B. Aubrey	B. Aubrey	16.3.83
Ch. Snow Queen	B	Caltonian Black Ambassador	Tara Pride of Hillerston	Mr Maclachlan	Mr Maclachlan	15.12.83
Ch. Hamason Red Renown	D	Ch. Hamason Red Rambler	Hamason Red Rosita	Mr & Mrs Robinson	Mr & Mrs Robinson	17.8.82

Name of Champion	*Sex*	*Sire*	*Dam*	*Owner*	*Breeder*	*Date of Birth*
1987:						
Ch. Duke of Ducks Hill	D	Royal Warrior	Lady Liza	Mr & Mrs J. H. F. Ward	Mrs Membry	14.12.82
Ch. Ashmoss White Wizard	B	Ashmoss Warpaint	Ginger Nut Lady	Mr & Mrs Phipps	Mr & Mrs Thompson	9.10.84
Ch. Jackstaff Heaven Sent	B	Lancstaff Kjells Namsos Noble	Miss Sunrise	Mr & Mrs S. K. Halifax	J. Kinsley	4.7.84
Ch. Jackstaff Prima Donna	B	Ch. Teutonic Warrior	Ch. Jackstaff Heaven Sent	Mr S. K. Halifax	Mr & Mrs S. K. Halifax	5.2.86
Ch. Wareland of Ironstone	D	Dyards Eager Lad	Tammy Shanto	Mr & Mrs Turnbull	Mrs Turner	4.11.84
Ch. Yuillstaff Dark Sultan	D	Ch. Martonger Rip Rap	Dark Secrets	Mr Yuill	Mr Yuill	26.9.81
Ch. Maljue Cutters Boy	D	Coal Cutter	Stockbull Peggy Sue	Mr S. Watson	M. Whiteley & J. Chappel	21.7.84
Ch. Lancstaff Roras Rosie Red	B	The Malasser Mauler	Jaunty Jane of Lancstaff	Mrs C. Atherton	Mrs C. Atherton	14.4.83
Ch. Crackerjack of Tridwr	D	Ch. Tridwr Dicey Riley	Tasha Valley Breed	T. Fletcher	G. James	10.3.83
Ch. Charlemagne of Judael	D	Whiptail Black Ike of Judael	Limelight of Judael	G. Earle	A. Enderwick & G. Earle	4.11.84

Ch. Rowenda Fearless Lad	D	Ch. Karjobri Black Pepper	Rowenda Northern Destiny	O'Brien, Patey & Rowe	T. Rowe	19.8.82
Ch. Leading Lady's Choice	B	Joline Sir Dan	Berith Leading Lady	Mr & Mrs M. L. Geens	Mrs K. Geens	13.12.85
Ch. Lendevs Dark Star of Barnard	B	Betchgreen Shillelagh	Lendevs Miss Prim	J. Bennett & D. Boyd	L. Devine	14.12.85
Ch. Rendorn Apollyon	B	Ch. Skean Dhu	Ch. Rendorn Devils Timpani	N. Berry	N. Berry	11.11.84
Ch. Belnite Marbillus	B	Belnite Black Warrior	Belnite Black Tulip	W. McKnight	W. McKnight	12.1.86
Ch. Reckless Lass	B	Reckless Lad	Abbeystaff Bit of Max	E. & I. Williams	S. Shepherd	9.11.83
Ch. Dosantors Molly Maguire	B	Dosantors The Gladiator	Dosantors Wicked Wave	J. Williams	Mr & Mrs D. Powell	10.10.83
Ch. Eastaff Ironsides	D	Ch. Black Tusker	Karjobri Miss Vanity	Baulter & Hedges	Mrs J. Shorrock	16.12.84
1988:						
Ch. Silver Bomber	D	Ch. Lawbury Cadiz Kid	Walswake Tigre Bianca	Mr & Mrs A. Hackett	G. Walton & B. Wakeman	18.1.84
Ch. Glynstaff Boris the Bold	D	Tommar the Chieftan	Andromeda's Wish	M. & G. Knowles	M. & G. Knowles	17.9.85
Ch. Zara the Pied Piper	B	The Big Fella	Martini Midnight Lady	Lee & Stafford	D. Wilson	6.7.86

Name of Champion	*Sex*	*Sire*	*Dam*	*Owner*	*Breeder*	*Date of Birth*
Ch. Rocky's Black Sea Eagle	D	Ch. Fulfin Black Eagle	Bearstaff Little Bunting	L. & E. Chamberlain	Mr & Mrs P. S. Edward	30.11.85
Ch. Indiana Acid Queen	B	Ch. Lawbury Spider Joe	Ironstone Evil Brew	Hanaway & Curd	Mr & Mrs T. Curd	14.10.86
Ch. Scarthwaite Diplomat	D	Ch. Ginnels Black Tuskyanna	Scarthwaite Appeal	Mr & Mrs L. Aspin	Mr & Mrs L. Aspin	20.6.85
Ch. Master Jay	D	Atomic White Wander	Inskillins Ronnies Chance	Mr & Mrs R. Williams	Mr & Mrs R. Williams	21.10.86
Ch. Rellim Black Ace	D	Ch. Eastaff Guardian	Rellim Deed I Do	Mr J. Miller	Mrs A. Hubery	10.9.85
Ch. Surestaff Aphrodite	B	Ch. Black Tusker	Constones Rio Rita	Mr & Mrs H. Coble	Mr & Mrs H. Coble	22.3.82
Ch. Zulu Warrior of Anselmo	D	Shaka Zulu of Red	Red Lady Claire of Durban	M. J. Frayne	D. N. Ryland	25.8.81
Ch. Skerry Dhu of Dumbriton	D	Dumbriton Jack to a King	Lady Emma of Balstruan	MacLean & Gilmour	R. A. Chessor	8.1.87
Ch. Lancstaff Sparbu Saga	D	The Malasser Mauler	Jaunty Jane of Lancstaff	Mrs M. A. Goddard	Mrs C. Atherton	25.1.85
Ch. Princess Papillon	B	Ch.Serrel White Lightning	Redstaff Princess	Plimley & Wolliscroft	H. Doughty	13.12.84

Ch. Hillenvale Destiny	B	Ch. Scarthwaite Coachman	Hillenvale Pandora	Mr & Mrs R. Naylor	Mrs J. Wolliscroft	22.11.82
Ch. Midday Wonder of Angelstaff	B	Ch. Angelstaff Blue Max	Diamond at Kentene	Mr & Mrs A. Taylor	Mr & Mrs Carlini	8.10.83

BIBLIOGRAPHY

The following books deal either wholly or in part with the Staffordshire Bull Terrier, his forbears, and the nefarious sports in which they engaged. All will prove useful and fascinating to the student of the breed. Many of these books are rarities and if in good condition can be obtained only at quite high premiums.

AIRY, JILL. *The Stafford Companion Dog*, n.d., SBTC of SW, 1979.

ARMITAGE, G. *Thirty Years with Fighting Dogs*, Washington, D.C., 1935.

ASH, E. C. *Dogs: Their History and Development*, London, 1927; *The Practical Dog Book*, London, 1930; *This Doggie Business*, London, 1934.

BARNARD, J. W. *The Staffordshire Bull Terrier*, Chesterton, 1939 (and reprints).

BEILBY, H. N. *The Staffordshire Bull Terrier*, Birmingham, 1943 (and later editions).

BRIGGS, L. C. *Bull Terriers*, New York, 1940.

BROWN, CAPT. T. *Biographical Sketches and Authentic Anecdotes of Dogs*, Edinburgh, 1829.

CAIUS, JOHANNES. *Johannis Caii Britanni de Canibus Britannicis, Liber Unus. De Rariorum Animalium, et Stirpium Historia, Liber Unus. De Libris Propriis, Liber Unus. Iam Primum Excusi*, London, 1570; *Of Englishe Dogges, the Diversities, the Names, the Natures, and the Properties.* (Translation by Abraham Fleming), London, 1576.

COLBY, J. L. *The American Bull Terrier*, Sacramento, California, 1936.

COMPTON, H. *The Twentieth Century Dog*, London, 1904.

DALZIEL, H. *British Dogs*, London, 1888–97.

DAVIS, R. H. *The Bar Sinister*, New York, 1903.

DAY, J. WENTWORTH. *A Falcon on St Paul's. Being a Book About the Birds, Beasts, Sports and Games of London*, London, 1935; *The Dog in Sport*, London, 1938.

DENLINGER, M. G. *The Complete Pit Bull Terrier*, Washington, D.C., 1948.

DITCHFIELD, P. H. *Old English Sports, Pastimes and Customs*, London, 1891.

DOWSETT, J. M. *Animal Life of Yesterday and Today*, London, 1936.

DRABBLE, P. *Staffordshire*, The County Books, London, 1948; *Black Country*, The Regional Books, London, 1952; *Of Pedigree Unknown*, 1964.

DRURY, W. D. *British Dogs*, London, 1901–3.

DUNN, J. *The Staffordshire Bull Terrier*, Cradley Heath, 1947 (and later editions).

EGAN, P. *Sporting Anecdotes*, London, 1820; *Life in London*, London, 1821; *Pierce Egan's Anecdotes Original and Selected of The Turf, The Chase, The Ring and The Stage*, London, 1827.

ELTINGE, S. *The Staffordshire Bull Terrier*, Santa Barbara, USA, 1986.

FAIRHOLME, E. G. and PAIN, W. *A Century of Work for Animals*, London, 1924.

FARMAN, E. *The Bulldog*, London, 1901.

FITZ-BARNARD, L. *Fighting Sports*, London, 1920.

FITZPATRICK, Sir p. *Jock of the Bushveld*, London, 1907 (and later editions).

FLEIG, Dr D. *Gladiatoren*, Rehenbach, 1974.

GLASS, E. *The Sporting Bull Terrier*, Battle Creek, n.d.

GLYNN, R. H. *Bull Terriers and How to Breed Them*, Oxford, 1936 (and later editions).

GORDON, J. F. *The Staffordshire Bull Terrier Handbook*, London, 1950 (and later editions); *The Bull Terrier Handbook*, London, 1957; *The Bulldog Handbook*, London, 1957; *Staffordshire Bull Terriers*, London, 1964. *Staffordshire Bull Terrier Owner's Encyclopaedia*, London, 1967.

GOVETT, L. A. *The King's Book of Sports*, London, 1890.

GRACE, Lady E. *Staffords in Eire*, Dublin, n.d.

HACKWOOD, F. W. *Old English Sports*, London, 1907.

HANNA, L. B. *Memories of the Pit Bull Terrier and his Master*, New York, n.d. (reprinted by Pete Sparks, Bladensburg, 1955).

HEALD, A. *Make Ready! Being some Notes and Queries concerning the Real Staffordshire Bull Terrier*, Northampton, 1936.

HOGARTH, T. W. 'The Bull-Terrier', publ. *Our Dogs*, n.d.; *The Coloured Bull Terrier and Colour Breeding*, 1932.

HOLE, C. *English Sports and Pastimes*, London, 1949.

HOLLENDER, Count V. C. *The Bull Terrier, And All About It*, Idle, n.d.; *The Bull Terrier*, London; *The Staffordshire Bull Terrier*, London, 1952.

HOMAN, M. *The Staffordshire Bull Terrier in History and Sport*. Liss, 1986.

HUBBARD, C. L. B. *An Introduction to the Literature of British Dogs*, Ponterwyd, 1949.

Hutchinson's Dog Encyclopaedia, London, 1935.

JESSE, E. *Anecdotes of Dogs*, London, 1846; *Researches into the History of the British Dog*, London, 1866.

JOHNS, R. *Our Friend the Bull Terrier*, London, 1934; *Smash Dog Fighting and Badgering*, London, n.d.

JÜNEMANN, W. *Der Stafford*, Bodensee, 1986.

KIRK, R. G. *White Monarch and the Gashouse Pup*, Boston, 1917; *Six Breeds*, New York, 1923.

LEE, RAWDON B. *A History and Description of the Modern Dogs of Great Britain and Ireland*, London, 1893–4.

LEIGHTON, R. *The New Book of the Dog*, London, 1907; *The Complete Book of the Dog*, London, 1922.

LOWSTUTTER, A. M. *Fighting Dogs of Other Years*, Berlin, 1921.

MAYHEW, A. *Paved With Gold*, 1899.

MAYHEW, H. *London's Labour and London's Poor*, London, 1851.

MEYRICK, J. *House Dogs and Sporting Dogs*, London, 1861.

MILLER, J. *The Staffordshire Bull Terrier Scrapbook*, Jarrow, 1985.

MONTGOMERY, E. S. *The English Bull Terrier*, Washington, 1946.

MORLEY, W. M. *The Staffordshire Bull Terrier*, Newton Abbot, 1982.

MORRIS, F. M. 'The Blue "Poll" Bulldog', *Kennel News*, 15th December 1905.

NIMROD (C. J. APPERLEY). *Memoirs of the Life of the Late John Mytton, Esq.*, London, 1935; *The Life of a Sportsman*, London, 1842.

ORMSBY, C. A. *The Staffordshire Terrier*, New York, 1956.

OSBALDESTON, W. A. *The British Sportsman*, London, 1792.

PHILLIPS, F. *The Staffordshire Bull Terrier*, periodical, Stourbridge.

REID, E. and Others. *Memories . . . of Staffordshire Bull Terriers*, London, 1975.

SCANLAN, R. R. *Book of Curs*, 1839–40.

SHAW, VERO K. *The Illustrated Book of the Dog*, London, 1879–81.

SLAUGHTER, F. *'The One' Dog and 'The Others'*, London, 1907.

SMITH, A. *A Scriptural and Moral Catechism . . . to Expose the Exceeding Sinfulness of Cruelty to the Dumb Creation*, Birmingham, 1833 (and other editions).

SPARKS, P. (Editor). *Your Friend and Mine*, various annuals, Vols 1 to 8.

STABLES, Dr g. *Our Friend the Dog*, London, 1883.

STOCKDALE, P. *Bull Baiting*, London, 1802.

STONEHENGE (*See* Walsh, J. H.)

STRATTON, R. *This is the American Pit Bull Terrier*, New Jersey, 1983.

STRUTT, J. *The Sports and Pastimes of the People of England*, London, 1801 (and later editions).

SWAIN, J. *Brutes and Beasts*, London, 1933.

TAPLIN, W. *The Sportsman's Cabinet*, London, 1803–4; *The Sporting Dictionary*, London, 1803.

TURNER, E. S. *All Heaven in a Rage*, London, 1964.

VESEY-FITZGERALD, B. *The Book of the Dog*, London, 1948.

VISAGIE, L. *The First 50 Years, Jubilee Booklet*, Pretoria, 1986.

WALSH, J. H. *The Dog in Health and Disease*, London, 1859; *The Dogs of the British Islands*, London, 1867.

WATSON, J. *The Dog Book*, London, 1906.

[WINDHAM, W.] *A Letter to the Right Hon. William Windham on his Late Opposition to the Bill to Prevent Bull-Baiting, by an Old Member of Parliament*, London, 1800.

WYNN, M. B. *The History of The Mastiff*, London, 1886.

YOUATT, W. *The Dog*, London, 1845.

BREED JOURNALS

The Stafford: (S.C.S.B.T.S.) Ed. Mrs Jackie James (0734) 415176
The Fiery Cross: (S.S.B.T.C.) Ed. Mr Danny Gilmour (041) 889 4027
Staffi: (S.B.T.C./Finland) Ed.
Stafford Bulletin (N.E.S.B.T.C.) Ed. Mr John Miller (091) 489 8087
Newsletters:

Ed. (S.B.T.C. of S.W.): Mr J. Holle (0792) 582597
Ed. (N.W.S.B.T.C.): Mr A. Bryden (0772) 715807
Ed. (N.C.S.B.T.C.): Mr R. Townsend (0742) 334438
Ed. (S.C.S.B.T.S.): Mr Laurie Ford (01) 841 4922

All these publications carry interesting information concerning activities in their regions and the editors can be contacted either by telephone or through their respective club secretaries.

INDEX

abcesses, 153
advertising puppies, 147–8
aglactia, 125
ailments, 152–8
Alaunt (Alan), 17–18
Alken, Henry, *26ff*, 32, *58ff*
Alleyn, Edward, 20
Alpaka Alf's Fancy, *58ff*
American Kennel Club, 43
American Pit Bull Terriers, 43
Anecdotes of Dogs, 16, 33
Annals of Sporting, 33, 34
Annie's Pal, 38
appearance, 52–3, 107
appetite perversions, 153
Archer, Mrs D.M., *90ff*
Ardblaster, 38
Armitage, George, 33
art, appearance in, 31–2
Ashtock Black Maria, Ch., *58ff*
asthma, 153

'B' line, 131
badger-baiting, 30–31, 38, *58ff*
balanitis, 153
Bandits Brintiga, Ch., 134
Bandits Fawn Dandy, *90ff*
bandogge, 17–18
Barnard-Jack, 37, 66–7
Barnes, B., *90ff*
bathing, 102
Baxter, A., 136
bear-baiting, 19–20
Beilby, H.N., 33, 39, 65, 131
Biographical Sketches and Authentic Anecdotes of Dogs, 33, 34
Billy, 29, 34
'Billy, Rose and Tumbler', *26ff*
Birch, Jack, 38
Birch's Monty, 37, 38
Bishop, Messrs T.B., 38
bitches, 112–13
  pre-natal care, 115–17
  post-whelping procedure, 122–3
bites, 153
Black Country, 36
black-and-tans, 55, 60
Blind Robin, 20
Blount, 33
Blue Paul, The, 40–41
blues, 60
body, *58ff*, 71–72
Boldmore Black Sabbath, Ch., *90ff*
Bolton, J., *90ff*
Boxley, H., 38
Brigands Bo'sun, 132
Boylan, W.A., 133
breeding, 107–138
  figure system, 129
Brightmore, J., 135
Brindle Bliss, 131
Brindle Bull, 35
Brindle Mick, 39, 131
Brindle Thelma, 38
brindles, 61, 62
Brinstock Glenagow, 133

British Medical Association, 157
British Veterinary Association, 155, 157
Brown, Capt. Thomas, 33, 34
Bryden, Dr A.S., 156
Bull Terrier, 41
bull-baiting, 20–23
bulldog, 17–23, 29, 32, 34–5, 65, 68, 147
'Bulldog Mars, The', *58ff*
Bulldog Pedigrees, 32
Burge Smith, G.W.R., 133
Bruce, Rev. Rosslyn, 131

'C' line, 131
Cairns, A.W.A., *122ff*
Caius, Dr Johannes, 18
cancer, 153
Camelford, Lord, 32
canine virus hepatitis, 152
canker, 153
Canterbury, Ned of, 20
Chalon, H.B., 32
Chaucer, 17
Chesson, R.A., *58ff*
Cinderbank Beauty, 38, 131
Clark, J., 32
Clarke, M., *90ff*
coat-colour, 55, 62
collars, 103
concussion, 153–4
conformation, 68–81
constipation, 154
Constones Tuscaloosa Sam, *122ff*
Constones Yer Man, *122ff*
Cooper, Abraham, 31
coughing, 154
Courcy Boxill, Mike de, 38
'Crib and Rosa', 31
Cross Guns Johnson, 37
Cruickshank, I.R. & G., 32, 33
Curd, T., *90ff*
Curfews White Orchid, Ch., *90ff*
Cuvier, F., 64
cysts, 154

De Canibus Britannicus, 18
Dee's Pegg, 38
Dee, Phil, 38
demodectic mange, 155–6
dew-claws, 87, 123
diarrhoea, 154
Dinkie, 38
distemper, 152
Dog Book, 33
Dog Breeder's Introduction to Genetics, The, 107
Dog, In Health and Disease, The, 64
Dog World, 139, 147
dog-fighting, 23–9, *26ff*
Dogs, 33
dogs and babies, 67–8
Dubourg, *26ff*
Dudley, G.A., 38, 137
Duke of Ducks Hill, Ch., *122ff*
Dunn, G.H. (Snowy), 39
Dunn, Jack, 38, 131
Dunn, Joe, 33, 36, 38

ears, 53–4
Eastaff Danom, Ch., 135
Eastaff Guardian, Ch., *122ff*
Eastaff Noire-Fille, Ch., *58ff*
Edward, 2nd Duke of York, 17
Egan, Pierce, 32–3, 34, 38
English Toy Terrier, 55
entirety certificates, 151
exercise, 97–9
Exchange and Mart, 147
export pedigrees, 151
eye-infections, 154

faults, 62–3
fawns, 61, 62
Fearless Joe, 37, 39, 131
Fearless Red of Bandits, Ch., 38, 101, *122ff*

feeding, 128–9
feet, *59*, 80–81
Field, T., 134
fights, stopping of, 103–5
fleas, 154
Fleming, Abraham, 18
follicular mange, 155–6
forequarters, 75–6
Forest, A., 38
Foxall, A., 38
Frankling, Eleanor, 107
Freden, 36, 38
freighting dogs, 149–51
fronts, *57*, 74–5

Game Flash, 136
Game Lad, 131
games, 105–6
Gentleman Jim, Ch., 38, 39, 131
gestation charts, 118–20
Gilmour, Danny, *58ff*
Ginnells Black Tuskyanna, Ch., *90ff*
Good Lad, 38
Gordon, John F., 33
Great Bomber, The, 38
Greaves, Mrs B., *122ff*
Grew, S., 38
Griffiths, A., 38
grizzles, 61
grooming, 101–2
Grosvenor, C., 38

Hackwood, 33
hand-rearing puppies, 123–5
Haraway and Carol, *90ff*
hard pad, 152
head, 53, *54*, 55, 70–71
Heald, Arthur, 38
Hentzner, 33
Hernias, 87, 155
Hill, Miss M., 38
hindquarters, 57, 77–9
Hinks, James, 41
hip dysplasia, 155
Hoggarth, D., 137
Holden, Fred, 36, 38
Holinshed, 33
Hollender, Count V.C., 33
Homer, L.E., 38
Hough, H., 38
house-training, 91–2
Howitt, *26ff*
Hurricane Freya, *26ff*
Hurricane of Judael, Ch., *26ff*
Hardwicke, B., 38

Icones Animalium, 17
immunisation, 98
India Doc, US Ch., *90ff*
Indiana Acid Queen, Ch., *90ff*
indigestion, 155
infestations, 154

'J' line, 131, 137
Jacco Maccacoo, 31
Jacko, 29
Jackson and Bowers, 32
jealousy, 67–8
'Jem Burns' Four Pets', *26ff*
Jesse, 16, 33
Jim the Dandy, 37, 39
Jolihem Dreadnought, Ch., *122ff*
Jones, Paul, 40
Judy, Capt. William, 43

Kennel Club, 15, 36, 37, 46, 49, 68, 108, 109, 139, 143–4, 151
kennelling, 99–101
Knight's Tale, 17

'L' line, 131
lactol, 124, 125, 126
Lady Rose, 38
Langdon, K.C., *90ff*
Langport Spearhead, Ch., *90ff*
Lassomine, 38
Latham, H., *58ff*

leads, 98–9, 103
Lee, A.M., *122ff*
Lee, Mrs C.J.H., *122ff*
leptospiral jaundice, 152
Lestom Boy, 38
lice, 154
Lincoln, Tom of, 20
line-breeding, 110
Lioness, 38, *122ff*
line-and-family breeding, 129-38
literature, appearance in, 32–3
liver-colour coats, 55, 60
Lloyd, Charlie, 43
London's Labour, London's Poor, 29
Lowe, Bruce, 130

'M' line, 131, 132, 133, 135, 136, 138
Maclean, Neil, *58ff*
McNeill, J., 135
mahogany brindles, 60
Major in Command of Wychbury, Ch., 38, 137
Major Mont, 101
Make Ready, 38
Mallen, Joe, 38, 39, 131
Mallen's Cross Guns Johnson, 37
Manchester Terrier, 55, 60
mange, 155–6
Marshall, Ben, 32
Master of Game, The, 17
Master of the Bears and Dogs, 20
mastiff, 16–19
mating, 110–15
Mayhew, Augustus, 29
Mayhew, Henry, 29
Melling, Harry, 38, *122ff*
milk-shortage, 125
Miller, Mrs T., 138
Miniature Bull Terrier, 43
Molossus, 16
monkey-baiting, 31
Morrison, James B., 40
mouth, 54–5, *56*

name, derivation of, 37
Nance the Fearless, 38
National Sports of Great Britain, 32
neck, 72
Nichols, 33

obedience-training, 92–5
Of English Dogges, 18
Old English Sports, 33
Old English White Terrier, 41
Orchid Beauty, Ch., *58ff*
origins, 15–19, 35
Our Dogs, 139, 147

Paddy, 43
pain, indifference to, 65
parvovirus, 152, 156–7
pasterns, *60*, 76
patella, 78
Paved with Gold, 29
pedigree, 107
Pedigree Nobility, 52
Pegg's Joe, 37, 38
Pepys, 33
Pilot, 43
Pit Bull Terrier, 35, 43
Pit Dogs, 35, 43
Pollott, J., *58ff*
Poole, S.W., 38
Pounds, V.H., *58ff*
Practical Dog Breeding and Genetics, 107
Priest, Horace, 38
Prince, Lew, 38
Procurator Pugnacium, 16
Pugnaces, 16
punishment, 99
puppies:
  delivery of, 117–22
  feeding, 128–9
  hand-rearing, 123–5
  selection of, 82–9

selling, 145–9
showing, 139–40
training, 90–97
weaning, 125–8

quality, 52

'R' line, 131, 134
Rafferty, 43
Rapparee Lady Luck, Ch., *90ff*
ratting, 29–30
rear, 76–7
Reckless Lass, Ch., *26ff*
registration, 109, 139, 144
Rellim A'Boy, Ch., 138
Researches into the History of the British Dog, 33
Ribchester Max, 131
RSPCA, 23, 29
Rubarths's disease, 152
Rum Bottle, 131

Sackerson, 20
sarcoptic mange, 155
scabies, 155
Scott, John, 32
scratch, 27–8
Shakespeare, 20, 38
Shaw, Mrs J., 39
Shaw's Jim, 37, 39
Shirley, S.E., 143
Shorrock, Mrs Joyce, *58ff*, *122ff*
Shoulder, P., *90ff*
Shoulders, 73–4
shows, 139–43
Silvers, F., 38
size, 62
Skerry Dhu of Dumbriton, Ch., *58ff*
Slater, A., 38
Smith, C.H., 33
Smith, Maurice, 38
soundness, 69–70
Southall, F., 134
Spanish Bulldog, 18
Sporting Anecdotes, 32–3
Sporting Magazine, The, 32
Sports and Pastimes of the People of England, 33
sprains, 157
Squires, *122ff*
Staffordshire Bull Terrier:
origins, 15–19, 35
name derivation, 37
Staffordshire Bull Terrier, The, 39, 65
Staffordshire Bull Terrier Club, 37–9
Advisory Council, 46, 47
Staffordshire Bull Terrier Handbook, The, 33
Staffordshire Bull Terrier Owner's Encyclopaedia, 33
Staffordshire Bull Terriers, 33
Staffordshire Terrier of America, 43–4
Standard, The:
Staffordshire Bull Terrier, 45–63
and breeding, 110
interpretations of, 50–63
original version, 45–9
1987 version, 49–50
Staffordshire Terrier of America, 43–4
stifles, *59*, 77–9
stings, 157
Stockdale, Top, 34
Stow, 33
strains, 157
Strutt, 33
Stubbs, George Townley, 32
stud dogs, 60, 111–12

tackle, 39
tails, *59*, 79–80
tasting, 27
teeth, 54–5, *56*

temperament, 113
Thirty Years with Fighting Dogs, 33
Thompson, Dr H., 156
Tittle, Alf, *58ff*
Top, 34
Topcroft Toreador, Ch., *58ff*
topping and tailing, 142
Tough Guy, 39, *122ff*
toxocara canis infection, 157–8
training:
  exhibition, 95–7
  house-, 91–2
  obedience, 92–5
  punishment, 99
Triton Judy, 38, 131
Trusty, 32

Undershot jaw, 55, *56*, 63, 147–8
United Kennel Club
  (Kalamazoo), 43

Vindictive Monty, 37, 38
Vindictive Montyson, 38

Wallace the Wizard, Ch., *122ff*
Walsh, J.H., 64
Ward, James, 32
Ward, William, 32
Warenne, William of, 21
'Wasp, Child and Billy', 32
Waters, Alec, *58ff*
Watson, James, 33
weaning, 125–8
Weaver, Matthew, 38
weight, 62
whelping, 116–123
whites, 61
Widneylandkim, 131
Williams, G., 38
Wood, J.W., 38
Wood and Hedges, *122ff*
Wolstenholmes, 32
worming, 127
Wystaff Warfare, Ch., 10

Yankee Terrier, 43